WEBSITE BRANDING FOR SMALL BUSINESSES

WEBSITE BRANDING FOR SMALL BUSINESSES

Secret Strategies for Building a Brand, Selling Products Online, and Creating a Lasting Community

NATHALIE NAHAI

Allworth Press

Library of Congress Cataloging-in-Publication Data is available on file.

ISBN: 978-1-62153-395-5

Printed in China

To my Boo

CONTENTS

THANKS

To my Boo—for your absolute faith, support, laughter and love. You mean more to me than words can say and I couldn't have done this without you.

To my parents—Ian Williamson and Francine Nahai—for your boundless support and love; for always providing an invaluable, stimulating arena for debate; for sparking an insatiable curiosity about the language with which we express ourselves; and for showing me the unbridled excitement and possibilities one can experience when logic and creativity collide.

To my brother and mental sparring partner—Paul Nahai-Williamson—for your wisdom and sharp wit, and for setting the bar so high. You are an inspiration to me.

To Berthe and Shapour—for your love and guidance, I am eternally grateful.

To my family—thank you for the joy you bring me, I love you.

To my teachers—Dad, for inspiring in me a delight in physics and science; Annette Vergette, for igniting a lifelong passion for psychology and the exploration of the human condition; Mr Butcher, for believing in me; Anita Gentry and Doc Harris, for a thrilling introduction to the beauty of the English language; and Trisha Davis, for encouraging me to follow my creative dreams.

SPECIAL THANKS

To Elie Williams, Paul East, Sarah Wild, Rachel Stock and the rest of the Pearson team—thanks for taking me on—and to Robbie Steinhouse, a heart-felt thank you for your kind introduction and friendship. To Ketan Raval and David Tennant-Eyles, for your generosity and support in the fabulous design of this book. To Edwin Williamson and Heather Holden-Brown, thank you for your help at the start of this project, and to my agent, Jacq Burns, for equipping me to play in this ring. I'd also like to thank Rob Teszka—a good friend and a brilliant academic—for volleying ideas with me over coffee and helping with my research. Araceli

Camargo—for showing me what can be achieved with a big vision, a great community and a fabulous mind—you rock. Nici Clements—for your unwavering friendship and support all these years. Richie Manu—for believing in me and opening up the door to living life on one's own terms. Sam Michel—for your exciting contributions to the debate on the psychology of online influence.

I'd also like to thank Fabian Stelzer and the EyeQuant team; David Stillwell and Stephen Haggard at Preference Tool; Jon Murphy and the guys over at Oban Multilingual; and Meabh Quoirin at Future Foundation.

THANK YOU TO EVERYONE WHO CONTRIBUTED TO THIS BOOK

Abdulaziz AlBaijan / Abigail Freeman / Adrian Harris / Alasdair MacGregor / Alastair Dryburgh / Alex O'Byrne / Ana Margarida Barreto / Anirban Saha / Barry Furby / Ben Slawson / Bex Lewis / Bill Mumford / Casper Blicher Olsen / Chris Murphy / Chris Nisbet / Cinzia Garoia / Dan Fox / Dan Gutierrez / Dan West / Dani Naydenova / Darren Shea / David Tennant-Eyles / Deb Swinney / Delfin Vassallo / Depesh Mandalia / Dominique Lim / Edward Phillip Bell / Ellie Parker / Esra Barlik / Eva Keogan / Farhan Rehman / Gabe Fender / Gaby Arjun Sharma / Gareth Hayes / Gemma Fountain / Geoff Kennedy / Graham Jones / Guy Buchan / Hedley Smith / Heidi Harman / Heli Rajasalo / Ian C Dowson / Isabelle Quevilly / Jack Murphy / Jade Tomlin / James Mawson / James Wood / Jamie Hancox / Janakiram Ganesan / Janice Learmond-Criqui / Jean Laleuf / Jim Allen / Jimmy Saruchera / John Cielik-Bridgen / Jon Ingham / Jonathan A. West / Juliet Chen / Kare Anderson / Karen Hawey / Kate Pierpoint / Kate Warwick / Katharine Robinson / Katie Kinnear / Katrina Padron / Kim Borrowdale / Laila Takeh / Lance R. Frizzell / Laura Hands / Lauren Stone / Luisfe Davalos / Mark Batchelor / Martin Talks / Mary-Ellen Mullally / Matt Cullin / Matt Lent / Matt Maltby / Meredith Marsh / Michael Britt / Michael Greer / Mike Teasdale / Mike Weston / Nadine Clarke / Noel Leeman / Olly Willans / Pablo Ettinger / Patrick Watt / Paul Levrant / Paul Rouke / Peter Cambell / Ralf Haberich / Ramon Bez / Rebecca Taylor / Remy Valette / Richard Hadley / Roisin Waite / Ross Andrews-Clifford / Sam Michel / Sameer Mohnot / Sangeeta Haindl / Servane Mouazan / Sheridan Flynn / Simon Fried / Simone Brummelhuis / Stuart McRae / Tamara Askew / Teresa Potocka / Tim Aldiss / Timothy Bosworth / Tom Bowden / W. C. Stevenson / Wesam Said / Will Sudlow / Zoe Hoster

PUBLISHER'S ACKNOWLEDGEMENTS

We are grateful to the following for permission to reproduce copyright material:

Figures

Figure on page 74 adapted from Maslow, Abraham H.; Frager, Robert D.; Fadiman, James, *Motivation and Personality*, 3rd, © 1987. Printed and Electronically reproduced by permission of Pearson Education, Inc., Upper Saddle River, New Jersey.

Screenshots

Screenshot on page 75 from http://www.mcdonalds.de/, McDonald's Promotions GmbH & Co. KG; Screenshots 8.1, 8.2, 8.3 from http://www.groupon.de, with permission from EyeQuant; Screenshots 9.1, 9.2 from Heat map of people looking at www.baby.com screenshot, http://www.objectivedigital.com, produced using a Tobii T60 eye tracker from Tobii.com by ObjectiveDigital.com; Screenshot on page 133 from United Breaks Guitars, www.youtube.com/user/sonsofmaxwell, with permission from Dave Carroll Music, http://www.davecarrollmusic.com; Screenshot on page 142 from Hudson River Tweet, http://twitpic.com/135xa, with permission from Janis Krums; Screenshot on page 148 from Evian Roller Babies International Version, http://www.youtube.com/watch?v=XQcVIIWpwGs, with permission from Danone and BETC Euro RSCG; Screenshot on page 163 from http://www.silvermanresearch.com/home/clients/, with permission from Michael Silverman; Screenshot on page 189 from Domino's Pizza Turnaround, http://www.youtube.com/watch?v=AH5R56jILag, with kind permission from Domino's Pizza LLC.

Tables

Table 3.1 from Internet World Stats (2011) Internet usage statistics: The Internet big picture. World Internet users and population stats.htm, available online at: http://www.internetworldstats.com/stats.htm (accessed 12 April 2012), Copyright © 2000-2012, Miniwatts Marketing Group. All rights reserved; Tables 5.1, 5.2, 5.3, 5.4, 5.5, 5.6 adapted from Geert Hofstede, Gert Jan Hofstede, Michael

Minkov, *Cultures and Organizations, Software of the Mind*, Third Revised Edition, McGraw-Hill 2010, ISBN 0-07-166418-1. © Geert Hofstede B.V. quoted with per-mission; Table 17.1 adapted from Effects of $9 Price Endings on Retail Sales: Evidence from Field Experiments, *Quantitative Marketing and Economics*, 1(1), pp. 93–100, p.94 (Anderson, E. T. and Simester, D. I. 2003), with kind permission from Springer Science+Business Media B.V.

Text
Epigraph on page 37 from Geert Hofstede, Gert Jan Hofstede, Michael Minkov, *Cultures and Organizations, Software of the Mind*, Third Revised Edition, McGraw-Hill 2010, ISBN 0-07-166418-1. © Geert Hofstede B.V. quoted with permission; Epigraph on page 109 from Dr Uri Hasson, interview in "What makes a masterpiece? Stories and film," television program, Channel 4, 7 January 2012, with permission from Uri Hasson; Epigraphs on page 114, page 124 from Are you selling the right colour? A cross-cultural review of colour as a marketing cue, *Journal of Marketing Communications*, 12(1), pp. 15–30 (Aslam, M. M. 2006), reprinted by permission of the publisher (Taylor & Francis Ltd, http://www.tandf.co.uk/journals); Epigraph on page 117 from reprinted with permission from Managing images in different cultures: a cross-national study of color meanings and preferences, *Journal of International Marketing*, pub-lished by the American Marketing Association, Madden, T. J., Hewitt, K. and Roth, M. S., 2000, 8(4), pp. 90–107; Extract on page 134 from United Breaks Guitars, www.youtube.com/user/sonsofmaxwell, with permission from Dave Carroll Music, http://www.davecarrollmusic.com.

Picture Credits
The publisher would like to thank the following for their kind permission to reproduce their photographs:
(Key: b-bottom; c-center; l-left; r-right; t-top)
Page 2–3 iStockphoto. Page 100 courtesy Simon Kimber. Page 102 (b) Alamy Images: Robert Ashton / Massive Pixels; (t) Getty Images: Jéan-Loup Gautreau / AFP / Getty Images. Page 103 www.imagesource.com: Nigel Riches. Image Source.

All other images © Pearson Education. Facebook is a Trademark of Facebook Inc.

In some instances we have been unable to trace the owners of copyright mate-rial, and we would appreciate any information that would enable us to do so.

ABOUT THE AUTHOR

Nathalie Nahai is an award-winning speaker and web psychologist. With a background in psychology and digital strategy, she is one of the few leading voices in this field to have both academic and hands-on experience in engineering online persuasion.

She lectures regularly on the subject of web psychology and works with businesses to increase their reputation, client base and profit online. Nathalie is also an esteemed member of #OgilvyChange, a new behavioral sciences practice that utilizes the latest thinking in cognitive psychology, social psychology and behavioural economics to create behavioural interventions in the real world.

You'll find her tweets @TheWebPsych and you can read her blog at thewebpsychologist.com.

INTRODUCTION

THE INTERNET—AN INALIENABLE HUMAN RIGHT?

> " *For many, Internet access is no longer a luxury, but a necessity; it has become an obligatory component for economic, political, cultural, and individual representation and empowerment.*
>
> E. B. WEISER, PSYCHOLOGIST[1]

The Human Rights Council of the UN recently ruled that any complete restriction of access to the Internet would be a breach of Article 19 of the International Covenant on Civil and Political Rights, "the right to freedom of expression."[2] In Cisco's "Connected world technology report" for 2011,[3] global research (in which 2800 people in their twenties from 14 countries were surveyed) found that 33 percent of young university students and employees consider the Internet to be as fundamental to their daily existence as air, water, food and shelter. Over 50 percent stated that the Internet was an "integral part of their lives" that they could not live without, while 40 percent of students globally said the Internet was more important to them than socializing with friends, going on dates, or listening to music.

For those of us who grew up in a pre-Internet age (I wonder if we will one day refer to it as PI, the next logical step after BC and AD), the fact that it now occupies a central space in so many of our lives is an absorbing one. Since its early 8-bit days, the web has blossomed into a global cornerstone of communication, without which many of us would feel isolated, cut off and alone. When our desire to be plugged in starts to trump even our offline social needs (the 40 percent of students mentioned above) it's a sign that there's something incredible going on. Whether we like it or not, the web has entangled us all—making some of us more influential in the process.

HOW TO USE THIS BOOK

Since we are increasingly using social feedback to inform and direct our purchasing decisions, it's vital for businesses to function transparently and deliver high-value solutions to clients' specific needs. Nowhere is this need more apparent than in the online marketplace, where the sheer volume of products and services available can overwhelm even the most experienced of users.

Presented with such a chaotic landscape of choices, as online consumers we pay most attention to those businesses and brands that we recognize and trust. While it helps to be a big player when competing for online clients, the most successful businesses succeed by following three fundamental rules.

THE THREE SECRETS TO ONLINE INFLUENCE

1 Know who you're targeting

To succeed online, you need an informed, intimate knowledge of your target market.

2 Communicate persuasively

You have to show your clients that you can meet their specific needs.

3 Sell with integrity

You must demonstrate that you can quickly and reliably deliver exactly what your clients want.

With this in mind, the book is divided into three parts. Within each you'll find real-world examples of the successful implementation of these influential techniques, the theories behind them and a "how to" guide that you can use today to achieve the online success you want.

PART 1

KNOW WHO YOU'RE TARGETING

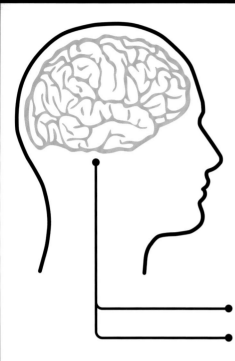

200 million billion
calculations per second

Do you believe in free will?

We become subconsciously aware of our intention to act **300** milliseconds after the relevant areas of our brain become active.

SYSTEM 1
Fast
Emotional
Unconscious
Intuitive
Automatic
FFF

SYSTEM 2
Slow
Analytical
Conscious
Laborious
Intentional
Rational

NEUROCHEMICAL ARCHETYPES p61

EXPLORER	BUILDER	NEGOTIATOR	DIRECTOR
dopamine	*serotonin*	*oestrogen*	*testosterone*

EXPLORER	BUILDER	NEGOTIATOR	DIRECTOR
Seeks risk and novelty	Sociable and loyal	Good with people	Driven
Independent	Friendly	Astute and introspective	Likes reason and logic
Unpredictable	Cautious	Patient	Tough-minded
Creative	Dependable	Compassionate	Competitive
Hedonistic	Methodical	Flexible	Goal-oriented
Sensual and fun	Hard-working	Facility with language	Problem-solver
Easily bored	Traditional	Diplomatic	Bold and blunt
Insatiably curious	Concerned with safety	OK with ambiguity	Uncompromising

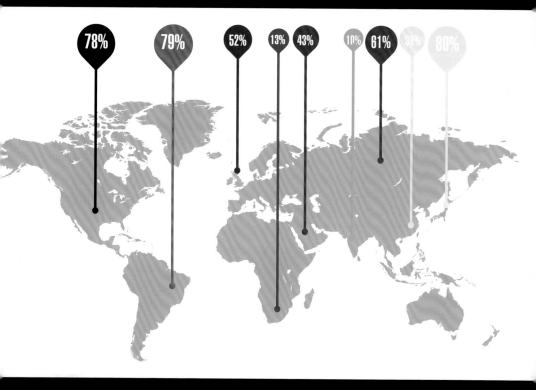

78%
79%
52%
13%
43%
10%
61%
38%
80%

p37 SOFTWARE OF THE MIND

HOFSTEDE'S 6 CULTURAL TRAITS

trait	score	country

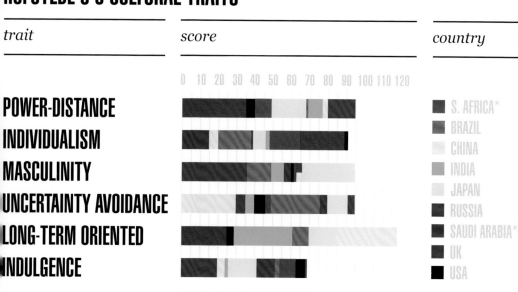

0 10 20 30 40 50 60 70 80 90 100 110 120

POWER-DISTANCE

INDIVIDUALISM

MASCULINITY

UNCERTAINTY AVOIDANCE

LONG-TERM ORIENTED

INDULGENCE

S. AFRICA*
BRAZIL
CHINA
INDIA
JAPAN
RUSSIA
SAUDI ARABIA*
UK
USA

*NO DATA AVAILABLE FOR LONG-TERM ORIENTED TRAIT

1 THE HUMAN BRAIN

AN INTRODUCTION TO YOUR BRAIN

200 million billion calculations per second.[2]

No, I'm not pitching you the latest supercomputer, I'm talking about your brain. Inside your skull sits a 3 lb (1.3 kg) mass of extraordinarily complex neural circuitry. Consisting of around 100 billion neurons, each with a 1,000 connections and a firing rate of 200 calculations per second, this singular organ is responsible for your every move, behavior and decision—and we're only just starting to discover how it works.

Despite the fact that we are constantly breaking new ground in this arena, our knowledge of the private life of the brain is still in its infancy. There are, however, some useful models we can use to help us understand how the systems within this complex organ might work. While researchers no longer think of the brain in the following terms (the reality is too complex to be reduced in this way), the primal, emotional and rational model outlined below is a helpful way of reminding us that the brain comprises multiple systems. If we want to convince someone of something, we need to target more than just one of these systems.

While we won't be going into too much detail here (we'll leave that to the neuropsychologists), this brief introduction will provide a framework from which to explore how we think, and how we can use this knowledge for greater influence online.

1 "THE PRIMAL BRAIN"

The primal brain is so called because it comprises the brainstem, which is thought to be one of the most primitive structures in the brain. Common to all animals (hence why it is nicknamed by many as the "reptilian brain") the brainstem is responsible for our basic vital functions, such as breathing, digestion, heart rate and blood pressure and it's also involved in regulating our arousal and alertness levels. Damage to this part of the brain can have profound effects on our sensory and motor processes, as well as our consciousness.[3]

You'll have no doubt heard of the freeze–flight–fight response (known colloquially as "fight or flight"). Well, this is where it happens. The brainstem's threat-response system is responsible for ensuring our survival and it's this system that helps us respond to imminent dangers in our environment. In day-to-day life, low-level threats usually result in freeze or flight, with other parts of the brain (such as the amygdala and hypothalamus) helping us determine the level of risk we face. To give you an example, I'm sure most of us can recall at least one occasion when we've mindlessly crossed a road only to freeze in the face of oncoming traffic. A terrifying moment at the best of times, but, when we find ourselves in positions of danger, the brainstem's threat-response system becomes highly triggered, initiating a violent response sequence: fight.[4]

Charged with the task of keeping us safe, the brainstem's aptitude for assessing new stimuli as potentially risky is the reason we tend to prefer things that are familiar—they seem safe. In a talk by Rory Sutherland on the subject of influence, he said that one of the best ways to sell a product is to make new things seem familiar, and to make familiar things seem new.[5] In the commercial world, failure to recognize (and capitalize on) this need can result in big losses. So, if you're thinking of taking established products from your own country into new, foreign markets, carefully consider whether you need to re-brand in order to ensure familiarity and good sales.

I mentioned that the brainstem is also involved in arousal and, as such, it also responds to opportunities for sex. While we all enjoy a bit of eye-candy, in an online setting using images that merely hint at sexual potential can be a great way of attracting users to your site. Whether they realize it or not, it's the reason even the most banal of websites use images of youthful, smiling faces to attract attention and sell their products.

2 "THE EMOTIONAL BRAIN"

The emotional brain comprises one of the most ancient and automatic areas of your brain—the limbic system. This can be found buried within the cerebrum and includes the amygdala, thalamus, hypothalamus and hippocampus.

The amygdala is largely responsible for our primitive emotional responses and is in charge of registering relevant stimuli in our surroundings (whether that's the threat of oncoming traffic or a burger when we're hungry). Research has shown that it even plays a role in our value judgements: we rely on its ability to decipher facial expressions to decide whom we should trust.[6] In an online context, where visual cues are crucial in forming our behaviors, it's this almond-shaped part of our brains that influences many of our purchasing decisions.

Above the amygdala sits the thalamus. This large area deep within the forebrain processes emotions such as happiness, sadness and disgust.[7] Sometimes nicknamed the "Grand Central Station of sensory processing," the thalamus acts as an interchange for information passing from all senses (except smell) to the cortical areas of your brain.

Together, the hypothalamus and pituitary gland control our visceral functions, body temperature and behavioral responses, and they are involved in our sexual responses, as well our feelings of pleasure and aggression.

Close by sits the midbrain, where we process the reflex of eye movements along with our posture and body movements. Within the midbrain you'll also find the ventral tegmental area. Packed with neurons that release dopamine (the neurochemical associated with pleasure, reward, risk-taking and motivation), it is responsible for relaying messages about pleasure to other parts of the limbic system. Much of the processing that happens in this area of the brain occurs beneath our conscious awareness, and it's this part that is often responsible for some of our more impulsive buying behaviors ... yes, that includes chocolate.

3 "THE RATIONAL BRAIN"

Responsible for our higher cognitive functions, the rational brain comprises the neocortex, which helps us to plan, organize and problem-solve. It draws inputs from almost all other regions of the brain, integrating this information to form the near and long-term goals that enable us to plan ahead.[8] The neural processes that underlie social learning and innovation are widely thought to reside here[9] and it is this area of the brain which is considered to be responsible for human language, abstract thought, imagination and even consciousness. While the neocortex is the defining feature that sets us apart from other mammals, it's the combined interaction between different regions that really makes us special.

When it comes to the human brain, the whole really is greater than the sum of its parts. So, if you want to be persuasive online, you have to target all three. This means creating a message that is arousing, emotionally effective intellectually compelling.

CASE STUDY Kiva

If you've never visited Kiva's microlending site, go and check it out now, and take a look at the landing page.

Nestled in a pale, neutral palette with fresh green accents, the first thing you'll notice when you arrive is the photo gallery of (mostly happy) faces, uploaded by people from all around the world.

As they blink into view across the full width of the page, you're greeted with a single, simple pop-up. On it, you see a woman's photo, her name, which country she's from, and a few lines that read, "A loan of $825 helps Alice to buy more cooking oil, sugar, eggs and other ingredients." You're invited to click through and "read their story," and at the bottom of the pop-up is a bright orange button emblazoned with the words "Lend now," with an option to browse all loans.

Once your attention has been pulled in by the movement and the faces, you may notice the strapline threaded across the top of the page, "Empower people around the world with a $25 loan." But just how does Kiva succeed in convincing such a large number of its visitors to take this action? Well, it boils down to a few key principles.

The human face is one of the most fundamentally compelling visual stimuli for our brains, to the extent that we'll scan our surroundings and perceptually group unrelated items if they so much as resemble a face (this is also the reason some of the most popular cars look like they're smiling when seen from the front).[10]

Once you've scanned Kiva's crowd (you may find yourself gravitating towards the most attractive face) and you've scrolled over a few photos to read their personal story (heart strings now fully engaged), your

▶

decision to donate will still need a bit of reasoning to back it up.

Luckily for you, there's a handy information box at the center of the page highlighting the fact that over 98 percent of loans are repaid, conveying to you that your investment is a safe one.

And, in case you were in any doubt, that same box shows you that over 4000 new lenders joined this week (and 129,265 "Liked" this on Facebook). So, if everyone else is doing it, you must be on to a good thing (social proof).

In just a few simple steps, Kiva has successfully managed to persuade the primal, emotional and rational parts of your brain that donating to them is an action worth taking. And, as a result of their ingenious strategy tailored to your brain, someone on the other side of the world will benefit.

MAKE THIS WORK FOR YOU

Target the primal brain

- **Sex, anyone?** One of the most effective ways of communicating directly to the primitive brain is through images—in particular, images that include cues for sex. I don't mean that you should be plastering pictures of naked models all over your website (unless, of course, you're in the porn industry), but even subtle cues can work wonders. We all know the feeling of excitement we get when we spot a beautiful face in the crowd and, in an online environment, our brains work in much the same way. Simply using images of attractive people on your website can be enough to entice users in, as can images of symmetrical faces (known to convey health, which makes for a good choice in reproductive partners).[11]

- **Hunger pains** Next up is food. Unless you're in the catering or events industries, it's unlikely that you'll want to use standalone food imagery on your website, but if you're selling your customers a lifestyle or something that will help improve it, then including beautiful-looking food in the images that you use can have massive appeal. It may sound facile, but the fact that food is one of the most popular image categories on social networking site Pinterest attests to the seductive nature of gastronomy—even when online.

- **Get moving** The primal brain also responds well to motion, which may account for the popularity of moving image sliders in current web design trends. With research showing that users aged 18 to 31 prefer web pages with a single large image and relatively little text,[12] we may be seeing a shift towards the hypervisualisation of online data, reflecting the preferred visual mode of the primitive brain.

- **Contrast** For our ancestors, the ability to make fast, sound decisions often meant the difference between life and death. Their brains evolved to respond to contrast and this quality still commands our attention today. It's for this reason that high-contrast information is so engaging. You need only look at our collective obsession with before and after photos to observe this phenomenon for yourself. Depending on what you're selling, you can convey the benefits of your product or service to online customers by using images that highlight scenarios of before and after, with and without, slow and fast and risky and safe. For instance, if you run a pharmacy and you want to promote your business online, you could use the pairing of risky and safe to highlight the benefits of using your pharmacy over others. Image one might show a customer in a long line of unhappy, uncared for customers, all waiting to pick up their scruffy-looking prescriptions from another pharmacy (risky). Image two might depict that same customer, but this time beaming as they receive expert, one-to-one advice from one of your professional, attractive-looking representatives (safe). It's a simple concept, but, when it comes to online persuasion, the principle of contrast is a powerful one.

- **It's a fine line between love and hate** Pop-up windows also work on the principle of contrast, but, as an ex-web designer, I have to say that most people hate these, so if you make a habit of using them you're more likely to irritate potential customers than entice them in. Where possible, avoid pop-ups like the plague.

- **End** The primal brain tends to respond to beginnings and ends, which may explain our positive bias towards end experiences[13]—why the last glorious mouthful of chocolate cake seems so much more

▶

enjoyable than the ones before. In an online context, this means that you have to prioritize your content. The product or service you wish to sell the most should be the first item your customers see, so make it count and position your products wisely.

- In scarce supply As we'll discover later (in Chapters 13 and 14), the primal system responds strongly to threats of scarcity, especially when it sees that other people are all clamouring for a particular item. This is why deal-a-day websites work so well and explains why telling your customers that they only have a limited time to buy (or a limited stock to choose from) can be a very powerful way of motivating them to buy. (Sending "final reductions" emails to loyal customers can elicit a sense of urgency and encourage last-minute impulse buys.)

- Keep it concrete If you're using text to communicate your message, make sure the language you use is familiar, friendly and concrete. The old part of the brain is self-centered and wants to know "What's in it for me?" It also prefers tangibles to intangibles, so if you're in the business of insurance, don't open a pitch by telling your customers what rates they can expect to pay per year. Instead, tell them how buying insurance from you can make their loved ones safe and protect them when their house burns down. Yes, it's dramatic, but it's tangible, meaningful and client-centered—and it works.

Target the emotional brain

Now you have pandered to the primal brain, your strategy should shift towards appealing to the emotional brain to deepen engagement. This is a theme we will be returning to throughout this book, so I will provide a brief introduction here.

- Empathy Whether you realize it or not, we're hard-wired to empathize. In 1992, a group of neuroscientists studying premotor neurons in primates made a startling discovery.[14] They were scanning the brains of macaques to observe which neurons became active when they picked up peanuts, when one of the researchers got hungry and inadvertently picked up a nut himself. Rather surprisingly, he observed that some of the same motor neurons that had fired when the monkey had picked up the nut were now firing as the monkey watched the researcher. It seemed as though the macaque's brain was activated in sympathy with the researcher's actions. This singular moment led to the discovery of mirror neurons, which are vital to our ability to empathise with others. They're the reason that we feel uplifted when looking at photos of happy faces and wince when we see someone trap their finger in a door. Online, the simple use of photos or videos conveying the emotional state that you want your customers to feel can have a significant effect on their perception of your brand. That's why so many businesses use images that feature groups of people having fun together, but, as we'll see later (in Chapter 5), when it comes to showcasing shiny happy people, it's not a one-size-fits-all solution. Rather, our cultures can have a dramatic effect on how we perceive others and there are certain differences you'll need to be aware of if you want to be persuasive online.

– **What's in a story?** Storytelling, the use of color and psychological principles of persuasion can also provide powerful ways in which to engage emotionally with others and, while I'm flagging it up now, we'll be exploring these strategies in greater detail later on in the book.

Target the rational brain

Once your customers are emotionally engaged, provide them with the rational support they need to justify specific actions.

– **Going with your gut** We all like to think that we're in control, which, for most of us, means identifying ourselves as rational people, but the assumption that humans carefully weigh up options before committing to a choice is shaky at best. The reality is that we tend to make choices based on our "gut" and only turn to our cognitive faculties after the fact, for a nice bit of post-rationalization. This is true both on- and offline and it's one of the reasons that putting items on sale is so effective. Knowing about this tendency doesn't make it any less

▶

seductive, either. I for one have lost count of the times that I've bought an item in a sale simply because it looks like a good "deal." Whatever stories we use to convince ourselves that we've made a sound choice, if you can provide your customers with some rationale to support their purchasing decisions, you'll be doing the work for them and making it easier for them to buy.

- **Authority** In an effort to make better decisions, we often look to people in positions of authority or expertise for guidance. While this strategy can serve us well (seeking medical advice when we're sick can save our lives), it's also very easy to exploit (dress someone up in a white coat and we're more likely to trust what they say).[15] As we'll see later, many of the strategies we employ (and justify) at a conscious level are heavily influenced by cognitive rules of thumb, which once identified, can be leveraged to shape and inform people's behaviors online.

2 THE PSYCHOLOGY OF DECISION-MAKING

> *Although we appear to have free will, in fact, our choices have already been predetermined for us and we cannot change that.*
>
> FRANCIS CRICK, NEUROSCIENTIST[1]

Before you jump straight in to specific, targeted influence techniques, it is vital that you understand some of the key processes that underpin our human decision-making. In the following pages you'll find a synopsis of some of the most recent insights from cutting-edge studies in the fields of neuroscience and psychology. This knowledge will arm you with the building blocks you need to understand and influence your global audience.

DO YOU BELIEVE IN FREE WILL?

Until recently, the study of human behavior and motivation was considered the domain of philosophers and psychologists. In the past few decades, however, advances in neuroscientific technologies—such as brain imaging (EEG, PET, fMRI), single-neuron measurement, the study of brain-damaged patients (to gather information on how the brain works), TMS and DTI—have transformed the way in which we explore and interact with the brain, allowing us to start building a picture of how and why we behave in certain ways.

This has led not only to dramatic advances in the field of neuroscience itself but also increasing interest from sectors that have much to gain from acquiring this new knowledge. We're witnessing the dawn of a new kind of business, one that utilizes neuroscientific research to aid marketing, advertising and film industries. If results are anything to go by, this is a trend that will only gain momentum as technology advances.

When it comes to making big decisions that affect our lives, most of us like to think we're in the driving seat, but in reality, surprisingly few of the decisions we make are actually within our conscious control.

So, which comes first—thought or action?

By using EEGs to monitor brain activity during decision-making tasks, researchers have found that we actually become consciously aware of our intention to act a full 300 milliseconds after the relevant areas of our brain become active.[2] It's then an additional 200 milliseconds before we actually express the behavior overtly, which means that our conscious experience of free will happens only *after* the neural events that caused it.[3]

Put simply, your brain knows what you're going to do before you do. You only experience the intention (that leads you to an action) after your brain is already committed.

If you know which specialized system(s) and unconscious processes are engaged during decision-making, you can use this knowledge to shape behavior.

THREE THINGS YOU NEED TO KNOW ABOUT DECISION-MAKING

1 Your brain thinks in parallel

Most of your brain's decision-making processes occur in parallel, without your conscious awareness. Since your brain comprises an interconnected neural network, it's not unusual for one process to influence another seemingly unrelated process, with startling results. Let me give you an example.

CASE STUDY Want people to like you?
Give them a hot drink

Imagine that you've signed up to take part in a study exploring personality. You head to a beautiful campus, walk up to the building where it's taking place and enter the lobby, where a research assistant greets you with her clipboard, two textbooks and a hot cup of coffee.

You walk together to the elevator and, during the ride up to the fourth floor, she asks you to hold her cup for a moment while she writes down your name and the time. You hand her back her coffee and exit the elevator, where she guides you to the experiment room and gives you a "personality impression questionnaire" to complete.

The assistant asks you to read the description of an anonymous Person A who's industrious, skillful, intelligent, practical, cautious and determined. Your task is to rate this person on a scale of ten personality traits for how friendly and warm you think they are. Now, if you had experienced the scenario above, you would have been much more likely to rate Person A as friendlier than some of your peers. Why?

The actual experiment began long before you started filling out the questionnaire. In fact, it started at the very moment the researcher handed you her coffee. Like you, half the participants were handed a hot coffee to hold, but the other half were given an iced one. The difference? The people who held the hot cup, even for just a few moments, rated Person A as considerably warmer (more caring and generous) than their cold cup-holding counterparts.[4]

From one seemingly insignificant act, the participants' brains had mapped across the physical sensation of warmth to their perception of someone's personality—highlighting a surprisingly powerful, subconscious halo effect between two seemingly unrelated experiences.

It's not just our physical sense of comfort that can influence our subsequent responses either. In another intriguing study, a similar effect was observed when two groups of students were asked to rate a set of cartoons on how funny they were.[5] The first group was asked .to hold a pen between their teeth without allowing it to touch their lips (picture a dog carrying a bone). The second group was asked to hold the pen with their lips, in much the same way that you might smoke a cigarette.

The results were striking: those students who had held the pen between their teeth rated the cartoons as much funnier than their pouting peers. The reason was simple. By clenching the pen between their teeth, students from the first group had effectively been engaging many of the muscles they would normally use to smile. This straightforward, physical act was enough to influence their emotional state to such an extent that even the cartoons they read seemed subjectively funnier. So, the next time you're feeling down and you need a pick-me-up, try putting on a smile.

In case you were in any doubt, these experiments prove that we are not rational beings, as classical economists would have you believe. In fact, the reality is that we are malleable, impressionable creatures, whose behaviors can be heavily influenced by our situations and surroundings, without us even being aware of it.

It's not just a question of faulty thinking. Recent research shows that bizarre behaviors (such as mapping across a physical experience to an emotional state) often have a neural basis. For example, the insula, the part of the brain responsible for processing physical temperature, is ▶

also involved in processing interpersonal warmth, which would explain why we sometimes conflate the two, as in the hot coffee example above. Interestingly, the insula also plays an active role in our social emotions, such as empathy, trust, embarrassment and guilt, and it is this very same area that lights up when we feel socially rejected or excluded.[6, 7]

The fact that our brains seem to automatically reconcile unrelated, parallel actions (in this case, feeling the warmth of a hot drink and rating a person for friendliness) highlights the extent to which our automatic, deeply embedded responses influence and override our conscious decision-making. This effect is so strong that it persists even when we've been forewarned that external influences are at play.[8] Whether we like it or not, we just can't seem to get the better of our irrational minds.

CASE STUDY Nestlé's ad for Pure Life Water

Released: August 2003
Advertiser: Nestlé SA
Brand name: Pure Life
Product: Pure Life Water
Agency: D'arcy Shanghai
Country: China

KNOW WHO YOU'RE TARGETING

Although we are not yet at the technological stage where we can directly transmit physical sensations (such as warmth, taste and smell) to an end user, we can elicit similar responses by presenting our target audience with images and sounds that evoke the same responses.

A perfect example of this can be found in Nestlé's 2003 advertisement for Pure Life Water,[9] in which we, the viewers, are primed for thirst by being shown an endless expanse of desert. By exposing us to this parched, dry landscape, the ad effectively engages our brains to respond as if we were in actual danger of dehydrating. Even though we're watching the ad from the comfort of our own homes, our brains perceive the threat as real and subconsciously react by experiencing a motivational state of thirst. That's when Nestlé lands its implicit knockout punch—drink our product and you won't die. Yes it's simple, but it's also devastatingly effective.

Clearly these findings have potentially huge implications, especially for those of us in the business of shaping consumer behavior online. If you understand how non-conscious, subliminal "priming" effects work, you can use this knowledge to guide the behaviors and decisions of those around you. Suffice to say, when it comes to online persuasion, this is a very desirable skill to possess.

For instance, if you want your customers to take a particular action (such as recommend your services to their friends) and you have an understanding of how they function and decide, you can engineer your user experience to encourage this specific behavior.

Although certain people might tell you otherwise (and I would be wary of those who do), when it comes to the art of persuasion, there is no silver bullet. There are, however, many principles that you can employ to significantly increase your chances of success, the most influential of which we'll be exploring in this book.

---

2 Your brain is specialized

You've no doubt heard the myth that we only use 10 percent of our brains. Let me ask you this: do you really think you could function if 90 percent of your brain was removed? The notion is utterly ridiculous of course, especially when you consider that just a small amount of damage (such as that caused by a stroke or Parkinson's disease) can leave people with devastating long-term impairments. Or perhaps you believe that we only use 10 percent of our neurons at any given time. Well, think again. Even when they are not firing action potentials themselves, our nerve cells may still be receiving signals from other neurons. The truth is that we still know relatively little about the brain and how it works, but it is highly improbable that we would have developed such a large and complex organ if it didn't provide a clear evolutionary advantage.

There is another 10 percent figure involved in the discussion about the brain. Around 10 percent of your brain's cells are neurons. Responsible for responding to external stimuli, these cells are considered to be the most active and important in the brain. The other 90 percent of it is made up of glia (Greek for "glue") cells, which until very recently were thought only to fill a supporting role, providing insulation, structure and nutrients to the all-important neurons.

In an exciting breakthrough in 2011, researchers from Tel Aviv University discovered that, far from performing a simple structural role, glia cells are in fact crucial to our brain's plasticity—that is, how it learns, adapts and stores information. According to PhD student De Pittà, "Glia cells are like the brain's supervisors. By regulating the synapses, they control the transfer of information between neurons, affecting how the brain processes information and learns."[10] So, even if we only used the 10 percent of our brains that consist of neurons, we'd still be stuck, since we need the other 90 percent—the glia—for the brain to function.

Neurologist Gordon reinforced these findings. In an interview for *Scientific American MIND*, he explained that "we use virtually every part of the brain, and [most of] the brain is active almost all the time."[11] In other words, if you were to scan your brain over 24 hours, you'd find most of its regions are continually active—over the course of the day you would have used around 100 percent of your brain.

While this completely debunks the 10 percent brain myth, it does highlight an important fact about the brain's functionality: it uses multiple specialized systems to accomplish specific tasks. Research shows neurons that perform similar functions tend to be found in clusters, which means, for any given activity, we'll engage particular areas of the brain. As we saw earlier, some of these areas compute similar but different experiences (such as physical temperature and interpersonal warmth) and it's not unusual for people who develop specific abilities to significantly alter the size and structure of parts of their brains. Allow me to give you an example.

CASE STUDY The London cab driver

If you've ever taken a black cab through London's labyrinthine streets, you'll probably share my sense of awe at their superhuman GPS powers.

Unlike other cabbies, London's finest are required to know the city streets by heart (or, more accurately, by brain) and must undergo two to four years of rigorous mental training in order to pass "The Knowledge" and gain their license. This is no mean feat. New drivers are required to memorize 320 "runs" (routes) in order to learn the 25,000 streets and 20,000 landmarks within a 6-mile radius of Charing Cross—a challenge that would leave most of us quaking in our boots (especially when you consider that only 50 percent of candidates actually pass).

This particular ability has long been a source of fascination to media and pop psychologists alike, so it was a welcome relief when, in the year 2000, a group of neuroscientists from the University of London decided to investigate it.[12] The researchers gathered a group of London cabbies and took structural MRI scans of their brains. What they found was extraordinary.

These particular taxi drivers had larger memory centers (hippocampi) than their peers. What's more, the longer they had been driving a taxi, the larger their hippocampi were—meaning that these drivers' brains were adapting and expanding to cope with the cognitive demands of their jobs.

Couldn't they have simply been born with larger hippocampi and subsequently become cabbies? In order to determine cause and effect, the researchers decided to follow a group of 79 taxi driver trainees for 4 years and monitor any changes in their brains.[13] At the end of the study, MRI scans showed that the brains of the successful trainees had indeed changed. The part of the hippocampus that facilitates expert navigation had grown significantly, but the area that dealt with new spatial memories had actually shrunk. So it would seem that super-skills are possible—at a cost.

This study proves that our brains are not only specialized, but they are also adaptable and can evolve within our adult lifetimes to deal with the demands of our everyday lives.

---

3 Your brain's dual-core system

 Cognition by itself cannot produce action; to influence behavior, the cognitive system must operate via the affective system.
     COLIN CAMERER ET AL., BEHAVIORAL ECONOMISTS[14]

In his book titled *Thinking Fast and Slow*,[15] Daniel Kahneman (an eminent Princeton psychologist, Nobel Laureate and godfather of Behavioral economics) proposed that our brains rely on a metaphorical "dual-core" system to process information and make choices. Kahneman's model suggests that our actions and behaviors are driven by two different but vital processing systems. One is automatic (emotional) and the other is controlled (cognitive).[16] These two processes can be roughly distinguished by where they occur in your brain,[17] and together they form the backbone of our decision-making processes. If we understand how each system works, we can use this knowledge to make better decisions and influence the decisions of those around us.

According to Kahneman, System 1 (thinking fast) is intuitive and automatic and generally operates below the level of our conscious awareness.[18] It is in this unconscious setting that we undergo different "affective" (emotional) states, many of which motivate impulse reactions and feelings such as hunger, fear, sexual desire and pain. These states can even have a bearing on the way we perceive and remember things and can affect everything from our ability to learn to the goals we choose to pursue.[19]

According to psychologist Zajonc,[20] these are the same processes that motivate us to approach or avoid something—decisions on which we depend to survive. It's this system that instinctively swerves the car when a child walks out on to the road as well as realizes the boss is in a foul mood the moment he enters the room. It's our hunch, our intuition and it informs almost everything we do.

System 2 (thinking slow) is altogether more analytical, deliberate and rational; it is the mode that we employ to reason about the world. It's the system we use to consciously work out a math sum or fill out a tax return and it's usually pretty labor intensive. We like to think that System 2 runs the show, but it is, by its very nature, a "lazy" system that has to cherry pick what it will and won't attend to—we can't consciously analyze everything all the time. In fact, these controlled processes tend to kick in when our automatic processes get interrupted. This can happen when experiencing a strong visceral state (someone wrecks your car and you're livid), when we encounter an unexpected event (your mother-in-law drops by unannounced and you have to put on a smile) or even when we come up against an explicit challenge (solving a cryptic crossword in the Sunday paper).

In reality, it's System 1 that's in charge. System 1 is also biased, but, most of the time, it works just fine. It runs on heuristics (cognitive rules of thumb) to make its decisions. For instance, employing the principle "you get what you pay for" tends to be useful when having to make decisions in general (since things that are more inherently valuable tend to be more expensive), but it's also open to exploitation, especially in the absence of System 2's more rational mind.

When it comes to decision-making, System 1 will continually generate feelings, intuitions and intentions, which, if endorsed by System 2, will turn into beliefs and actions.

This interplay works well until we're asked to respond to something that violates our normal understanding of the world (a flying pig) or requires greater cognitive attention (your end-of-year report). At this point, it's System 2 that steps in, helping us to weigh up the facts (pigs can't fly, it must be an illusion) and respond appropriately (laugh it off).

Thinking v. feeling

 Where thought conflicts with emotion, the latter is designed by the neural circuitry in our brains to win.

RITA CARTER, SCIENCE WRITER[21]

Good decision-making is not just a question of pitting our rational minds against our intuition. Our thoughts are often strongly influenced by our feelings and, when pushed to explain the rationale behind decisions we've made on a "hunch," we tend to post-rationalize.

In reality, emotions are hard to control at a conscious level, so they tend to drive the choices we make—even when those choices fly in the face of logic. Yes, it's unsettling, but it comes down to human evolution: the emotional systems in our brains seem to have strong connections to our cognitive systems, so our emotions exert a great influence on our thoughts (as opposed to the other way round).[22]

If I asked you to picture someone "blind with rage," what image would spring to mind? Perhaps a mad, ax-wielding murderer—the archetypal villain and staple character of horror movies. Perhaps you would picture a wild, drunk soccer fan, red in the face with a dangerous look in his eyes—a man beyond the reach of reason. I am, of course, stereotyping to make a point, but this curious turn of phrase (along with others, such as "love is blind") hints at the enormous power that emotions can have over us, both in altering our subjective experience of the world and our capacity to respond to it. What's interesting is that it's not just extreme feelings that can alter our judgements—emotions of all kinds can influence the way we think and behave. For instance, if something makes us sad, we're much more likely to recall other sad memories and perceive risks as threatening, but make us angry and we're much more likely to take risks in the belief that they will pay off.[23]

While what we have looked at so far illustrates the effect that our emotions can have on our behaviors, the interplay between emotions and cognition actually goes both ways. For instance, the sense of pain you might experience from breaking your arm would probably feel quite different depending on whether you had injured it for a "good" cause (protecting your friend in a bar fight) or a "bad" cause (being mugged on your way home from work).

In fact, in one study, psychologists found that our feelings for a loved one can actually help to anaesthetise us against real physical pain. In a simple experiment, a team of psychologists from UCLA asked 25 women to look either at a photo of a stranger, their partner or an object while they received a painful heat stimulus to their forearms. Intriguingly, the women reported experiencing less pain while looking at photos of their partners, than when they were looking at pictures of an object or a stranger. Simply looking at a photo of their loved one reduced their physical pain![24]

While it may seem a bit voodoo, this dramatic effect illustrates the extent to which our physical, emotional and psychological processes are intertwined and it is for this reason that we are considering them here.

Beyond making us feel good or bad, emotions play a vital role in how we make decisions. When it comes to thinking about the things we want—whether it's a new Porsche 911 or better health—we're very good at rationalizing our emotions and persuading ourselves that what we *want* to happen *will* happen. This state of "motivated cognition"—the glitch in our systems that makes so-called "miracle cures" and Ponzi schemes seem so alluring—is also one of the main reasons so many of us turn to phony remedies or solutions when all else fails.

On the plus side, though, it may also be the reason why the placebo effect is so powerful. The truth is that, much of the time, we're haplessly unaware of why we make certain decisions. In fact, when we're asked to analyze why we prefer one object to another, this very process of rational introspection can actually block our emotional response and lead us to make poorer choices.[25] So, the next time you're considering making a purchase, it may be better to weigh up your options and then go with your gut.

In an online context, it pays to remember that we are emotional creatures and that if we want to engage with and influence our online audience we'll have to appeal to both their emotional and rational minds.

3 WHO'S ONLINE AND WHY?

No man is an island, entire of itself.

JOHN DONNE, POET[1]

As technology continues to advance at close to an exponential rate, it probably won't surprise you to know that more of us are going online, for a growing number of reasons. What you may not know is what this audience looks like or what they're doing. In the following pages we'll take a quick, concise look at who's online and why—this is your chance to identify any demographics that you might be missing out on.

At this point I must add that, due to the fluidity of online growth and markets, this small section of the book will inevitably be subject to change and the statistics presented herein will require revision as time elapses. I have included these pages to illustrate the changing face of online demographics and to highlight the importance of periodically analyzing your target audience. The more accurate your understanding of who is online, the more likely you will be able to identify and convert new customers.

WHO AND WHERE?

While more of us are going online than ever before, global penetration rates do still vary. To find out how much bang you'll get for your buck in different countries, take a look at the rates in Table 3.1.

Table 3.1 Global usage of the Internet[2]

Region	Penetration (% of population)	Growth (% 2000–2011)
North America	78.6	152.6
Canada	81.6	
USA	78.3	

Table 3.1 Continued

Region	Penetration (% of population)	Growth (% 2000–2011)
Oceania/Australia	67.5	214.0
Russia	61.5	
Europe	61.3	376.4
Norway	97.2	
Sweden	92.9	
Austria	74.8	
Germany	67.4	
UK	52.7	
Portugal	50.7	
France	50.3	
Italy	35.8	
Spain	30.7	
Latin America/Caribbean	39.5	1205.1
Brazil	79.2	
Mexico	36.9	
Middle East	35.6	2244.8
Israel	70.4	
Saudi Arabia	43.6	
Asia	26.2	789.6
Japan	80.0	
Hong Kong	68.7	
China	38.4	
India	10.2	
Africa	13.5	2988.4
Egypt	21.7	
South Africa	6.8	
World average	32.7	528.1

HOW?

Going mobile

At the Mobile World Congress 2012, Google's Head of Mobile Sales, Jason Spero, announced that around 1 billion of us now primarily access the Internet through a mobile device. With global Internet penetration rising above 30 percent, around a third of humanity is now officially online and more mobile than ever before (when organizations start announcing that more of us now own a mobile phone than a toothbrush,[3] you know something's going on).

While Internet access still varies greatly from one country to the next (97 percent in Norway versus 10 percent in India[4]), the rise of mobile Internet use in less affluent countries has led to a shift in how some of us are accessing and using the web. In fact, in Africa, mobile banking has become so popular that in December 2011 IBM signed deals worth $200 million to provide technology services to five Kenyan banks.[5] With more of us going online to shop, check our emails and socialize, the growth of mobile access looks set to continue.

Trends in technology are often led by the young and this current shift towards m-commerce is no exception. In the USA, nearly twice as many "millennials" (consumers currently aged 16–34) consider online shopping to be a vital convenience than older respondents,[6] and over 60 percent of students and young employees worldwide now consider their mobile device (laptop, smartphone, tablet) to be "the most important technology in their lives."[7]

Even children's entertainment is taking a hit, with more youngsters switching from TV to mobile Internet than ever before.[8] Gone are the days of sitting at home in front of the box, these mini consumers expect us to meet them on their terms and on their platform of choice. Failing to do so would be tantamount to business suicide.

Where the youth lead the way, the rest of us follow. If you're an Apple fan, it will come as no surprise that the number of Europeans who now own an iPad nearly doubled in 2012.[9] Although the UK currently leads this trend as the largest and fastest-growing European market, Italy, France and Germany are close behind, with the USA and China leading the global picture. In fact, when it comes to the cult of Apple, there seems to be no sign of it stopping. Yes, each device they launch is more seductive than the last, but the phenomenal success enjoyed by the iPad stems not just from its portability but also from the level of interactivity and onscreen aesthetics it affords its user. That and the fact that you have to physically stroke the thing to get it to work.

But looks aren't everything and, in a recent study, the BBC (online division) and Starcom MediaVest found that tablet owners consume a greater breadth and depth of news than their non-tablet-owning peers.[10] It seems that the device we use can, in fact, alter our level of online engagement. So, if your customers are connecting with you via a tablet, chances are that its interactive, visual nature will encourage a deeper level of engagement than that enjoyed by their desktop computer-using peers.

Go mobile

Whether your customers are reaching out to you via phone, tablet or laptop, if·you really want to influence them, you have to engage with them on their terms, in the most persuasive format possible. This means deploying websites and digital products that are tablet- and mobile-friendly. With more than half of us accessing social networks via our smartphones on a near daily basis,[11] making your business accessible through both mobile devices and social media sites is crucial if you want to get in front of a younger demographic.

If you think you can get away with ignoring the mobile market, think again: in the USA alone, half of all smartphone owners completed purchases via their phones while at home, with one in three making a purchase from their phones while actually in a store.[12] Whether we like it or not, the power of the mobile consumer is growing—a fact that is reflected in our preference for uncluttered, easy-to-navigate websites. This leaning towards design simplicity indicates that we're already tailoring online shopping experiences to touchscreen devices—after all, who wants to spend hours pecking away at a screen trying to get a website to respond?

WHY?

Shopping

Online shopping has got us flocking to e-stores in droves. In December of 2011 alone, Europeans spent a total of 19.3 million minutes on websites like Apple.com, Amazon and Otto Gruppe (Germany).[13] This Christmas surge marked a new chapter in online shopping, reflecting a growing acceptance of and trust in Internet transactions.

In the USA, deal-a-day websites are on the rise, attracting swathes of affluent mobile users, a third of whom gross a household income of $100,000 or more.[14] If you're thinking of going mobile, now's the time—this market has deep pockets and, as we'll see later in the book, the gamification (applying game design thinking to make applications more fun) of online shopping can be an exciting and lucrative way to engage your customers and boost your sales. (Incidentally, if you're wondering what time your customers are going online to shop, Wednesdays at 4 p.m. tend to be particularly busy, seeing an increase in shopping of 75 percent,[15] and evenings between 8 and 10 p.m. attract an influx of buyers across a whole range of categories.)[16]

Gamification is not the only way in which the face of online shopping is changing. Beyond the endless gossip and stalking opportunities that social media provides, our social sprawl is also influencing the way in which we buy.

Gone are the days of the silent consumer—we now expect communication, excitement and preferential treatment from our brands before we commit to them. We've moved firmly from the realm of one-night stands to full-on relationships and those businesses smart enough to court us properly might well earn our love for life.

Ever the ones to blaze a trail, when it comes to leveraging social principles to further their agenda, Facebook is king. In a bid to make marketing more inherently social, Facebook releases apps (such as Ads with Friends) that rely on the power of social proof (our tendency to follow the behaviors of the group) to persuade us to buy (see Chapters 13 and 14). From its track record, it's clear to see that basing your marketing strategies on the principles of social psychology not only works but can also generate millions of dollars in the process.

In fact, research by consumer insights giant Nielsen Wire found that social ads actually generate a 55 percent lift in recall compared with their non-social counterparts. Bolstered by the fact that most of us trust recommendations from personal acquaintances (with around half of us trusting consumer opinions posted online), this finding highlights the fact the social marketing can deliver a phenomenal return on investment.[17]

MAKE THIS WORK FOR YOU

Access all areas

I know this sounds obvious, but if you're selling products directly from your website, make sure that it renders well across all devices. This means making it text-light and easy to use.

Consumers want to be able to see what they're buying before handing over their cash, so make sure your product images are of a high enough resolution to look great whether on a 15-inch screen or a handheld smartphone. This can often mean getting your developers to create two sites—one for mobile devices and one for larger screens—but, if your market is predominantly mobile, then it's an investment that's well worthwhile.

Research, socializing and entertainment

Despite what you might think, it's not just social media and online shopping that are drawing the crowds. Checking our emails and searching for information remain the staples of online activity, with over 90 percent of us going online for these two reasons alone (USA).[18]

News and information sites enjoy a huge amount of traffic, with the largest European audiences coming from users aged 25 to 34.[19] While this younger group is certainly the biggest, engagement levels actually increase with age, peaking with people aged 55 and over.

When it comes to access, more tablet and smartphone owners are using their devices to research products (80 percent) than purchase them (41 percent[20]), and simultaneous consumption of TV and tablets is becoming the norm[21] making information junkies of us all. The fact that Google now handles over 1 billion search queries every day[22] indicates a truly unquenchable thirst for knowledge.

That being said, when it comes to "searching" behaviors, not all are created equal. Researchers have found that men spend on average 20 minutes more on news sites than women, possibly because the ladies are otherwise occupied updating their Facebook profiles and pinboards. I'm not being sexist here— many believe that Pinterest's sharp rise to fame is due to a heady combination of gossip and social media—a cocktail that has earned it the title of being the "first major social networking site to be driven by women."[23] While Pinterest's three founders are all men, its US members are overwhelmingly female (enjoying themes such as crafts, interior design and fashion), in comparison to the distinctively male majority in the UK (with interests ranging from venture capital, design and web stats to PR).[24]

Whatever gender differences exist across certain social platforms, it seems that we simply can't get enough of networking. When a species collectively spends 6.7 billion hours on social media in one month alone,[25] chances are it's because they're hard-wired for socialization.

It turns out that we are. The fact that we are the descendants of highly social ancestors may go a long way to explaining why our species has thrived where others have failed. It may also explain why the lure of Facebook and Twitter is simply too strong for most of us to resist. After all, if even our neural networks are cooperative, what chance do we have of coming away from social media unscathed?

Even the youngest among us are at it. In a study carried out by the London School of Economics for the European Commission,[26] half of the UK's 9- to

12-year-olds were said to be online, dropping to 38 percent Europewide. With more youngsters being granted access to mobile devices at an increasingly early age, it's likely that this figure is set to rise. In fact, we're already seeing boys and girls refer to the Internet before making any purchases, and research shows that boys are more likely to seek this kind of validation than girls. They're also more likely to be influenced by the reviews and comments they find online.[27] It's no coincidence that this influx of younger netizens has risen alongside the popularity of social online gaming. What is surprising is the fact that these gamers are coming from the world's emerging markets.[28]

Wherever we come from and however our social platforms evolve, we can be sure of one thing—as long as humans are driving technology, we will continue to exploit it to meet our social needs. For those of you smart and brave enough to harness it, social media can offer you a way to connect with your online audience like never before.

MAKE THIS WORK FOR YOU

Socialize

If you're not already using social media to engage with your customers, now's the time. As we'll see later in the book (Chapter 12), going social can be a great way of building your reputation and boosting sales—and it doesn't have to be labor-intensive to get results.

Where possible, socialize your products/services by allowing users to share them across their preferred social platforms. A great tool for integrating this functionality into your website can be found on ShareThis. com[29] and you can streamline your social efforts by checking out which networks (Twitter, foursquare and so on) your users prefer to use.

You can also generate influence by taking advantage of the human penchant for research. Writing regular articles on a specialist subject is a great way to build your reputation and add value to your brand. Not only will it boost your website's ranking in search results but it will also establish you as an expert—you'd be surprised at how many new clients you can attract simply by writing a good post.

4 WHO ARE YOU TARGETING?

> *You have brains in your head. You have feet in your shoes. You can steer yourself any direction you choose. You're on your own. And you know what you know. And YOU are the one who'll decide where to go.*
>
> DR. SEUSS, OH, THE PLACES YOU'LL GO![1]

Before you can successfully ascertain your target audience, you have to have a clear understanding as to the purpose and identity of your business (for example, my core purpose in my consultancy, The web Psychologist, is to empower people to become more influential online). If you have never developed a marketing strategy or if it has been a while since you updated an existing one, you may find it useful to complete the questionnaires provided here.

Take a few moments to carefully consider each question below. The answers you provide (in particular to those regarding your target market) will directly determine how you'll implement the principles in this book to influence and successfully engage with your online audience.

WHO ARE YOU AS A BUSINESS?

1 What are your core values as an individual?

2 What compelled you to start/join your business?

3 What are your company's core values?

4 What specific need(s) do you solve?

5 What is your primary goal for your business?

6 Who are your competitors?

7 How do you differ from your competitors?

8 What is unique about your service/product?

9 What would happen if you did not provide this service/product?

10 What would you like to gain from the knowledge within this book? *(For example, make more money, increase your market share, become a key influencer within your field, enhance your reputation.)*

WHO IS YOUR TARGET MARKET?

1 What is the age range of the customers who want your service/product?

2 Which gender would be most interested in this service/product?

3 What is the income level of your potential customers?

4 What level of education do they have?

5 Is this a service/product they need or is it a luxury item?

6 How will they use this product/service?

7 What do your customers value most? *(Easy availability? Low price? Personalized attention? Special features?)*

8 Is this an impulse buy or something they are saving for?

9 Where do they get most of their decision-making information? Do they research the Internet, newspapers, books or television?

10 Where are your clients located? Locally? Globally?

Now that you have identified the key elements of your identity as a business and the potential profile of your target audience, let's take a look at how this knowledge sits within the wider context of cultural quirks and the global marketplace.

5 CULTURAL QUIRKS

> *Those designers who better understand the preferences for their target online audience are more likely to achieve success in highly competitive online markets.*
>
> DIANNE CYRA ET AL., PSYCHOLOGISTS[1]

Whether or not you're aware of it, your culture forms the foundation of your behavior, your thoughts, even your feelings.[2] It informs and influences the language(s) you speak, the art you enjoy and the music you listen to. Culture shapes the social norms that you adhere to, the attitudes you express and the beliefs that you hold. In short, it is "a shared set of values that influence societal perceptions, attitudes, preferences, and responses."[3]

This crucial form of cultural transmission is as old as humanity itself and you can observe it in action today. Travel to any community in the world, and you will find people sharing and teaching their culture's social map to one another, shaping the values and behaviors of generations to come. It is this vital pro-cess that distinguishes one society from the next and differentiates your culture from that of your fellow humans living on the other side of the world.[4] In an online marketplace, it is your insight into the cultural sensibilities of your audience that will determine how much influence you can wield.

GLOCALIZATION AND ADAPTATION

> *Glocalization: A global outlook adapted to local conditions.*
>
> PROFESSOR ROLAND ROBERTSON, SOCIOLOGIST[5]

In a globally connected world, we're no longer simply exposed to elements from within our own culture—for the first time in our history, huge swathes of the Earth's population are now being exposed to the cultures of our neighbors, near and far. The very fact that Google Translate is used hundreds of millions of times a week in over 52 different languages[6] hints at the fact that we're living in increasingly globalized times. This has led to some fascinating dialogues and to some even more fascinating research.

One of the intriguing effects of this interconnectedness can be observed in local communities that have adapted to online globalisation. Rather than allowing themselves to be assimilated into a generic online culture (as many predicted would happen), many communities have, instead, co-opted foreign values and incorporated them into their own modus operandi. They have effectively taken neutral online tools and adapted them to fit their cultural needs, creating a "glocalization" effect.

It's not just local cultures who are doing the adapting—some of the most successful companies have been taking advantage of this phenomenon for years, by designing culture-specific websites to target markets from different countries with power and precision. In fact, there is research dating from as early as 1995 that documents the effectiveness of this strategy[7] and, as more of us gain access to the Internet, this is a trend that is surely set to continue.

Although glocalization plays a large role online, it's interesting to note that this phenomenon isn't just web-specific. A friend of mine once told me a story about a business he had set up, selling small, portable motorbikes to rural communities in India. He had started the venture in the hope of providing an essential, affordable means of transport to people in isolated areas, and it turned out that these bikes were a big hit.

After watching his business grow for a while, he decided to go back to India and visit some of the communities to whom he'd sold these bikes. What he found when he got there was quite unexpected. Instead of using the motorbikes for transport, many of the communities were using the engines to power their water pumps and irrigation projects.

On making this discovery, our businessman changed his product to reflect the needs of his local market and, in so doing, revolutionized his business, making a lot of money in the process.

Why is this story relevant? Well, the success of any business rests on its ability to engage and respond to its target market. Equally, if you wish to be influential online, you must research your audience and understand their culture. Yes, even if that culture is your own. This critical knowledge will provide the foundations you need to build your online business and secure its future success.

One of the most high-profile companies to have successfully glocalized their brand is Coca-Cola—it now supplies over 3,500 products to more than 200 countries worldwide.[8] Its branding and marketing has been so successful that the name "Coca-Cola" is recognized by 94 percent of the world's population and is now the most widely recognized word after "OK." (Intriguingly, in China, the characters for Coca-Cola mean "delicious and happy" and, in Hong Kong, Coke is sometimes served hot as a remedy for colds.[9] Who knew?!) While we can't all be the next Coca-Cola, the online success its enjoyed does illustrate the importance of a strategic, reflexive marketing approach as well as a good product.

The lesson here? If you respond to culture, you can influence it, too.

Not only does Coca-Cola glocalize its product packaging and websites, but it even tailors its drinks to the taste preferences of the countries it's supplying. The Coke you order in London on a hot summer's day (we do get hot summers on occasion) will be physically different from the Coke you might drink while on vacation in the Seychelles. While the company that produces the Coke is the same, the target market in each country is different, so, therefore, is the product.

It's a perfect example of sophisticated supply and demand and this short story demonstrates it beautifully. In Papua New Guinea, Coca-Cola had long been a popular drink, but, without much access to refrigerators, it had been served warm, off the shelf, for decades. Wanting to boost its sales, Coca-Cola decided to introduce refrigerators to all its vendors and, for the first time, Coke was served cold.

What happened? Sales plummeted. Despite the soaring popularity that ice-cold Cokes enjoyed throughout the rest of the world, in Papua New Guinea the refrigerated version of this drink simply wasn't the norm. Coca-Cola learned its lesson, removed the refrigerators from its vendors and returned the warm Coca-Cola-selling market to its natural balance, restoring its sales and customer satisfaction in the process.

It's not just offline that Coca-Cola glocalizes its product. Take a look at the following screengrabs of its websites throughout the world to see some design glocalization in action. (I originally screengrabbed these when I'd just started writing this book and have since had to replace all the images as the sites have been updated. The most interesting change was to China's website, which had previously been in HTML and justified to the top left of the screen. While the new design is still relatively simple, perhaps its increased interactivity reflects the growing Internet access and broadband speeds available in China.)

The bottom line here is that if you want to run a successful, global online business, you need to adopt a diverse, evidence-based range of targeted design strategies as part of your focused marketing program. This will empower you to establish a desirable brand image in the minds of all your clients, wherever they may be.

Coca-Cola's Caribbean website

Coca-Cola's Chinese website

Coca-Cola's German website

Coca-Cola's Italian website

CULTURE: "SOFTWARE OF THE MIND"

> *Culture is defined as the collective mental programming of the human mind which distinguishes one group of people from another.*
> PROFESSOR GEERT HOFSTEDE, PSYCHOLOGIST[10]

What I hope to have demonstrated with the case study of Coca-Cola is that global success is dependent on catering to cultural sensibilities. It's easy to get lazy and design a "one size fits all" website or engage in the social media channel that's native to your own country—but if you want to influence a global audience, you need a more targeted approach.

The following pages will provide you with a breakdown of six different psychological dimensions that influence (and identify) a culture's preferences and traits and we'll look at how you can apply this knowledge online to improve the performance of your website and digital strategies.

In 1990, having researched the cultural traits of over 70 countries for more than four decades, Dutch psychologist Professor Hofstede released his magnum opus—a seminal book titled *Cultures and Organizations: Software of the Mind.*[11] Originally published in 1991, this hefty work provided a concise, evidence-based view on how national cultures differ in their tolerance of ambiguity, inequality and their preference for assertiveness versus modesty. Hofstede's work focused on the essential patterns of thinking, feeling and behaving that we express by late childhood and provided a unique insight into the way in which different cultures manifest themselves through the values, symbols, rituals and narratives they hold dear.

These cultural dimensions appear to be hundreds, even thousands of years old and research shows that they have even remained stable during the huge technological shifts of the past 20 years. It is likely that the characteristics of the most traditional cultures will continue to remain constant and relevant even in the midst of our new, globally connected era.

In the following pages we'll explore the six dimensions in turn and identify how you can use this information to generate online influence within the specific culture(s) of your target market:

1 Power Distance

2 Individualism v. Collectivism

3 Masculinity v. Femininity

4 Uncertainty Avoidance

5 Long-term Orientation

6 Indulgence v. Restraint.

1 Power Distance (PDI)

The first dimension, power distance, deals with our cultural attitudes towards inequality. It measures the extent to which the less powerful members within our society will expect and accept unequal power distribution.

Countries that have a high power distance index (PDI) tend to experience huge divides between the richest and the poorest (in both salary and status), their institutions usually have tall hierarchies and political power is centralized. Russia is a good example of this—it sits among the top 10 percent of the most power distant societies in the world and its predilection for dictatorial leadership (and the societal inequality that follows) is reflected in a whopping PDI score of 93.

Countries with a low PDI, however, tend to place a higher value on equality, possessing flatter institutional hierarchies and smaller differences in status and salaries. In the UK, for instance, we have a low PDI of 35, reflecting a culture that (despite having a monarchy) strives to minimize inequality with institutions such as the NHS and housing for all. Weirdly, this number is actually lower among the higher classes, flying in the face of our historical class system and underlining what we like to think of as a very British sense of fair play. To see where different countries rank, see Table 5.1.

Table 5.1 Global PDI rankings

	PDI score	Country
High Power Distance	95	Saudi Arabia
	93	Russia
	81	Mexico
	80	China
	77	India
	70	Egypt
	69	Brazil
	68	Hong Kong
	68	France
	64	Africa (E)[12]
	63	Portugal
	57	Spain
Moderate Power Distance	54	Japan
	50	Italy
	49	Africa (S)
Low Power Distance	40	USA
	39	Canada
	38	Australia
	35	UK
	35	Germany
	31	Sweden
	31	Norway
	13	Israel
	11	Austria

In the interests of brevity, the selection of countries listed in Table 5.1 represent a summary of a much larger inventory[13] (For a comprehensive list, visit www. geerthofstede.eu.)

High Power Distance score

What to do if the majority of your audience comes from a country with a high PDI score.

- **Order, order** Emphasize order within your website by clearly defining the hierarchy of content and using social roles to organize information. You can do this by restricting access to certain areas of the site according to the seniority of your users (such as making a director's forum password-protected and available only to those with the relevant level of authority).

- **National pride** Use cultural and national symbols that reflect the social or moral order of your target audience, such as specific colors, metaphors and national icons. If you were designing a website for a Chinese audience, this might include using colors from the Chinese flag (red and yellow) and a symmetrical design that matches the aesthetic of the national architecture.

- **Speak as you're spoken to** If you're using social media to engage with a high-PDI market, be very careful to observe the cultural mores. Breaking rank and using overly familiar language with people whom you don't know can be problematic, especially when it comes to business.

- **Stamp of approval** The use of endorsements from experts and authority figures can be very persuasive and, where relevant, official stamps and certifications can add a much-needed level of credibility for high-PDI consumers.

MAKE THIS WORK FOR YOU

Low Power Distance score

What to do if the majority of your audience comes from a country with a low PDI score.

- **Keep it clean** Your customers will expect transparency, disclosure and equal access to the content on your website. The exception to this rule is if you have certain areas that are for paying subscribers only, in which case the ability to subscribe to that section should be made available to all.

- **Web-thinking** Countries with a low PDI are more likely to search laterally for the information they want, which may explain why non-hierarchical platforms such as YouTube, Twitter and Pinterest tend to come from developers in low-PDI countries. When high-PDI populations adopt such platforms, the resulting tension (between the flat social structure of the online world and the strict hierarchy of the offline society) can lead to violent and extreme reactions from that country's established political powers, such as those witnessed during Iran's Green Revolution and the Arab Spring.

- **Meritocracy rules** While people from low-PDI countries do respond to the heuristic of authority, they are much more likely to respect someone whose merit is based on academic or professional credentials rather than inherited (class or caste) status. They are also more likely to value the opinions of their fellow citizens. Therefore, if you wish to add credibility to your website, include endorsements from experts and testimonials from happy customers.

2 Individualism v. Collectivism (IDV)

This dimension addresses the degree to which a culture's members are interdependent and looks at whether people define their self-image in terms of "I" (themselves) or "we" (the group).

Cultures that score highly on individualism (IDV), such as the USA, UK and Australia, tend to have loose-knit communities that prize autonomy and expect people to take care of themselves. Societal responsibility only extends as far as one's immediate family and friends and people tend to have a high level of geographic mobility. In the USA, for example, there is limited free healthcare, insurance rates are high and businesses expect their employees to be self-reliant. In fact, in the business world, transactions between strangers are the norm and hiring decisions tend to be based on a person's individual merit. Like Americans, people from individualist countries value freedom, personal time and challenge, and are likely to be motivated by extrinsic factors such as the end of year bonus or a bigger salary.

China, however, has a very low IDV score (20), reflecting its cultural preference for larger, cohesive social networks, in which the needs of the group are placed before one's own. In collectivist cultures like this, an individual's preferences and behaviors will be heavily influenced by the opinions of his or her family, friends, peers and wider social group.

Non-conformity can result in rejection, leaving individuals "rudderless and with a sense of intense emptiness,"[14] which may be why there was such a media storm when Google refused to allow its Chinese Google+ users to use pseudonyms (vital in protecting their users' real identities).

In collectivist cultures, physical conditions are important and intrinsic rewards, such as mastery and the acquisition of skills, are strong motivators. With regard to business, employers tend to offer their employees a high level of protection in exchange for loyalty and relationships are often at the center of hiring policies.

See Table 5.2 for a selection of IDV rankings.

Table 5.2 Global IDV rankings

	IDV score	Country
Highly Individualist	91	USA
	90	Australia
	89	UK
	80	Canada
	76	Italy
	71	France
	71	Sweden
	69	Norway
	67	Germany
	65	Africa (S)
Moderately Individualist	55	Austria
	54	Israel
	51	Spain
Collectivist	48	India
	46	Japan
	39	Russia
	38	Brazil
	30	Mexico
	27	Africa (E)
	27	Portugal
	25	Egypt
	25	Hong Kong
	25	Saudi Arabia
Highly Collectivist	20	China

Individualism

What to do if the majority of your audience comes from a country with a high IDV score.

- **Reward your users** Motivate users to take specific actions by encouraging a sense of personal achievement. This system of reward is one of the reasons behind the popularity of games such as SimCity, in which the player's success depends on his or her ability to complete certain goals within a certain timeframe. Although less exciting, LinkedIn employs a similar, personalized reward system: it uses a progress bar to encourage members to complete their profiles.

- **You're unique** Individualist cultures tend to view difference as exciting, so focus on communicating what's new and unique about your business. What's your unique selling point? How are you different from your competitors? What makes you a game-changer?

- **Give them a challenge** Competitions can be a great way to engage with an individualist audience and promote your business. Giving your users a sense of challenge and a tangible call to action can help create rapport and establish a sense of excitement around your brand.

- **Causing a ruckus** In terms of the language you use, cultures with a high IDV score tend to respond well to controversial speech and extreme claims. These audiences quite like being shocked (it's practically requisite for viral videos) and, as long as you don't overstep the mark (and can back up any legal claims), it's a great way to connect with your market.

- **In it to win it** When using images on your website, appeal to the individualist by including happy images and material symbols of success. While we all want to feel loved and that we belong, one of the reasons lifestyle ads do so well in individualist countries is they get us to buy into their vision of autonomous success—the fast car, big house, beautiful body ... Since individualist cultures tend to favor youth, you can reflect this bias by using photos of young, attractive individuals to draw people's attention.

▶

- **Private eye** People from individualist cultures tend to be more comfortable with sharing information that differentiates them from the group, so if you wish to collect data from this kind of audience you can request it overtly. Furthermore, such cultures tend to rely on media outlets as their primary news source, so if you're going to promote your brand it can help to run a public media campaign alongside your social media strategy.

MAKE THIS WORK FOR YOU

Collectivism

What to do if the majority of your audience comes from a country with a low IDV score.

- **Group dynamics** Relationships are at the heart of collectivist cultures, therefore if you wish to engage this audience, you need to approach them en masse and provide them with a service or platform that they can use collectively.

- **Morality** Whereas individualist cultures tend to value truth and science over a fixed sense of morality, in collectivist cultures it is important to respect the moral tenets and social sensibilities of your audience. As a rule of thumb, any communications and campaigns you launch should emphasize relationships and honor the traditions and history of your audience's culture.

- **Represent** When using images to sell your products and communicate your brand, you can increase their impact by using photos of your product taken in the context of the group. In some collectivist cultures (such as Iran and some Arab countries), it is forbidden to show images of women, and overt expressions of happiness may be frowned on. So, unless you want to alienate your market, make sure you do your research beforehand.

- **There's no "I" in team** With regard to language use, collectivist cultures tend to speak in terms of "we" and, in some cases, drop the "I" from sentences altogether (for example in Spanish, "I love you" is "te quiero," as opposed to "yo te quiero"). In fact, English is the only language in which "I" is capitalized. So, when you're engaging with a collectivist audience, make sure you reflect this in your language. If in doubt, ask a native speaker to write your copy for you or employ the services of a company like OBAN Multilingual,[15] who do a fantastic job of "glocaliz-ing" website content for businesses with a global client base.

- **Wisdom comes with age** Collectivist cultures tend to favor the wisdom and experience that age brings, so if you wish to come across as authoritative and knowledgeable, it may help to bear this in mind. You can boost your perceived credibility through association, by includ-ing images and testimonials of older citizens and established industry leaders.

- **Keep it private** With regard to personal information, cultures with a low IDV score tend to protect information that differentiates them from the wider group. When requesting user information on websites, make sure that you only ask for the bare minimum and provide clear cues as to the security and privacy of your site (see Chapter 19). You need to assure these users that their information is safe with you and that it won't be passed on to any third parties.

3 Masculinity (MAS) v. Femininity

This dimension tends to raise eyebrows, but only if you're from a "masculine" cul-ture. So, if your society is of a masculine persuasion, prepare for some political incorrectness.

Based on traditional gender roles, Hofstede describes "masculine" cultures as ones in which people express distinct (stereotypical) gender roles—that is, women are tender, modest and focused on quality of life and men are tough, assertive and concerned with material success. "Masculine" societies like Japan favor assertiveness, heroism and achievement and measure success through material rewards (apparently they like the bling). In terms of business, these countries can be highly competitive and enjoy a good challenge. They value their earnings and career advancement and strive for recognition.

"Feminine" cultures, however, such as Norway and Sweden, favor a much more blurred, pick-and-mix attitude towards gender roles, preferring a society in which quality of life and tenderness towards others is encouraged in everyone. With a much stronger focus on relationships and consensus, "feminine" societies orientate towards the home, social cohesion and a good standard of life for everybody. They value cooperation and employment security and tend to provide more willingly for the weak.

Where would you expect your country to rank on this scale? See Table 5.3 to find out.

Table 5.3 Global MAS rankings

	MAS score	Country
Highly Masculine	95	Japan
	79	Austria
	70	Italy
	69	Mexico
	66	UK
	66	Germany
	66	China
	63	Africa (S)
	62	USA
	61	Australia
	60	Saudi Arabia
Moderately Masculine	57	Hong Kong
	56	India
	52	Canada
Neither Masculine nor Feminine	49	Brazil
	47	Israel
Moderately Feminine	45	Egypt
	43	France
	42	Spain
	41	Africa (E)
	36	Russia
	31	Portugal
Highly Feminine	8	Norway
	5	Sweden

Masculine

What to do if the majority of your audience comes from a country with a high MAS score.

- **Free the inner explorer** When designing your website's navigation, give your users greater control and the ability to explore. If needs be, you can create multiple levels of sub-pages and, as long as your content is engaging, this can encourage users to spend longer on your site.

- **Rich media** Enrich your website's offering by using interactive features such as animations, videos and graphics. Motion is a great way to catch attention and masculine cultures respond well to exciting, active user experiences.

- **Role-play** Traditionally, masculine societies tend to like clear-cut roles and distinctions, so make sure your audience can understand quickly and explicitly whom you are targeting—in terms of their age, gender and status. For instance, if you're selling pharmaceutical products to China, where the medical profession is dominated by women, you may wish to use images of female doctors. If, on the other hand, you were selling these products to the USA, photos of male doctors would better reflect your audience.

- **Playing games** If you want to gamify your website's user experience, this is your market. Take a look at Coca-Cola's website for Japan[16] (the highest scoring culture for masculinity) and you'll see it has loads of moving parts and game elements to keep its market engaged and interested. Masculine cultures are competitive and enjoy challenges, especially goal-orientated ones. Running limited-time offers and competitions can work well, not only for attracting new clients but also for establishing your business as engaging and exciting.

Feminine

What to do if the majority of your audience comes from a country with a low MAS score.

- **Quality of life** When you're targeting a culturally feminine audience (and I don't necessarily mean a female one), emphasize the core qualities of your offering in terms of how it can benefit the wider group. Focusing on relationships and how you can improve people's quality of life will help you to connect more deeply with your audience and boost your credibility.

- **Don't project** If you come from a traditionally masculine culture, be careful not to project your concepts of gender roles on to any characters or images you might use in your branding or website content. Always do your research first and, when in doubt, ask the locals what they associate with each gender before building these traits into your messaging.

- **Keep it collaborative** Mutual cooperation goes a long way with this audience, so asking your customers to provide valuable feedback in return for information or a free trial can be a great way of engaging with them and improving your product/services. You can also take advantage of this by building in a customer support forum, in which your clients can share tips, experiences and advice. It shows that you care about the community and that you're committed to providing a collective space for support.

- **Pretty social** Make your website visually appealing by reflecting your audience's aesthetic preferences. Uncluttered sites tend to work well and, if you're using images select those that emphasize relationships, collaboration and the wider community.

4 Uncertainty Avoidance (UAI)

The uncertainty avoidance index (UAI) measures how uncomfortable we are with ambiguity. The truth is that none of us can predict the future, and when it comes to accepting this reality some cultures find it easier than others.

In fact, our ability to deal with ambiguity has even been related to specific structures in the brain. During a study commissioned by Colin Firth (yes, *that* Colin Firth), a group of neuroscientists from UCL discovered that Conservatives had more grey matter in the amygdala (see page 6), whereas Liberals had more in the anterior cingulate cortex (part of the brain responsible for cognitive flexibility).[17] Based on these findings, the researchers proposed that individuals who have a large amygdala would be more sensitive to fear and disgust and would therefore be more inclined to hold Conservative beliefs. Although it is tricky to establish which came first, the brain structure or the belief, it is fair to say that people differ greatly in their ability to deal with the unknown, and the culture to which we belong can have a huge impact on our overall perspective.

For instance, in countries with high UAI scores, such as Portugal and Russia, people tend to feel threatened by uncertainty and deal with this discomfort by erecting rigid codes of conduct and adopting strict beliefs. These cultures tend to fear the unusual and perceive unorthodox ideas or behaviors as dangerous. Rates of suicide, incarceration and alcoholism are typically quite high in these societies.

People from such cultures often expect organizations and relationships to be clearly predictable and easy to interpret. They tend to be emotionally expressive and "talk with their hands"[18] and aggressive displays of emotion are not uncommon. Formality and punctuality are important and strict rules and rituals are *de rigueur*.

In contrast, cultures that are uncertainty *accepting* tend to be adaptable and entrepreneurial and dislike the kinds of uncompromising institutions and laws favored by uncertainty avoidant nations. It is in these cultures that you can expect to find a great amount of innovation and liberalism, coupled with a high caffeine intake, a higher rate of heart disease and the belief that emotions should be understated.

Although I am, of course, biased, to my mind it is no coincidence that Sir Timothy Berners-Lee, inventor of the World Wide web and the first truly universal language of HTML, hailed from one of the most uncertainty accepting countries in the world—the UK. Well known for their "stiff upper lip" and unrelenting ability to "muddle through," the British are typically quite comfortable with ambiguous situations. Perhaps this is why the UK comprises one of the most multicultural and secular societies in the world (which, if you score high on UAI, you may not see as such a good thing).

When it comes to relating to your audience online, the degree to which it avoids uncertainty can make a big difference to the way in which it will respond to your website. The key here is to understand your customers' tendencies and behaviors so that you can make it easy for them to relate to you. After all, good rapport and affinity are the foundations of influential relationships. See Table 5.4 to see where countries are in the global UAI rankings.

Table 5.4 Global UAI rankings

	UAI score	Country
High Uncertainty Avoidant	104	Portugal
	95	Russia
	92	Japan
	86	France
	86	Spain
	82	Mexico
	81	Israel
	80	Egypt
	80	Saudi Arabia
	76	Brazil
	75	Italy
	70	Austria
Uncertainty Avoidant	65	Germany
	52	Africa (E)
	51	Australia
	50	Norway
	49	Africa (S)
	48	Canada
Uncertainty Accepting	46	USA
	40	India
	35	UK
	30	China
	29	Hong Kong
	29	Sweden

MAKE THIS WORK FOR YOU

Uncertainty Avoidant

What to do if the majority of your audience comes from a country with a high UAI score.

– **Less is more** Navigation should be clearly structured and labelled, the user journey predictable and assuring. Pop-up ads and links that open up in new windows should be avoided and it is wise to limit your users' choices to the essentials. Any non-vital information is likely to be seen as redundant and misleading, so try to keep your website uncluttered and formal.

- **Clarity is key** Any images you use should clearly reflect who you are as a business and what products or services you offer. Again, avoid ambiguous imagery and, if you are using photos of people, make sure that their roles or status are clearly visible and that these reflect the expectations and norms of your market.

- **Keep it simple** When in doubt, keep it nice and simple. Use clear language to communicate with your audience and avoid using ambiguous terms. Carefully selected metaphors can be a great way to clarify your message and communication should also remain fairly formal.

- **Careful communication** In high-UAI cultures the use of social media can be a source of contention, so before you engage in any tweeting, make sure that it's appropriate. Unwanted communication can damage your reputation and your business.

- **Plan ahead** If you want your users to follow a particular path of action, give them an overview of what they can expect to reduce any ambiguity. Providing a clear sitemap can be a welcome addition, as can tips to help reduce any user errors. FAQ sections are particularly useful.

- **Paint by numbers** You can also reduce ambiguity by using color, font sizes and typography as identifying markers on your website. For example, if you sell a wide range of electrical goods, you could make the information easier to digest by color-coding home appliances blue and music-related goods red (see Chapter 11 for information on cultural meanings of color).

MAKE THIS WORK FOR YOU

Uncertainty Accepting

What to do if the majority of your audience comes from a country with a low UAI score.

- **Tell it to me straight** Uncertainty-accepting cultures tend to enjoy open-ended dialogue and communicating in plain language. If this is the audience you're targeting, use social media to connect informally with your customers but avoid expressing yourself in overly emotional terms. The flexibility and intimacy inherent in platforms such as

▶

Pinterest, Twitter and Facebook can work well with this market, and can make a dramatic difference to levels of customer engagement.

- Risk-takers Low UAI-scoring cultures tend to frown on overprotection, preferring instead to roam free and take greater risks when browsing. This is reflected in the aptly named platform StumbleUpon,[19] an American-born platform the *raison d'être* of which is to help its members discover new, exciting websites and content from across the web.

- It's complicated With regard to content, uncertainty accepting societies don't mind a bit of complexity. A wide choice of content, actions and choices appeal to this audience's sense of adventure, though when it comes to getting users to pursue one particular course of action, the best results are still achieved by being more directive (see Chapter 18).

- Layer your information In such cultures, navigation tends to be structured into dropdown menus, allowing for easy chunking of information and a larger number of sublevel pages. Providing a search box on your website can give these explorers the freedom they need to find what they're looking for, while linking out to other web content and pages is standard practice.

5 Long-term Orientation (LTO)

Here we examine the human search for virtue. Based on Confucian dynamism, this dimension was added in 1991 and was developed from the combined work of Geert Hofstede and Michael Bond.

Cultures with a long-term orientation (such as China and Hong Kong) tend to base their values around Confucianism and consider truth to be relative and context-dependent. These cultures usually believe that acquiring skills, getting an education, working hard and being frugal earns a virtuous life. Achievement comes from being patient and persevering and saving for the future is considered a worthwhile investment. The family is seen as the blueprint for all social organizations, meaning that the older and more male you are, the greater authority you wield. Unlike Western philosophy's golden rule—"do unto others as you would have others do unto you"—long-term-orientated cultures opt for the more pacifist precept of *not* treating others as you would *not* like to be treated.

In contrast, short-term-orientated (typically Western) cultures, such as Spain, enjoy living in the moment and like to achieve quick results without too much concern for the future. Keeping up with the Joneses is an important motivator, as is the search for "absolute truth," and these cultures tend to have a great respect for traditions. Here, the golden rule does apply and people are encouraged to find personal fulfillment through creativity and self-actualization. See Table 5.5 to see where other countries are in the global LTO rankings.

Table 5.5 Global LTO rankings

	LTO score	Country
Long-term Orientated	118	China
	96	Hong Kong
	80	Japan
	65	Brazil
	61	India
Short-term Orientated	44	Norway
	39	France
	34	Italy
	31	Australia
	31	Austria
	31	Germany
	30	Portugal
	29	USA
	25	Africa (E)
	25	UK
	23	Canada
	20	Sweden
	19	Spain
No data available	34	Africa (S)
	36	Saudi Arabia
	7	Egypt
	38	Israel
	24	Mexico
	81	Russia

MAKE THIS WORK FOR YOU

Long-term Orientated

What to do if the majority of your audience comes from a country with a high LTO score.

▶

- **Practicality** Your market is likely to be pragmatic and adaptable, tending to value websites and content that offer practical value.

- **Be flexible** Since punctuality is not usually a strong point, any webinars that you might give should be made available afterwards so that those who missed the beginning (or the whole thing) can still access your content.

- **Relationships are important** People will assess your credibility based on your connections and reputation. By creating and nurturing good relationships with your audience, you can create brand advocates and boost your reputation via word of mouth. Choose your associations wisely.

- **Education** Long-term-orientated cultures tend to value the acquisition of skills, so a great way to promote your business is to offer free training and materials that your market will actually find useful. This shows that you value them and relies on the principle of reciprocity to encourage your visitors to become paying customers (see Chapters 13 and 14).

- **It's in the stars** Since these cultures typically express a natural ease with "discovering the fated path,"[20] website navigation can be less structured and outbound links that open up in new windows can be used to direct clients towards particular actions.

- **Long-term benefits** If you are looking to persuade clients to try or buy your particular products, underline their practical use and long-term benefits. Since high-LTO cultures tend to save more, offering solutions in which you take smaller recurring payments can be a good way to reduce the pain of outright purchases.

MAKE THIS WORK FOR YOU

Short-term Orientated

What to do if the majority of your audience comes from a country with a low LTO score.

- **Give us some stats** This audience prefers the certainty of facts over subjective, unsubstantiated claims. If you are selling a product that will save people time, money and effort, provide the evidence.

- **Ratings** Facts and figures are more likely to persuade this market than anecdotes alone, so if you are including testimonials on your website, give them quantifiable credibility by providing your customers with the option of a five-star rating system (like the ones you find on Amazon).

- **Instant download** Immediate gratification is a strong motivator for low-LTO cultures, so reward your clients with content they can access at the swipe of a finger. If your product is digital (such as Adobe's Creative Suite), provide clients with the option to purchase it for immediate download as well as making a hard copy available.

- **Trendsetters** Short-term-orientated cultures tend to follow social trends and rituals, whether it's spending a month's salary on those new Laboutins or going down the bar on a Friday night with your friends. You can capitalize on this by reflecting such trends in your advertising material and website content where appropriate, such as using photos of people wearing this season's must-have jeans, or showcasing videos of your products with the most popular music playing in the background. (If you're going to use other brands' products in your content, make sure you get the relevant permissions beforehand—the last thing you want is a lawsuit!) A quick note of caution: the kinds of trends that your market follows will also depend on factors such as their age, gender and income level, so make sure you have a clear idea as to which trends are important to this specific group before you mirror these back in your messaging.

- **Listen in** People expect instant results and, with social media now firmly embedded into our everyday lives, this applies to customer support, too. If you don't know what your clients are saying about you, it's time to start listening. Services such as Repskan[21] can help you monitor social media channels for client chatter and enable you to gauge customer sentiment, nipping any negative feedback in the bud. Managing your audience's concerns in a swift manner will help ensure happy customers and a gleaming reputation.

6 Indulgence v. Restraint (IVR)

This final dimension does what it says on the can. It measures the extent to which our society allows us to have fun and enjoy life through the free gratification of our natural drives.

People from high-indulgence cultures, such as Mexico and Sweden, tend to feel that they have personal control over their own lives, which may explain why they are generally happier, more optimistic and extrovert than their restrained counterparts.

While indulgent societies tend to be loose knit, the people within it place a high value on friendships and leisure time and the percentage of people who feel healthy is generally high. Unsurprisingly, there's a positive relationship between indulgence and national wealth and those of us from indulgent cultures are less likely to value moderation or the concept of moral discipline.

In contrast, restrained societies tend to believe that gratification should be regulated and suppressed, which is usually achieved by the enforcement of strict social norms. While these communities tend to be tightly knit, there's a lower percentage of people who feel very happy or healthy, alongside a general perception of helplessness due to lack of autonomy. People tend to be more pessimistic, neurotic and cynical and death rates from heart disease are higher.

It stands to reason that restraint is more likely to be the norm under poverty and, in restrained societies, people tend to value frugality and moral discipline over leisure and friendships. According to Hofstede, "social restriction not only makes people less happy but also seems to foster various forms of negativism."[22]

See Table 5.6 to see where countries are placed in the global IVR rankings.

Table 5.6 Global IVR rankings

	Score	Country
Indulgent	97	Mexico
	78	Sweden
	71	Australia
	69	UK
	68	USA
	68	Canada
	63	Austria
	63	Africa (S)
	59	Brazil
	55	Norway
	52	Saudi Arabia
	48	France
	44	Spain
	42	Japan
	40	Germany

	Score	Country
Restrained	33	Portugal
	30	Italy
	26	India
	24	China
	20	Russia
	17	Hong Kong
	4	Egypt
No data available	n/a	Africa (E)
	n/a	Israel

MAKE THIS WORK FOR YOU

Indulgent

What to do if the majority of your audience comes from a country with a high IVR score.

– **Friends with benefits** Indulgent cultures tend to use the Internet for private socializing and personal use and generally have greater contact with people of other nationalities. If you want to engage with this group, make your interactions fun and personally rewarding by giving away entertaining freebies that people will share with their friends (if you haven't heard of "iPint," the famous beer-drinking app by Carling, go check it out—it's the perfect example of this sort of thing).[23]

– **Free as a bird** Debate and freedom of expression are important, so if you are making claims about your product or services, be prepared to back them up. People expect frank and honest discussion, so any customer care or advice you offer should reflect this.

– **Gender bender** Successful advertisements work because they get their audiences to identify with the characters in the ad—whether on a billboard, website or video (think Lynx ads for geeky pubescent males). When you're pitching to an indulgent culture, gender roles tend to be more loosely prescribed, so it's wise to steer clear of stereo-types. Instead, have some fun and give your audience a range of models to identify with.

▶

- **Give us a smile** Indulgent cultures tend to be more optimistic and perceive smiling as friendly, so use joyful, extrovert people in your images and videos. Humor and comedy can also work well, especially when it comes to promoting your business through word of mouth.

- **Spicing it up** Sexual norms tend to be less strict, so you can play with this to add some spark to your branding, apps or campaigns. While this can be a great way to deliver a bit of light-hearted entertainment, obviously such a strategy should only be employed if it is appropriate to your market. I wouldn't advise using sexy images of bikini-clad twenty-somethings to sell children's books (unless their dads are doing the buying!).

- **If the price is right** High-indulgence cultures tend to be wealthier, so take this into account when you are pricing your products and services.

MAKE THIS WORK FOR YOU

Restrained

What to do if the majority of your audience comes from a country with a low IVR score.

- **Care in the community** Selling your products or services on the promise of personal gratification is a bad idea. Instead, focus on how your offering can work within the norms of your target culture to benefit the community. For example, if you sell Internet solutions, highlight its security features and practical applications—adapt the way you pitch to reflect the needs and expectations of your audience.

- **Money saver** Restrained cultures tend to be frugal, so use discount codes, sales and limited offers to attract attention and business. Consider how your product or service will save people money and make this one of your key messages.

- **Proceed with caution** Gender roles tend to be strict, so when it comes to engaging your audience be careful whom you target and how. As we saw earlier, in some restrained societies it is completely unacceptable to show images of women at all, so if your target audience is female you may have to think of creative ways in which you can engage with them visually.

- **Shiny happy people** Smiling can be seen as suspect, so, again, be careful with the images that you use. If you are a global brand, glocalize your website by toning down any extrovert claims, images or features and, when in doubt, err on the side of formality.

- **Spare the rod** Similar to uncertainty-avoidant cultures, restrained societies favor structure and discipline. Reflect this in your website by providing clear, structured navigation and a user experience that is predictable and consistent. If you are taking online payments, highlight the security of the transaction and don't request additional information unless absolutely necessary.

- **Formality** Customer support should follow a formal process and Live Chat services are probably unwise. I would advise against using social media as a means of engagement with restrained cultures, as this may be perceived as improper and intrusive.

6 INDIVIDUAL DIFFERENCES

 Always remember that you're unique. Just like everyone else.

ALISON BOULTER

GENDER

We've seen how our brains and culture can influence our behaviors, but what about other individual differences?

There is a lot of research to suggest that our gender plays an important role in our behavior and activities online. For example, when it comes to privacy, women tend to be more concerned about third-party access to personal information than men and they are more likely to protect their privacy in a proactive way than they would have a decade ago.[1] Interestingly (and possibly as a result of this), women are also more likely to use modest photos,[2] provide inaccurate personal information[3] and blog anonymously[4] than men.

When it comes to social network sites, some other interesting gender patterns emerge. Men are more likely to reveal their phone number[5] and address,[6] whereas women are more likely to actually read the site's privacy policies and change their privacy settings accordingly[7] (personally I think this is to do with avoiding online stalkers more than anything else). Despite the fact that women express a greater concern for their online privacy than men, they are still more likely to join a social network,[8] be more active within it,[9] and open their profiles to a larger number of friends[10] than their male counterparts.

In terms of why we use the Internet, there is evidence to suggest that males tend to go online for a wider variety of reasons than females and their primary activities revolve around entertainment and leisure (yes, this does include porn). Unsurprisingly, they are also the heaviest users of online videos.[11]

Women, however, go online primarily to socialize and, to a lesser extent, find educational assistance.[12] Although men tend to use the web more than women, it's actually women who are the more prolific users of emails[13] (and, as we shall see in Chapter 19, women also seem to have greater levels of anxiety than men when it comes to shopping and engaging online).

It's not just our gender that can have a marked effect on our Internet activities. Far from being a product of our environment or gender, a growing body of research suggests that our personalities (and behaviors) are profoundly influenced by our neurochemical "type." If this is true, then the audience we attract online will respond to very different things depending on their specific type.

WHAT'S YOUR NEUROCHEMICAL ARCHETYPE?

You'll remember that we touched briefly on neurochemicals in Chapter 1. In this section we're going to delve a little deeper and discover how you can use this to engage more persuasively with your online audience.

In 2009, renowned biological anthropologist Helen Fisher published a book—*Why Him? Why Her?*[14]—on the subject of personality and romantic relationships. Although I would have opted for a better title (*My Neurochemical Romance* perhaps?), the book itself is a real eye-opener and revolutionized the way I perceive personality.

Fisher proposed that our personalities are a product of our genes and neurochemicals and suggested that our temperament styles fall into one of four archetypes:

- Explorer
- Builder
- Negotiator
- Director.

Although we're each a mix of all four, most of us will express a primary and secondary type, typified by the prevalence of a particular neurotransmitter in the brain. Why is this important for online persuasion? Well, if you can ascertain what "type" of personality your service or product is likely to attract, you can design your website and user experience to specifically target and attract this type. Have a look at the brief descriptions below—which one sounds most like you? Which type(s) does your business attract most?

Explorer

You may have heard of dopamine—the "reward" neurochemical we tend to associate with pleasure and risktaking. Similar to adrenaline, this chemical affects our emotional experience and is responsible for the high you get from drugs such as cocaine.

As you might have guessed from the name, Explorers have a very active dopamine system, which is why they tend to seek out novelty and take risks. They enjoy life in the fast lane and choices made on the spur of the moment, their insatiable curiosity tending to lead them on exciting adventures. This is the kind of person who decides they need a break and the very next day they're on a plane to Brazil. Naturally restless and on the go, Explorers tend to be independent and unpredictable, which is why their lives can seem so action-packed to those looking in. Often regarded as hedonistic, this playful type is usually creative, sensual and fun, but can become easily bored if forced to adopt a daily routine.

The online Explorer

The online Explorer is more likely to seek out new, unusual experiences and so creating a website or sending out a tweet that is playful and intriguing can work wonders with this type.

Submitting your website to discovery engines such as StumbleUpon is a great way of reaching out to new Explorers since it works on the principle of curiosity.

Websites that deal in high-octane sports and novel experiences, such as Zombie Boot Camp[15] and Aqua Sphering, are likely to have a natural appeal to this group and can be made more inviting by adopting language and design that excite the senses. Explorers tend to be impatient, so avoid using anything that takes an age to load as they'll simply click away. If you want to encourage interaction, providing content that demands a higher level of engagement (such as videos, interactive games and moving sliders) is sure to appeal.

In terms of social media, foursquare, Twitter, and Instagram are great stomping grounds for Explorers as they require little time to use and can be accessed on the trot.

This group tends to respond well to last-minute deals and competitions (if they're exciting enough), so engaging with these customers by pushing the adrenaline button can be an effective way of attracting their attention.

Once you've got them, keeping Explorers around is a case of updating your content regularly and throwing in a few curve balls to spice up the mix. Once you've embedded yourself firmly in their psyches as a thrill-provider, you will be able to engage with and influence this market more easily.

Builder

The Builder's sociable, loyal and friendly personality is influenced by the serotonin system—if dopamine is the accelerator that drives risky behavior, serotonin is the brakes.[16]

Networkers by nature, Builders are most comfortable in social situations (you'll find plenty of them at social events and on social media platforms) and they tend to attract devoted groups of friends and peers.

Unlike Explorers, this group is not easily bored and their cautious nature allows them to be dependable, methodical and hardworking. Security and structure are important to Builders and they think in concrete terms, which means they are often traditional in their values. This is the kind of person who meticulously plans vacations a year in advance and emails the itinerary (and all three contact numbers) to family and friends in case of emergency.

The online Builder

The Builder's need for structure and rules also translates to online preferences. If your website is targeted towards this type, special care should be taken to ensure that the navigation and sitemap are logically organized, clearly labelled and easy to follow.

Builders are not impulsive and like to plan ahead, so if you want to influence this target demographic, you have to put in the time and effort. Invest in developing a relationship with this group by interacting with them on their platforms of choice: Facebook—a rich social experience in a structured environment; and LinkedIn—it adheres to a clear, formal structure and provides information that people trust.

Social proof (see Chapters 13 and 14) can be a particularly powerful way of shaping a Builder's choices and behaviors and you can appeal to the wider group by socializing your products/services. Builders are also concrete thinkers, so make sure any metaphors or examples you do use are tangible (for example, "Our ISAs are as safe as houses").

Since this type is the most traditional of the four, it is important to respect their personal beliefs and boundaries—especially in the public arena of the web. Communications should be friendly and clear, but not invasive—and risqué jokes or links should be avoided. With regard to websites, if you want to make the online purchasing process more appealing to Builders, including a clearly marked progress bar during checkout can be a great way of structuring the experience and reducing uncertainty:

1 basket	2 welcome	3 details	4 delivery	5 payment	6 completed

As a rule of thumb, if your content is useful and clearly structured and you use the right social channels to build relationships and boost trust, you'll attract more business from online Builders.

Negotiator

High in oestrogen, the Negotiator is any man or woman who is naturally gifted in the art of handling people. Psychologically astute and introspective, this type tends to read others easily and is typically patient and compassionate.

Negotiators have a facility with language and creativity and like to consider things in context when weighing up a decision. Comfortable with ambiguity, they are flexible and diplomatic, but can sometimes find themselves swayed by others, subject to the social forces of the group.

That being said, negotiators are socially savvy and their ability to theorize and assume different points of view makes them particularly accommodating –but it can also lead towards rumination and an inability to make decisions.

The online Negotiator

Online, the Negotiator is likely to be interested in creative nooks (such as Pinterest and StumbleUpon) and any social hub that provides a deeper level of insight into the psychological workings of friends and family (Facebook). Since the Negotiator tends to consider all factors and possible outcomes before making a decision, converting this type into a paying customer requires that you present a united front. User reviews, social recommendations, product information and photos should paint a positive, cohesive picture in order to persuade a Negotiator to buy.

Since Negotiators tend to shy away from confrontation, customer service should be designed to open up a dialogue and provide support—failure to do so can result in negative social media chatter and a dent in your reputation. When it comes to your website, greeting Negotiators with a creative design and an intuitive user experience will win you brownie points. You can also improve website engagement by including a search function, as this will give your Negotiators the flexibility to find what they're looking for on their own terms. Since this group is instinctively perceptive when it comes to people, the use of videos as a means of communication can give them a "gut sense" for who you are and encourage a deeper level of engagement. A word of advice: make sure that whomever you put in front of the camera is naturally comfortable there as Negotiators are excellent cue-readers and can typically read a lot into the slightest body or facial movement.

Director

Traditionally associated with men, testosterone is the driving force behind the Director archetype. Although we may think of this neurochemical as typically male, there are plenty of full-blooded female Directors out there (I count myself among them) and they are often marked by a searing drive for success.

This is a tough-minded, competitive and goal-orientated type—one that can be relied on to take decisive action even in difficult circumstances. The least social of the four, Directors are often bold and say what they mean, preferring reason and logic to the more socially empathetic tendencies of the Negotiator.

Not afraid to follow unpopular lines of enquiry in the pursuit of truth, Directors can sometimes seem rude and uncompromising to those who don't know them.

They tend to have a great ear for music and a natural facility with understanding rule-based systems which, combined with their ability to focus in on specific tasks, make for great problem-solvers.

The online Director

The Director's goal-orientated temperament and disinterest in casual socializing can translate to a lack of social engagement online. So, if this sounds like your target audience, social media may not be the best way to connect with them. I've noticed this in my own use of social networks. While I do have a Facebook account, I rarely update it and I use it for the sole purpose of staying current about upcoming events. Rather than using what I perceive to be indiscriminate social platforms, I prefer the functional, focused interaction I get through Twitter (as a news feed) and LinkedIn (for new business opportunities).

If you're aiming to engage with Directors, you're better off communicating with them directly via email or LinkedIn than through any of the major social platforms.

This personality type will evaluate your product/service in terms of how it can help them achieve their goals and compete better. Since Directors make their decisions swiftly, you have a short window of time in which to convince them to buy what you're selling (or listen to what you're saying). Make it count. Directors strive to be the alpha (fe)male, so any message that focuses on success will be attractive, as long as your claims are substantiated by evidence. With regard to websites, the use of authority figures and experts can be a great way of conveying your status as a heavyweight and a good track record is likely to encourage this group to engage.

THE FIVE SENSES

You don't need to be a scientist to notice that we experience and interact with the world through our different senses. While there are many ways in which we can explore our environments, by and large we tend to gather information through our three primary senses ("modalities"): visual, auditory and kinaesthetic (physical)—and, to a lesser extent, through our olfactory (smell) and gustatory (taste) senses.

While there is debate as to whether some of us tend to express a preference for one particular sense over another, in my experience I've noticed that people do seem to vary in the way in which they choose to consume information and interact with one another. For instance, I prefer working with visual stimuli and like to explore visual media in great detail, whereas I have friends who seem to prefer interacting with their environment in a more auditory way—listening to podcasts, going to lectures, "reading" audiobooks.

If you're interested in finding out how you might process information, think back to a particular holiday and notice what memories spring to mind. Do you see pictures? Hear sounds? Remember any particular sensations, tastes or smells? You may find that you encode and recall memories in a more visual or kinaesthetic way. For instance, my memories tend to consist of images and voices and rarely anything else, but some of my more foodie relatives have the uncanny ability to call to mind the flavour of incredible dishes they had abroad decades ago as kids.

While we all use all our senses (I'm sure you will have experienced the weird feeling of being instantly transported back to an early memory from simply smelling a particular scent), we do seem to prefer some senses over others and it is this piece of knowledge that you can employ to reach a wider audience online. For instance, people who prefer visual media are more likely to use Pinterest or the media-rich Facebook as their primary social platform, whereas someone who enjoys a more auditory interaction may well turn to SoundCloud for inspiration.

The bottom line is this: whatever your preferences and online habits are, make sure you make your online presence as accessible to your market as possible, by analyzing your audience's preferences and meeting it in its preferred modality.

AGE

Of the different factors that influence how we interact online, age is a fascinating one. You need only turn on the TV (if you still use one!) to get a sense of the stereotypes we perpetuate, such as those expounded in commercials that depict our older citizens as technologically naïve. While advertisers necessarily push their own agendas, their power lies in the ability to capture and play on the zeitgeist and the views we hold as a society.

When it comes to influencing your market, these sorts of assumptions can land you in hot water—not least because some of the myths that are perpetuated (such as "older people don't go online") simply aren't true and, in some cases, are completely opposite to the behaviors we're witnessing in reality. In New Zealand, for instance, there seems to be no difference between the amount of time spent online by older and younger age groups, possibly due to the fact that older users generally have higher incomes and therefore better access.[17] In a study carried out in Turkey, researchers found that older employees (aged 40 and over) actually reported higher Internet use than their younger colleagues, averaging more than three hours a day.[18]

The important point here is that we can't trust snap judgements or stereotypes. To really know our audience we must do our research. For instance, research has found that, while there is a correlation between the age of users and their ability to use the Internet, it's actually a person's level of education that is the most important factor in determining how digitally literate he or she is.[19]

While most of us learn how to use the Internet via trial and error, if someone consistently makes the same mistakes but still manages to achieve what they want, they have no reason to develop their digital literacy—meaning that they will remain digitally stunted. This may not sound important, but if your services or products are targeting a client base that is limited in its ability to use the Internet (whether through lack of practice or lack of access), this will naturally dictate the parameters within which your site can yield the most influence.

That being said, the majority of global Internet users do seem to be young and, as more and more people are born into an online world, the prevalence of Internet use and our facility with it are surely set to rise. Research is already finding generational differences in the ways in which we consume online information, with Generation Y (18–31-year-olds) preferring web pages that include a main, large image, a search feature, pictures of celebrities and relatively little text.[20]

Yes, this has led to exasperated cries from various corners that we're "dumbing down" our kids and reducing our attention spans (and goodness knows how many other untold ills), but the truth of the matter is that, if we are to really engage with our online audiences, we have to meet them on their terms. Only then can we shape and influence the way in which they interact with us. Even then, it's a two-way process.

COMMUNICATE PERSUASIVELY

When you talk

1 MIND the brains of communicator and listener

are trying to be coupled
merging as one

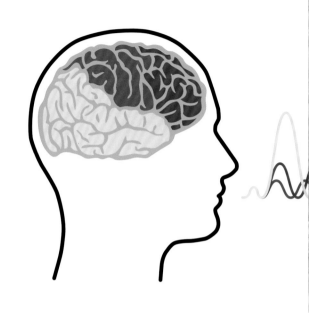

MEDIA p80

WEBSITE	IMAGES	VIDEOS	SOCIAL MEDIA
target and test	*attract*	*communicate*	*engage*

Have a clear purpose	Beauty is universal	Tap into emotion	Have a clear identity
Target your audience and meet their needs	Use faces to engage with visitors and direct their gaze	Tell stories	Target the right people
Create a community	Mystery is alluring	Nostalgia is persuasive	Use social validation, reciprocity and social proof in your campaigns
Update your content	Our brains enjoy visual metaphors	Neurologically optimise your videos	Become valuable
Clear calls to action	Use exaggerated images	Embed commands	Own up to mistakes
Simplicity rules		Stop an image to attract attention	Converse and convert
Attention is a resource			

The mind meld

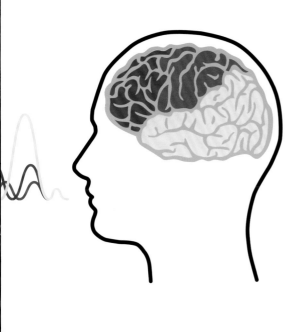

2 PEOPLE engaged in a story - both brains fire in **identical patterns** of neurological activity

Did you know...

in individualist countries women and men differ

in their perception **of a website's** attractiveness **and usability?**

Colors
Fewer levels
Uncluttered

VERSUS

Flashy
Interactive
Animated

Your website's appeal
can be measured in two ways:

AESTHETIC
culture-specific
attractive
visually appropriate
harmonious
and elegant

DYNAMIC
universal
attention-grabbing
colorful
fun to use and
interactive

7 BASIC PRINCIPLES

> ❝ Persuasive communication is "any message that is intended to shape,
> reinforce or change the responses of another or others."
> GERARD MILLER, SOCIAL PSYCHOLOGIST[1]

Communicating persuasively may be a tricky art to perfect, but when it's done properly, the payoff can be huge, which is why marketing campaigns continue to siphon off huge amounts of corporate money every year.

If you want your message to reach and influence your target audience there is one golden rule you must follow: tailor your communication style to the medium you're using. For instance, if you're launching an email campaign, research shows that we're more likely to forward an email that makes us feel good, that's media-rich (includes audio/video/visual information) and, surprisingly, that's greater in length.[2]

Whatever the medium, a campaign's success (its ability to influence) will always depend on several key factors:

- the clarity of the message and call to action

- the amount of time and hassle required to complete the task

- the credibility and usability of the website where the action takes place.

In a nutshell, a good campaign will have a clear message, be hassle-free and be easy to act on. When it comes to being persuaded by a source of information (whether it's a person, news station or website), we tend to respond most positively to people we perceive as likeable, similar to ourselves and credible.[3, 4]

As deceptive as it may be, it's not uncommon for big businesses to meticulously engineer characters in a bid to get us, the consumers, to buy into their message. You'll have no doubt come across this in commercials: the friendly, well-dressed "lawyer" who tells you you're entitled to compensation or the attractive "doctor" who informs you this particular brand of diet pills is safe. "It's just an actor," I hear you say. Well, yes, it is, but, even if that actor has never set foot in a legal practice or medical college, the fact that he or she *looks* the part is often enough to convince our subconscious that we can trust the information they're spouting (more on this when we cover authority in Chapter 14).The ability to manufacture persuasion is a powerful one and its success hinges on the accuracy of your demographic data.

These kinds of commercials work because they exploit your brain's uncanny ability to pick up "appearance cues." Which, when combined with a person's level of attractiveness, can dramatically influence the degree to which you will consider someone credible.[5]

This particular foible was highlighted in an ingenious study conducted back in 1979, when a group of confederates asked some students to sign a petition. Quite unsurprisingly, it turned out that the most successful petitioners were also the ones who were rated the most attractive.[6]

Although we now live in a dramatically different era, when it comes to attraction very little has changed. Our freshly airbrushed world is a living testament to our quest for beauty, and it is this impulse that lies behind some of the most influential communication techniques known to humankind.

As clichéd as it may be, sex sells. Freud was right when he said that man was motivated by his biological drives for self-preservation and a bit of "how's your father." Don't believe me? Take a look at the press coverage for any motor show and tell me that for most red-blooded males the main attraction isn't more cleavage than cars.

HIERARCHY OF ONLINE NEEDS

While sex is one of our most powerful motivators, when it comes to online behaviors there is a whole range of forces at play.

You may have come across Maslow's famous hierarchy of needs—a five-stage theory that explains the drivers of human behavior. This model proposes that we are driven by five kinds of "deficiency needs":

- our physiological need for food, warmth and water
- a sense of safety
- a desire for love and friendship
- a sense of accomplishment and self-esteem
- a desire for self-actualization.

The fifth component, a "being need," is self-actualization, which is the driving force behind our desire for self-improvement. Maslow called this fifth need a "metamotivator," typified by some of our most beloved icons, such as Ghandi and Einstein. While these exceptional people did seem to possess a driving force many only aspire to, the truth is that, as a species, we will often go to great lengths to achieve a sense of self-actualization.

So it is online. The Internet can fulfill many needs—from the tawdry to the divine. Whatever your desires, the web is an amazing place to satisfy them. That is what makes it one of the sweet spots where influence can happen.

In a highly saturated marketplace, it's tricky to rise above the noise and get your message heard. If, as research suggests, the key to successful communication rests on meeting the expectations and desires of your users,[7] then this hierarchy of needs can provide a powerful framework with which to engage your customers—whatever the level.

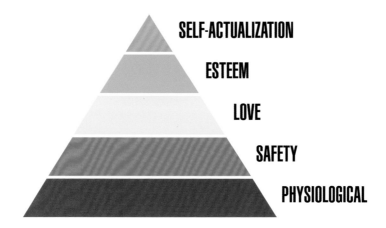

1 Physiological

Our first, most basic need is for physical well-being. If we are fed, watered, clothed and protected, we can move up the hierarchy towards loftier goals.

You can appeal to people's basic instincts by using imagery that speaks to them at a subconscious level. For instance, you may have noticed that most fast-food chains tend to use red and yellow in their outlets and branding to attract attention and stimulate appetite[8] (more about this in Chapter 11). What's interesting is that they also do this online. If you take a look at McDonald's German website below, you'll see that the company has used a color palette that is predominantly red (this is only the case in certain countries, however—like Coca-Cola, McDonald's websites are culture-specific).

As we saw earlier in Nestlé's water ad, the fact that our brains find it difficult to discern between real and imaginary threats can be used online to devastating effect. As can the suggestion of sex. Remember that fabulous Cadbury's Flake commercial from the 1980s? The one where a beautiful, scantily clad woman sits at her window suggestively biting into her Flake while the phone rings off the

Source: http://www.mcdonalds.de

hook? Chances are if you do remember it, the only thing that will spring to mind is the money shot—the bit where she bites. The simple fact is that we're primed to respond to opportunities for sex, even if that "opportunity" is just on a screen.

MAKE THIS WORK FOR YOU

Pleasure and pain

As a species we are hard-wired to move towards pleasure and away from pain. If you run a reputable business, you may wish to steer clear of the old heuristic "sex sells," but you can still take advantage of our basic physical needs in a number of ways.

Many businesses use clever videos to highlight the physical, comfort-related benefits of using their services. This is fairly easy to do if you're selling something like chocolate or ice cream, for instance, and the advertising world is full of examples that play on the sensuality of food to encourage us to buy (modern ads for Magnum ice creams are a great example).

Doesn't this only work if you're selling basic products? Well, no. If your business trades in intangibles, such as software or insurance, you can still capitalize on this principle—it just requires a slightly different tack.

As we saw in Chapter 1, the contrast principle can provide a great way of highlighting what's great about your product/service. This can be as simple as showing a "before" picture of someone in discomfort (I don't mean anything extreme here—a mild expression of worry will do!), followed by an "after" picture of that same person using your product and looking happier. You can even do this in your tagline. A great web design agency I know (WeMakeWebsites)[9] uses this principle beautifully when pitching to clients: "We make websites, so you don't have to." This simple phrase captures both the "pain" involved in having to design a website and the relief you'll feel by having someone else do it for you.

It's basic, and it works.

2 Safety

Early humans who were unable to find adequate shelter would have been viciously ripped from the genetic pool by hungry predators. Thankfully, for most of us this is no longer the case, but our desire to feel safe remains strong and, in a digital world, this evolutionary hangover can be expressed through our desire for financial and informational security. As we shall see later, one of the greatest barriers to e-commerce adoption is lack of trust, so if you wish to be influential online, it is vital that you earn the trust of your users by taking concrete steps to assuage their fears.

MAKE THIS WORK FOR YOU

Safe and sound

To create a sense of safety, provide your customers with opt-out boxes and additional information about how their data will be used. While we will look at this particular topic in greater detail in Chapter 19, I will add here that cues such as color, official logos and secure payment symbols can help your customers to feel safe, as can providing a direct, easy way for them to contact you (and, no, a call center in India will *not* do).

3 Love

This level reflects our need for meaningful relationships and the desire to belong. The urge to connect is universal and strong and, as in the pre-industrial era, good relationships remain the foundation for good business. Your power to influence depends largely on your social standing, reputation and whom you know. Gone are the days where businesses can hide anonymously behind their websites—social media have banished such practices to the past and we are now dancing to an altogether more transparent tune.

MAKE THIS WORK FOR YOU

A sense of belonging

Our desire to belong is the singular reason that social media exist. This deep-seated need for social validation and community is one of the most crucial tools in online influence, especially for young and collectivist demographics in which *non*-conformity can lead to painful ostracisation from the group.

It is this same desire that has spurred the rise of the viral video phenomenon. A video will only go viral when enough people send it to their peers and people only tend to share videos they think others will like. In a bid to gain standing or prestige within our respective groups, we share content that we think is valuable and, if it's deemed compelling enough, our peers then spread it out to their networks in a bid to acquire some social status along the way.

Use this online by finding out what your customers like and will want to share with their friends. Also, as your business depends on their loyalty, give your clients some love. Showing that you appreciate their feedback and comments, whether good or bad, can go a long way towards building good relationships. More importantly, it will make your customers feel valued—and, as anyone will tell you, a customer who feels valued is more likely to stick around in the long run.

4 Esteem

This element reflects our need for positive self-regard, whether we achieve it through association (when your team wins the cup), group identity (you're a Mac or a PC) or reputational capital (you've earned your stripes).

Online, it is this drive for self-esteem that fuels many of our social and community-based activities. Those of us trying to grow armies of Twitter followers will know this feeling all too well: it's the delight you experience when you gain new fans and the sinking feeling you get when you lose some.

This desire for prestige is what motivates some people to contribute to forums, literally spending hours of their time answering questions and helping others. It's feel-good "altruism" at its best, but how can you harness it online?

MAKE THIS WORK FOR YOU

Feeling good

If self-esteem can be gained through a sense of achievement, give your clients some calls to action that they'll feel good about. Several of my favorite blogs often host polls in their sidebars and I'm usually happy to complete them. Why? Because I enjoy the feeling of giving something back to a website that provides me with great stuff to read (reciprocity in action). Not only that, but interacting with these websites in this way makes it feel more like a two-way relationship and, yes, that makes a difference.

You can also offer your customers a sense of prestige by rewarding them with special access to certain areas of your site. It won't cost you much, and rewarding your customers' loyalty this way will make them feel good and show that you value them.

5 Self-actualization

While this is the most ethereal and possibly immeasurable of needs, the desire to self-actualize and feel a sense of accomplishment is a powerful one. Websites that encourage people's sense of creativity and connectedness tap into this drive and it is at this level that many successful charities operate.

Sites such as Pinterest, Tumblr and Flickr are great examples of this: they all provide a platform for people to share images for the sheer beauty of it. Although some may consider these services pointless (debates rage about the difficulty of monetizing such platforms), the fact that people are flocking to these sites from all over the world points towards their intrinsic value. We are by nature aesthetic creatures who have evolved to commune and share with one another. Therefore, any service that provides us an easy way in which to do this is bound to garner a lot of attention.

MAKE THIS WORK FOR YOU

A helping hand

Most of us want to achieve our potential, so if you can help some of your customers along the way to reaching theirs, they'll thank you for it.

The single most important thing I appreciated during the writing of this book was the untold generosity of the countless websites that shared their insights, trend forecasts and white papers with me online. They didn't *have* to make their knowledge open to the public, but because they did, much of their research has made its way into these pages and into your hands. In helping me to reach my potential, they not only gained my loyalty but also earned a platform for their work and a whole new audience in the process.

If you don't know what would help your customers, ask them. Whether it's via Twitter, LinkedIn or in your newsletter, first thank your customers for connecting with you and then ask them what they're struggling with, what they need from you. This personal, direct approach can have a real emotional impact and, although you won't get a response from everyone, the answers that you do receive will be worth their weight in gold. If you know what your customers are trying to achieve, you (and your business) can help them get there.

8 YOUR WEBSITE

> *In the case of an Internet vendor, the website is perhaps the only way a firm communicates with its customers. Therefore, its appearance and structure encourage or discourage a consumer's purchase intentions.*
>
> SANDY CHEN AND GURPREET DHILLON,
> INFORMATION MANAGEMENT[1]

When designing your website, there is a multitude of factors that can influence your visitors' actions and behaviors. Everything from a website's graphics and layout to its ease-of-use affects a visitor's click-through rate.[2]

How can you even *begin* to compete with the sheer volume of videos and images that bombard us every time we go online? The fact that we are becoming increasingly "aestheticised"[3] highlights the importance of careful, considered design. When it comes to websites, success boils down to just two things:

- *who* will be using your website

- and *why*.

According to psychologist Marcel Gommans and colleagues, a good website "has to be designed for a targeted customer segment."[4] This means that its very foundations should be based on a thorough analysis of its target market. Yes, it does take time and money to get it right, but, as investments go, this is one of the best you can make (you'd be surprised how many big businesses get this bit wrong).

One of the fundamental reasons that online businesses fail is because of their lack of research. In this chapter we'll look at some of the more universal principles that you can leverage to design a persuasive website.

One of the biggest barriers to gaining new clients is lack of trust, so your ability to establish credibility online can make or break your business. This can be influenced by the context of your message, the medium through which it's delivered and the actual characteristics of your visitors.[5]

As well as contributing to a richer user experience, certain design features have also been found to increase trust, including branding and the ability to provide user feedback.[6] When shopping online, we're more likely to return to a website if we like its design and functionality,[7] all of which suggests that you can (at least to some extent) manufacture satisfaction and e-loyalty by engineering your website's aesthetics in a particular way.

AESTHETICS

Over the decades, centuries and millennia, our view of what makes something attractive has changed dramatically and frequently. From Reuben's voluptuous beauties to today's size zero models, aesthetics remain dynamic in nature. However, there are certain objective qualities that seem to remain constant throughout.

For example, you may already know that, as a species, we find symmetrical faces more attractive (think Tyra Banks and George Clooney) than those which aren't. What you may not know is that this preference for symmetry also extends to other visual media, from simple black and white geometric shapes[8] to websites themselves. In fact, in a recent fMRI study, psychologists discovered that the specific areas of our brains that become active when we're making an aesthetic judgement about beauty also light up when we're judging something for symmetry.[9]

This may not sound particularly exciting, but it shows us that there is a neural relationship between symmetry and beauty—which means that using symmetry in the design of our websites can be a great way of making them more universally attractive.

By symmetry I don't mean to say that if you split a website down the middle you should find a perfect mirror image on each side. Rather, the visual components within the right and left of the page should be well balanced.

Colors are another strikingly influential design component, especially since they seem to evoke particular emotions and associations in us.[10] For instance, if I asked you to picture a color that was "fresh," what color would spring to mind? What about if that color was "aggressive"? "Calming"? Chances are (if you're Western) that you'd have thought of green, red and blue, in that order. We use emotive words to describe colors all the time and, though we may rarely give it a second thought, science is starting to find real evidence for the psychological, emotional and even physiological influences that color can exert over us (we'll be exploring this in greater detail in Chapter 11).

Gender differences

Some research suggests that men and women differ in what they consider beautiful and how they make those judgements. For example, when asked to judge the aesthetic merits of a piece of work, one study found that men are more likely to scan from top left to bottom right, whereas women will do the mirror opposite (top right to bottom left).[11] That said, any research that explores gender differences should be treated with caution, since many of the differences they claim to observe are often influenced by myriad factors.

In the online world, though, there do seem to be significant gender differences in our perceptions of website attractiveness and usability,[12] especially in more individualistic cultures such as North America.[13] It brought a smile to my face to read that men generally prefer websites that are more "flashy," interactive and animated. Women on the other hand tend to be attracted to a website's colors[14] and to designs that are clean and uncluttered (women also seem to prefer sites that have fewer sub-page levels to trawl through).[15]

Whether it's the design of a site or the greater level of risk that women experience while shopping online,[16] there is evidence to suggest that women generally view websites more negatively than men.[17] Many seem to view the computer environment as "masculine," which, some researchers suggest, may contribute to a sense of disempowerment among women.[18] Other research suggests that men tend to report "a more satisfying online shopping experience than women."[19] This may be linked to the greater anxiety and lower self-efficacy that women report feeling when using a computer.[20]

Whether male or female, website satisfaction is a tricky thing to measure. Some psychologists suggest that a satisfying website is one that is "sticky," whose combined qualities "induce visitors to remain at the website rather than move to another site"[21] (this is commonly referred to as "bounce rate" in SEO parlance, which you can track via tools such as Google Analytics). Customer satisfaction can also be influenced by an individual's level of web skills (which can depend on factors such as age and location) and involvement with the product (how much they want it).[22]

Why does all of this matter? Well, if you know the needs of your customers and the barriers that prevent them from engaging, you are in the perfect position to assuage any fears and give them what they want. Once your customers can sense that you are reliable and trustworthy, they are more likely to give you their business and recommend you to others.

Good research leads to clearer communication, greater satisfaction and more influence.

Cultural differences

> " *Aesthetic effects begin with universal reactions, but these effects always operate in a personal and cultural context.*
>
> VIRGINIA POSTREL, CULTURAL CRITIC[23]

Since our sense of aesthetics tends to be subjective, it makes sense that a range of factors, including our culture, gender, age and class, would also influence our response to online visual information.

On the flip side, we might expect our brain's hard-wired arousal responses (to movement and bright colors, for example) to be more universal.[24] If you add to this the fact that we prefer and trust things we consider to be "like" us,[25] you'll start to see the benefits of designing your website to match the aesthetic values of your target group.

In 2010, a group of psychologists carried out a study to investigate the influence of culture on the way that we respond to a website's aesthetics.[26] They tested a range of websites for their appeal and found two main (and universal) dimensions that underpinned a site's overall attractiveness:

- aesthetic appeal
- dynamic appeal.

The first measured a website's attractiveness—whether it was visually appropriate, harmonious and elegant. The second measured a website's ability to arouse the user's attention—whether it was colorful, interactive, fun to use and created impact.

The researchers found that, while a website's aesthetic features were influenced by cultural differences, its dynamic impact was universal, meaning that if you present your website's information to match the aesthetic values of your target group, you will be more likely to grab its attention and trigger the appropriate emotional response.

Although culture does seem to influence our preferences in the design, content and usability of a website (as well as the meanings we extract from any metaphoric images used), these preferences also vary according to the genre of website being viewed.[27] When you consider the sheer volume of visual noise your website has to contend with, your ability to design to the cultural preferences of your audience can mean the difference between rising to the top or sinking into obscurity.

A common language?

> Although it is true that English was the main medium of the early Internet, it is increasingly the case that the Internet is now a communication space for other language communities.
>
> DAVID BLOCK, PROFESSOR OF LANGUAGES[28]

While we have just seen the advantages of culture-specific website design, at the time of writing, English is still the prevailing language online—but only by a whisker.[29] Since its humble beginnings using a text format (ASCII) that could only accommodate the Roman alphabet, Internet technology has changed beyond recognition. In 1998, it was estimated that around 75 percent of all websites were in English; by 2003, this number had plummeted to around 45 percent.[30] Although the exact numbers are difficult to ascertain, it looks as though the days of an English-speaking Internet are now over.

With over 100 million non-English speakers online, and legions of Chinese- and Spanish-speaking users growing by the second, it's easy to foresee a time in which websites will no longer be written in a universally accepted language, but in the mother tongue of their designers.

The availability of increasingly accurate online translation tools is making it easier for us to access a truly global web and countries that embraced the Internet early on now routinely offer their website content in both their national language and English. While it may be tempting to go for the easy option of online translation, if you are serious about really engaging with a global audience, your best bet is to have your text written by a native speaker. Not only will that person have a natural familiarity with the idioms and turns of phrase of the language but you willl be saved the embarrassment of literal translations that simply do not make any sense. Whatever method you decide to use, the message is clear: if you want to reach a global market, English may not be enough to get you by.

AVATARS

We've travelled a long way from the pixelated, static avatars of yesteryear. With our ever-increasing connection speeds and sense of cultural connectivity comes a growing demand for high-quality, instantly engaging rich media.

In the world of e-commerce, more and more businesses are turning to Live Chat platforms and animated avatars to engage with their customers in new ways. Researchers investigating the impact of such platforms and the use of embodied virtual agents (EVAs) are providing some exciting new insights into how businesses can profit from integrating these into our online platforms.

Broadly speaking, an EVA is a virtual, autonomous, human-like agent, whose characteristics tend to reflect real humans.[31] EVAs usually perform different online tasks, such as inform your customers about a new product or provide advice and customer support. They can range from a truly interactive agent, with whom you can dialogue, to a simple video of a person who appears to welcome you, as if stepping out from the website itself.

The purpose of an EVA is to establish a sense of rapport and familiarity with your users. Its success largely hinges on the quality of information you have gathered about your users and what will appeal to them. It goes without saying that his or her physical appearance should match both your audience's characteristics and expectations. Once you know what your clients' common traits are you can incorporate them into the design of your avatar. For example, if you attract mostly well-dressed, high net worth females over the age of 50, then it's obvious that your EVA should also be a well-dressed female over the age of 50.

This kind of mirroring extends beyond appearance and includes characteristics such as tone of voice, the language used and non-verbal cues, such as body language, posture and clothing.

As bizarre as it may sound, there is strong evidence to suggest that we tend to interact with avatars as if they were real people,[32] and the more natural they appear to be, the more naturally we behave towards them.[33] The fact that we all share an innate need for human connection is not enough in itself to warrant the use of EVAs on a business website, but, as technology improves, it does point towards a time in which this particular form of interaction will likely be widespread and very useful in the process of engaging and retaining new customers.

MOTION

When it comes to effective interface design, motion is one of the key components that can either add to or detract from your viewers' overall experience. Although several millennia separate us from our hunter-gatherer ancestors, their lives on the savannah still affect ours today. Though we no longer hunt, we remain evolutionarily primed to respond to movement. In an online context, it can be a distraction to our visual attention,[34] and can mean the difference between the success and failure of your site.

This topic is of particular importance if your website hosts banner ads. If you do use these, make sure that the ones you accept don't clash with or detract from the design and content of your website. If the ads are too distracting, they will discourage your viewers from returning to your site.

When you consider that most of our online activities tend to occur in parallel (for example, when you multitask, chatting online and checking your emails) and that the human brain has limited short-term memory and attention spans, you'll see the importance of streamlining your clients' user experience so they are not having to perform conflicting concurrent tasks. Bombard your viewers with too much distracting content and you'll decrease their ability to process the information on your website.[35]

E-COMMERCE

Whether you already have an established online presence or you're just starting out, it's crucial that you understand and deliver what's most important to your customers. Not only will this deepen your understanding of your market, but it will also set you apart from your competitors.

Part of being influential online is knowing how to give people what they want, so that you can create good client relationships and boost your reputation. One way in which you can do this, is by delivering high-quality service.

In a study by Zeithaml *et al.* a group of Internet shoppers were interviewed to see what they valued when judging the quality of service on a website.[36] As well as a site's overall aesthetics and responsiveness, the researchers found that ease of navigation was crucial, as was the site's flexibility, reliability and efficiency. Personalization was also important, as was the sense of security, privacy and assurance while visiting the site.

Another influential factor was "price knowledge": how easily customers could determine an item's shipping, total and comparative prices during the shopping process. Despite what you might think, you don't have to have the lowest prices to attract customers. Instead, by making it easier for people to understand what they're paying for and why, you can maintain a high quality of service while providing a transparent pricing structure that your clients can trust (more about this in Chapter 17 on Pricing and Value).

INFORMATION ARCHITECTURE

Information architecture basically means how you organize the information on your site. Since the majority of us go online in order to seek out specific information,[37] it's vital that you understand the principles of best practice so that you can structure your website for maximum impact.

The role of well-presented information is to reduce the cognitive load that you place on your users when they visit your website. A simple way to do this is to signpost the most important information so that your users can navigate to their area of interest as quickly and easily as possible. Websites that succeed in this are more likely to reduce their bounce rates and retain their customers for longer, which means they have a greater amount of time to influence users towards a particular outcome.

In the late 1990s, two psychologists investigating this subject proposed four categories of information quality that can significantly affect the impact of your website's information.[38] The first quality, *intrinsic*, refers to information that is accurate and reliable, in and of itself. The second quality, *accessibility*, does what it says on the box—the information is easy to locate. The third quality, *representational*, relates to information that is concise, interpretable and easy to understand. The fourth quality, *contextual*, is information that is relevant and provided in a timely manner.

All four of these qualities can improve your customers' user experience, but you can also make your information easier to understand by adopting a coherent design throughout your website.[39] This means that the pages within your site should be consistent with one another, so that users know what to expect as they navigate from one page to the next.

Oftentimes, the landing page (home page) or blog section of a website will be different from the rest, which is fairly standard practice, but once your customers navigate further into your website, all your pages should be consistent in their layout.

Yes, you would think this is common sense, but there are still scores of businesses that have inconsistent and confusing websites, placing an unnecessary cognitive burden on their users[40] and alienating would-be customers in the process.

While I am advocating an internally standardized approach to web design here, there are (as ever) exceptions to the rule and, in some cases, a break in the expected flow or design of a website can be used to dramatic effect. By interrupting someone's expectations and natural behaviors, you can draw immediate attention to particular information and elicit powerful calls to action. This tactic should be approached with caution, however, and I wouldn't recommend it unless you have a really good reason for doing so and an experienced design team to pull it off.

(Incidentally, while you may not necessarily use sitemaps yourself, it is useful to include one on your website for users who want a detailed overview of your website's structure.)

USABILITY

With regard to website usability, the "structure which makes sense to the user will often differ from the structure used internally by the data provider."[41] Since your target is the end user, it's vital that your website is structured in a way that your customers will understand. While it is true good design and clear navigation can boost e-satisfaction,[42, 43] when it comes to usability, a website whose hierarchy of web pages and information "feels natural and well structured"[44] is likely to be user-friendly and engaging.

Although functionality is, of course, important, research shows that first impressions (especially aesthetic ones) can also influence a user's *perception* of your website's usability.[45] Since initial impressions are surprisingly consistent,[46] it pays to make sure you get it right.

On the whole, however, most websites follow similar conventions with regard to general structure. For instance, you'll usually find navigation bars across the top of a page, the logo in the top-left corner[47] and contact information in the footer. Why does this matter? Well, when it comes to influencing your customers online, part of the equation is how to make their lives easier so that they can focus on the important (influential) elements of your website. By making your site easy to use, you are, in effect, giving your customers more mental space to take in the information that really matters.

It's not just standardization that can improve the comprehensibility of your website. When it comes to web design, a picture really is worth a thousand words. Sites that use images to capture their users' attention and convey a particular message tend to be much more persuasive than plain text sites.[48] If your market is predominantly male, research shows that you'll get a better level of engagement if you throw some video and interactive media into the mix.[49] While there is still some debate as to whether or not the fold (the bottom of the screen) makes a big difference to usability, evidence suggests that it's preferable to provide all your important information above the fold so that your customers can capture it all in one go without having to scroll.[50]

It should go without saying, the most persuasive websites tend to be the ones that are well designed and easy to use—that's a no-brainer—but when it comes to getting people to take *action*, it's the interactive sites that win out. These particular websites simply provide more mechanisms for online advocacy (such as e-petitions and comment sections) and it is this level of interactivity that has the biggest impact on getting people to take positive action.[51]

The type of website you own will also inform the structure that your users expect from it. In the 1990s, Hoffman and his colleagues identified six primary types of commercial websites:

- incentive site
- online storefront (such as www.liberty.co.uk)
- search agent (Google)
- Internet presence (flat ads, information and image sites)
- shopping center (such as Amazon)
- content (sponsored, fee-based sites and searchable databases).[52]

While things have changed a lot since then (especially with the advent of social media), these six types still provide a useful framework for categorizing your website to help inform its design and service dimensions. For example, if your website provides digital products and services, the quality, reliability of your information (and how easy it is to search through) will be vital to your site's success.[53] If, however, your website sells physical products that you actually have to deliver, factors such as security, privacy, ease of use, fulfillment, and reliability become more important.[54, 55]

MAKE THIS WORK FOR YOU

Design a killer website

- **Purpose** Whatever the purpose of your website, this should be clearly communicated by its design.[56] Whether your website provides personal, commercial or recreational services, by employing an aesthetic that reflects its *raison d'être*, you can improve your users' experience. This kind of congruent design also helps to boost your website's perceived trustworthiness, since customers can count on your navigation to be reliable and consistent.

- **Meet their needs** Analyze your target audience and tailor your website to their needs and beliefs.[57] We all want to feel connected, valued and understood. By taking the time to research your audience and design your website to meet its needs, you can create a sense of subconscious rapport with your users, making them feel safe and, therefore, more likely to buy.

– **Clear messaging** Present your key messages clearly and concisely. Simplify the amount of information your users have to process by making use of case studies and analogies to communicate your services.[58]

– **User experience** The more comfortable, easy and enjoyable it is for your users to navigate your website, the more satisfied they will be. By understanding who your users are, you can structure your website according to their level of Internet expertise (it makes a difference whether they're novices or digital natives).

– **Intrinsic information** A good website will provide accurate information that is updated as and when necessary. This doesn't just apply to blogs, but to any website that delivers information about a service, contact details, products and so on that require updating. Yes, this includes you.

– **Accessibility** Make it easier for your customers to find what they're looking for by including a simple search box in the header of your website. It should go without saying that your word count should be kept to a decent minimum (no one likes to be greeted by a sea of words) and your headers should be clear and succinct (you'd be surprised how many businesses don't do this). Your navigation should follow the same rules and, where necessary, you can use dropdown menus to order your information and keep visual clutter to a minimum.

– **Representational information** Unless you run a very niche online business or forum, the information on your website should be friendly and easy for most people to understand. This means making sure you include explanations for any jargon you use, as well as providing concise descriptions of any products or services you may be offering. A great way of adding clarity to your information is through the use of examples, images and footnotes. To ensure that your content is accessible, make sure you label content correctly for users who have visual impairments.

– **Search engine optimization (SEO)** It's imperative that the content on your website is well organized, accessible and search engine-friendly. This means that all your page headings and page content (images, videos and text) should be labelled appropriately. For example, if you're including an image of a new water-saving device that you've just launched, its title should describe it as such—that is "New water-saving device." Make sure that the written content you do have is succinct, brief and contains the keywords and headings most relevant to your service/products.

- **Contextual information** If you provide customer service directly through your website (through instant messaging or Live Chat services), make sure you know when your clients are likely to get in touch so that you can be on hand to respond swiftly. For example, if you are a company specializing in hand-piped chocolates (a product close to my heart) and you're based out of the West Coast USA, you may have customers coming online and asking for your help hours before you've even woken up. In this case, it can pay to have someone on hand to respond to these customers and provide the support they need in a timely manner. For websites that cater to a global audience, contextual information can include subsites that represent different countries, making it easier for new visitors to find the portal that's right for them.

- **Coherent design** Make your user experience flow by ensuring that your website is internally consistent. Different countries have different norms for standard web design practice, so make sure you research your market, observe the relevant norms and present a website the pages of which are consistent and easy to navigate. By complying with local web conventions, you can make it easier for your users to cognitively "map" your website and find what they're looking for more easily. If you need help designing culture-specific websites, OBANMultilingual[59] provide great service in this arena.

- **Interactivity** The most successful websites are interactive.[60] Where relevant, encourage users to comment on your blog, rate your products, interact with you (via Live Person for example) and upload (appropriate) user-generated content to your website.

- **Moving images** One of the most powerful ways to convey a message quickly and with impact is to use images. We're evolutionarily primed to respond strongly to faces and movement, so engage with your visitors is by integrating a moving image slider or video into your home page.

- **Keep updating your content** Keeping your visitors up to date with your news and products/services will communicate how active you are and encourage users to keep returning to your site. Maintaining an interesting blog will also allow other sites to quote your articles and link back to your site. This can provide you with a good boost in terms of your search engine optimization (SEO) and can also increase customers' engagement by giving them the opportunity to comment on your posts.

- **Call to action** This is the bit where you tell your site visitors exactly what you want them to do. By providing a clear call to action, such as "try this new service free for 30 days" or "sign up to our newsletter," you can direct people's attention towards a singular outcome and increase conversion rates. To make it easier for your visitors to take the desired action, you can use blocks of "hot" colors (such as bright pink, yellow, orange or red) to highlight the message and provide clear links and buttons in the margin on every page, located where everyone can see them clearly.

- **Create a community** Providing and actively maintaining Facebook pages or Twitter feeds can provide a much-needed space for your customers to interact. Enabling your clients to connect, share tips and swap stories can be a great way to foster a strong client community. It also creates a group identity and can generate a healthy buzz around your business.

- **Target your audience** If your target market is women (either partly or entirely), make sure you engineer your website so as to boost your perceived trustworthiness and credibility to minimize any sense of risk (for more information, please refer to Chapter 19).

- **e-satisfaction** Beyond simply looking good and making yourself understood, by greeting your customers with a website that is well designed and easy to navigate, you can actually manufacture e-satisfaction.[61, 62]

In order to get the most from this knowledge, you need to put the relevant principles into practice and test them on your target audience. One of the best ways to do this is to launch a beta site and monitor your visitors' responses. By gathering user feedback, you can then utilize this information to fine-tune your website's design and iteratively evolve its aesthetics, user experience and functionality. You can repeat this process until you are happy with the level of engagement and return on investment that you're getting.

PUTTING IT INTO PRACTICE: EYETRACKING

Eye tracking is the process of measuring where we're looking, in what sequence and for how long. Harnessed correctly, it can be used to predict where people will look when they hit your landing page.

There are some great resources out there that you can explore to optimize your website. The best are often the most expensive, and no one wants to spend more than they have to on developing a site. In terms of accuracy, live eye-tracking trials carried out on members of your target market tend to provide the most insightful information, but they are also time-consuming and can take a vast amount of preparation and investment to run well.

This is where neurotechnology comes in. We all want to improve our websites' usability and conversion rates, but measuring the visual impact of your site can be tricky at best, especially when even the professionals disagree on how this should be achieved.

Imagine for a moment that I give you a piece of white paper with a single red dot in the top-right corner. I could predict with 100 percent certainty that your gaze would be immediately and involuntarily directed towards the dot, regardless of your age, gender or ethnicity. Why? Well, ask color psychologists and they might say it's because this highly saturated red is stimulating your limbic system. Ask designers and they might say it's due to the placement of the dot on the page.

The truth is it's a combination of many factors and, as trivial as this example may be, it shows there must be predictable mechanisms that govern our eye movements; mechanisms tightly intertwined with our visual structure of the world.

Recent advances in technology now make it possible to predict how people will respond to websites without ever having to set foot in a focus group. One tool in particular does this surprisingly well.

Unlike many of the pseudo-scientific tools crowding this market, EyeQuant is an in-browser platform and its algorythms are derived from neuroscientific models of human attention. Based on the work of three of the world's leading attention researchers (professors Koch, Itti and König), EyeQuant can predict, with *over 90 percent accuracy,* where people will look within the first few seconds that they visit your website. How? By using the data gathered from over 500 live eye-tracking trials to simulate how our eyes will respond to statistical image features (such as color contrasts, luminance, shapes, forms and the positioning of design elements).

All you have to do is upload a snapshot of your website to the EyeQuant platform and the program does the rest. It automatically weighs and evaluates each visual feature within a computational model of human attention and shows you how the design can be improved to optimize your site.

This is particularly powerful technology that not only speeds up the optimization cycle itself but also saves you huge amounts of time and money in the process—and can have a dramatic effect on your bottom line. Allow me to give you an example in the following case study.

CASE STUDY Groupon

Whether you're a dedicated fan or have yet to use it, you'll have no doubt heard of the discount shopping website Groupon. Despite a few wobbly moments, this international site has attracted a huge consumer base throughout the world and, in 2011, its German site underwent a neuro-technological makeover. Following a simple, iterative procedure, Groupon used EyeQuant to optimize its landing page and increased the sign-up rate by a massive 52 percent.

In the first test depicted below (see Figure 8.1), it became apparent that users were focusing on the logo and images when visiting the site, but were completely ignoring the text, sign-up form and call to action.

Figure 8.1

Source: http://www.groupon.de

Figure 8.2

Source: www.groupon.de

So the designers made some changes (see Figure 8.2): they increased the contrast between the background color and the main page; reduced the size of the footer banner and aligned its content; and simplified the design, layout and color scheme of the page itself.

Having tweaked the design, they ran the test again and found that the users' gaze was now being directed towards the text. While this was an improvement on the initial landing page, it showed that users would still be skipping over the sign-up form and special offers, which were the whole point of the site. So, they made some more changes.

As you can see from the final version (see Figure 8.3), the designers shrank the banner even further and aligned it with the call to action, placing it firmly in the best perception path for anyone visiting the site. This simplified landing page was now drawing attention in all the right places: the logo, text and call to action. When it launched, Groupon's freshly optimized website was greeted with a 50 percent increase in the sign-up rate. The neurotechnology had done its job and had done it well.

This simple case study illustrates what a huge impact the application of a few principles can have on a user's website experience. It also shows that knowledge by itself is not enough—in order to really engage your audience, you have to test these principles in action. EyeQuant provides a great platform with which to do it. After all, what would a 50 percent increase mean for your business?

Figure 8.3

Source: www.groupon.de

While the human visual system is too complex to capture in a few rules of thumb, there are nonetheless some ground rules you can follow to design a successful website. Here are a few tips sourced by the guys over at EyeQuant to help you on your way.

MAKE THIS WORK FOR YOU

Keep it simple

- **Simplicity rules** There is a reason products such as Google Search and the iPad are so successful: beyond their elegant, minimalist designs, they provide a simple, almost foolproof user experience. Your website should be no different. Make the first few seconds count by showing your users what you're about, how you're providing value and what they need to do next.

- **Attention is a resource** Your users' attention is a finite resource, so use it wisely. Every bit of information on your website will consume a certain amount of attention, so the more design elements you include, the more competition there will be. In order to minimize the cognitive load, you should stick to a clear attentional hierarchy. Do your users really need to be able to see the full navigation menu at all times? Do they need a cluttered sidebar on every page? Again, simplicity rules.

– **Rules are silver, testing is golden** When it comes to the success of your website, testing is vital—and I don't just mean as a one-off. Carrying out repeated tests along the way can mean the difference between a trickle of visitors and a veritable downpour. In this day and age, if you want your business to succeed, relying on your "best guess" isn't an option. Since the online environment makes it possible for you to test every single one of your marketing and sales efforts, you really have no excuse not to succeed. To find out more about how to test effectively, check out Bryan Eisenberg's book, *Always Be Testing: The complete guide to Google Website Optimizer.*[63]

9 YOUR IMAGES

> *A picture is worth a thousand words.*
> FREDERICK R. BARNARD, MARKETER[1]

All websites and online content are necessarily visual in nature and there are certain rules you can apply to make your visual media more influential to your online audience.

While we all have a different take on what's beautiful and what's not, research suggests there are universal principles that underpin our overall sense of aesthetics. World-renowned neuroscientist Professor Ramachandran and philosopher Hirstein[2] explored this and found there are indeed rules for the ways in which we process aesthetics.

If our visual preferences are hard-wired, then they are also predictable, which means, if you know the visual triggers that elicit a deep, primal response, you can use this to influence your viewers' experience.

THE UNIVERSAL APPEAL OF BEAUTY

Professor Zeki, considered by many as the founding father of neuroaesthetics, claims to have discovered the formula for beauty. In a study using MRI scans, he found that a specific part of our brain (the medial orbitofrontal cortex) becomes active when we see or hear something beautiful (when we see something ugly, it's the amygdala that lights up).[3] Associated with pleasure and reward, this particular area seems to respond universally to beauty—which means that we could conceivably use it to measure the "attractiveness" of elements such as website headers, typography and images. It doesn't take a neuroscientist to see how this could be very useful indeed.

In another study, two researchers set out to discover if we exhibit any *global* preferences in aesthetics—but, this time, with regard to paintings.[4] Komar and Melamid canvassed millions of participants worldwide and found most of us prefer to look at blue landscapes that include national icons (such as our country's flag). They also found we like paintings that depict children playing, with the exception of one country—France—whose participants collectively preferred to see naked women. While I'm not advocating the use of naked women to lure in your French viewers (though I'm sure it would be effective), these results do reveal some deep-seated, subconscious preferences that dramatically affect our responses towards visual media. For instance, we'd rather look at natural environments than those influenced by humans[5] (we seem to share a universal preference for our ancestral savannah) and we tend to be irresistibly drawn towards images that contain a certain quality of mystery about them (such as a partially obstructed view).[6]

PERCEPTUAL PROBLEM-SOLVING

Our primitive ancestors depended on their keen senses of sights and smell to keep them alive: identifying potential predators, prey, mates and sources of food and water. Their ability to *perceptually group* together those slow-moving yellow dots amid the green foliage of the trees, so that they recognized the outline of a moving lion, meant the difference between life and a rather grisly death.

Of course, life is different now, and you're unlikely to face life-and-death situations online. Yet, our visual system has developed out of this basic need to recognize salient features in our environment and we still like to engage with images that challenge and puzzle us today.

Consider the classic Dalmatian illusion below. Initially it just looks like an abstract array of black dots on a white background and, for a while, your brain will simply scan the image, trying to discern any visible pattern. Until, suddenly, you see that there is a Dalmatian walking in the dappled shade of trees!

In that tiny "aha" moment, you get a tingly, gratifying sense of satisfaction. This reinforcing jolt of excitement highlights the primitive connection between your visual system and the limbic, emotional part of your brain, so that once you've spotted the dog, it becomes impossible to "un-see" it. Now that your brain has successfully made sense of the picture, it's damned if it's going to go back to its previous, uncomfortable state of ambiguity.

It's for this reason that we find mysterious, ambiguous images so frustratingly irresistible. The less obvious the puzzle, the more it piques our interest—and the greater the satisfaction in solving it. With our attention spans diminishing by the second, this technique is great for grabbing people's attention and holding it there.

Source: Gregory, R. (1970) *The Intelligent Eye*, McGraw-Hill.

Ever the leaders in psychological wizardry, Apple uses this principle worldwide every time it opens a new shop. The simple act of hiding something behind an archetypal red curtain is a powerfully seductive one, as anyone who's been to a burlesque show can attest.

Even though it's an extraordinarily simple trick, the fact that a bit of ink and some board can literally shroud a store in mystery and quicken our desires to see what's inside should drive home the point that mystery works (as abhorrent as this may be to our rational minds).

Source: Courtesy Simon Kimber.

NOT JUST A PRETTY FACE

Another odd visual phenomenon is the *peak shift effect*. Our brains get a kick out of seeing exaggerated images and caricatures of real-life things.

From ancient cave paintings to Disney animations, every culture through-out history has created art that represents life through symbolic, hyperbolic forms.Why? Because we have limited attentional resources, so are hard-wired to prefer "supernormal" stimuli. If we extract only the key, defining features of a subject (such as the slim waist, full bosom and round hips of a reclining nude) our brains can ignore any superfluous information and instead focus on the salient features. In fact, neurons that specialize in facial recognition actually fire more rapidly and strongly in response to caricatures of people's faces than when looking at the real thing.

PERCEPTUAL GROUPING

Besides this penchant for distortion, our brains are also hard-wired to iden-tify and link related features into one single object (such as the yellow dots of the lions among the trees). We tend to lump together items that are the same shape, color, luminance or saturation, as well as items that are close together.

As we saw in the case study on Groupon's use of eyetracking technology at the end of the previous chapter, our ability to chunk information based on its visual properties can have a dramatic influence on where we look. In an online context, too, this has significant implications for the persuasiveness of our websites and the images that we use.

If you have any experience of design, you'll be well aware of the impact that *contrast* can have on attracting people's attention. Since high-contrast areas are usually rich in data, your brain will automatically be drawn to these regions to help it make sense of the world. This is why camouflage is so effective—it relies on our brain's natural bias towards contrasting visual stimuli to magically "disappear" the person or animal that is hiding.

WHAT'S WRONG WITH THIS PICTURE BELOW?

Source: Yéan-Loup Gaut reau/AFP/Getty Images.

Another odd characteristic of our visual system is that we show an intense dislike of unusual vantage points. Our brains like to be able to generalize visual information, so when we see something that doesn't tally with our expectations, it throws us. While this particular ploy goes against our aesthetic preferences, if used cleverly, it can be a uniquely powerful way of grabbing and maintaining someone's attention, as our brains will usually puzzle over these kinds of images for as long as it takes us to figure out what's going on. If this particular trick isn't your cup of tea, you can also draw on *visual metaphors* and puns to attract your viewers' attention (see below).

Source: Robert Ashton/Massive Pixels/Alamy.

Fundamentally, we enjoy discovering implicit, hidden similarities between seemingly disparate items—so much so that some of our most treasured artists have used this principle in their work. Take a look at Picassco's *Bull's Head* (1943)—using just a bicycle seat and handle bars—and you'll see at first hand the fabulous pull of this trick when applied as a conscious technique.

LESS IS MORE

Now for a really odd one. If I asked you to tell me which of the three images below elicits the strongest response from the limbic (primitive) part of your brain, which one would you choose?

Source: www.imagesource.com Nigel Riches. Image Source.

Surprisingly, it's actually the cartoon-like line drawing on the right that sets your limbic brain firing. Research has shown that a sketch or outline drawing elicits a much stronger response from our brains than a fully colored photograph.

This may seem profoundly bizarre, since in the real world we're surrounded by real faces every day, but, when you recall that our brains have limited attention, it makes sense that a pared-down image would be easier to digest than a complex one. In this case, the black and white line drawing provides only *one* source of information for the brain to absorb, so we read it quickly.

It's not just the content of a face that we attend to. Let's play a game of spot the difference and look at the heat maps taken of the website Baby.com. The areas marked in red are the parts that attract the most attention, so there's obviously a clear difference between the images in Figures 9.1 and 9.2. What makes the text in the second image so much more engaging?

Figure 9.1

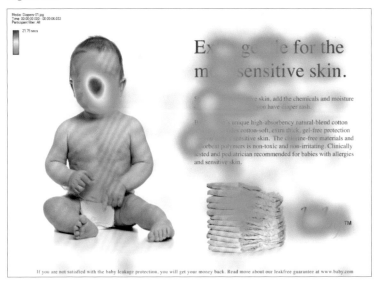

Figure 9.2

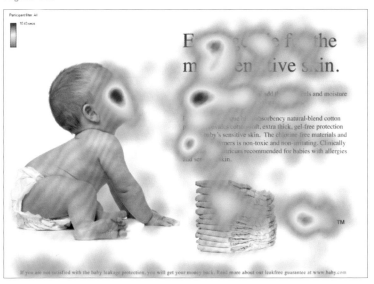

Although the content of the text is identical in each image, in this A/B split test carried out by ObjectiveDigital.com using a Tobii T60 eye tracker from Tobii. com,[7] website visitors who saw the version of the website shown in Figure 9.2 consistently engaged more deeply with the content on the page than they did with the content on the page shown in Figure 9.1. Why? Because that's where the baby was looking.

Evolutionarily speaking, it makes perfect sense. Our survival as a species has always depended on our ability to read and respond to social cues. Whether it's the tilt of someone's head, the direction of their gaze or their pointed finger, we're primed to subconsciously pick up these signals and respond to them accordingly.[8] That is why we'll always gaze in the direction someone's looking.

MAKE THIS WORK FOR YOU

Picture perfect

If you're using images to attract (and direct) people's attention within your website, make sure you A/B split test each iteration to maximize impact. While pictures can add a great deal of richness to an otherwise plain design, they do place a demand on your viewers' attentional resources. If used incorrectly, they can actually end up competing against other important elements within your site. When optimizing the psycho-visual design of your site, the principle elements to consider are:

- luminance

- contrast

- color

- content placement

- typography

- use of images

- hierarchy of information

So, the next time you're dealing with a design issue—whether you're deciding between photographs and illustrations or choosing the animation style for your next video—think twice about the elements you're using and what impact they will have. Whatever you decide, make sure you test it properly, too—you might be surprised at the results.

10 YOUR VIDEOS

 One minute of video is the storytelling equivalent to reading 1.8 million words.

DR. JAMES MCQUIVEY, FORRESTER[1]

THE RISE OF PARASOCIAL RELATIONSHIPS

In one study, people reported that when they were feeling lonely they would tune in to watch their favorite TV show, which would make them feel better. This pseudo-social behavior appeared to ward off feelings of low self-esteem and rejection—simply thinking about their favorite program was enough to increase people's sense of belonging.[2]

These parasocial relationships may seem unnatural and one-sided, but the sense of connection we develop with our favorite fictional characters follow a similar pattern of growth that you'd expect to find in a normal relationship. With increased exposure, and as time passes, we become more and more enthralled and emotionally invested in the dramatic lives of our fictional friends.

It isn't just the lonely who exhibit these behaviors either, it's all of us.

I experienced this first hand when one of my favorite orators and writers, Christopher Hitchens, died of cancer. I had become accustomed to going online to watch Hitchens lecture and debate and, over time, had begun to feel a sense of connection with him. The acute sense of loss I experienced at the news of his death took me completely by surprise. It was, to my mind, utterly irrational—sure, I had read Hitchens' books and seen him give speeches, but I'd never actually met the guy. Yet, the sense of loss was real and more profound than I was expecting. Judging by the explosion of tweets, shared stories and memorial videos that ensued, I wasn't the only one who felt this way.

I'm sure most of us can recount similar stories, but the reason I'm writing about it here is to highlight the emotional power that video (and the characters within it) can have over us.

A LITTLE NEUROSCIENCE GOES A LONG WAY

If you've had your ear to the ground, you'll know that the field of neuroscience has been generating a lot of buzz. Not least because there are tell-tale signs that neuroscience is starting to unlock the secret workings of the mind.

In a fascinating television series for Channel 4, *What makes a masterpiece?*[3] Matthew Cain, the culture editor for *Channel 4 News*, set out to investigate whether neuro-imaging and the nascent field of neuro-aesthetics can identify what makes a great story or film.

In one experiment, volunteers were wired up to EEG machines to measure their brain activity as they watched a series of films.[4] The researchers decided to measure three types of activity in the brain: attention, emotion and memory. They kicked off their experiment with a classic horror, *Jaws*,[5] then an action thriller, *The Bourne Identity*,[6] and ended with an unashamedly romantic comedy, *Love Actually*.[7]

If you had to place a bet on it, which of these three very different films do you think had the most impact on our London audience? Well, if you guessed the action-thriller or the rom-com, you'd be wrong.

Despite the dated special effects and the rubber shark, *Jaws* blew the other two movies out of the water, with an average effectiveness rating of 6.5 out of 10. Despite being over four decades old, the original narrative plays so well on our primal fears of confined spaces, wild animals and the dark that we still can't help responding to it today.

Though the rapid-fire sequences and dramatic chase scenes of *The Bourne Ultimatum* may *look* flash, when measured for overall effectiveness it only scored 5.5. While attention levels were high (you have to really concentrate to follow the visuals), emotional engagement remained low. Despite a hit at the box office, this flick is unlikely to experience the same shelf-life enjoyed by *Jaws*.

As for the rom-com (which scored 5.9), the low emotional engagement of female viewers suggested that they actually found the film more awkward than romantic. A word to the wise.

Although most of us will never direct a blockbuster, this research shows that there are certain psychological principles at play in high-impact films. Once you have identified and understood these principles, you can use them to create emotionally resonant videos that your users will pay attention to and remember long after they've seen them.

Let's consider TV commercials for a moment. Think of your favorite commercial—perhaps one from your childhood. Which one stands out?

I remember with startling fondness the Milky Way ad, in which the red car and the blue car had a race (did you hear the jingle as you read those words?). The commercial still makes me smile to this day and, when it made a comeback to our screens, every time it played I was transported right back to my childhood home, where I would sit watching TV cross-legged on the floor.

Why was this particular ad so effective? How could that short, jingly animation evoke such a nostalgic emotional response? TV advertisers have mastered the art of the ultimate short story and now they're using neuroscience to create the maximum impact in a short window of time.

According to Paul Newton of Neuro-Insight,[8] "Advertising execs are now using science to sex up retail goods and products."[9] In order to get more people to remember their products, advertisers are increasingly investing large budgets collecting neurodata to scientifically engineer their ads for maximum brain impact.

CASE STUDY Birds Eye fish fillets

Picture this scene for a moment. A man dressed in casual blue clothes strolls barefoot along a beautiful expanse of beach. As he walks, a soothing melody drifts in the background and the sound of the sea fills the air. He starts talking directly to you, about the Southern Pacific ocean and the sheer abundance of Mother Nature. While he walks, a seagull flies up to his left and, as the camera pans out over the blue landscape, the whole scene pauses. The music is suspended and only the man continues to move. In that moment he asks you, "Wouldn't it be good if you could … simply capture this moment?" After a brief pause, the music starts again and the scene around him comes back to life, and you're greeted by the image of a box of Birds Eye Fish Fillets.

What you've just pictured is the original version of a Birds Eye commercial. In a bid to make the ad more persuasive, researchers used neuroscientific data taken from brain scans to produce a second, psychologically optimized version. Into this second ad, they inserted an additional scene: a school of fish swimming through the sea, with the sun shining through the water behind them. As in the original ad, we see the man walking along the shore, talking about Mother Nature, with the music drifting in the background, but, this time, as the whole scene starts to slow down, it's a school of fish that are in the freeze-frame (not the seagull with the landscape, as in the original version). After a brief pause, the camera then cuts back to the man on the beach and, as we watch, the music returns and the whole scene moves as it did before. Then, as in the original ad, you're greeted by the image of a box of Birds Eye fish fillets.

The difference? One short, seemingly insignificant scene: the school of fish, which relates directly to the product Birds Eye is trying to sell. This tiny addition resulted in a 40 percent increase in recall of the commercial and contributed to a significant boost in sales. The psychology behind this effect is deceptively simple. Stopping a moving image is a powerful way of engaging the brain and highlighting to our subconscious that this is something we should pay attention to (and remember).

This technique, combined with the blue color, distant views and open skies (all of which elicit a very positive, primal response from our human psyches), makes for a very persuasive video indeed.

Incidentally, while it wasn't mentioned in the experiment, the advertisers behind this video also used a subliminal linguistic technique to influence its viewers. Did you spot it?

"Wouldn't it be good if you could … *simply capture this moment.*"

By unnaturally splitting the sentence into two fragments, the man in the scene is effectively giving you what's known as an *embedded command*—a technique widely used by hypnotists to elicit certain behaviors in their clients. In commanding us to "Simply capture this moment" (the effect of which is further enhanced by the slowing down and suspension of the music in the background), we're compelled to pause and *really* "capture" the school of fish the advertisers are presenting to us.

If even the smallest of differences can increase sales from a commercial and neuroscientific methods can help us find them, just think what you could do if you put some of these principles into practice.

WHAT'S IN A STORY?

> *Communication is one act, in which the brain of the communicator, and the brain of the listeners are trying to be coupled, and merging as one.*
> DR. URI HASSON, PSYCHOLOGIST[10]

The story is one of the oldest and most powerful forms of communication known to humankind. In one experiment, Dr Hasson and his team at Princeton University set out to investigate exactly what goes on in our brains when we tell, and listen to, a story. The researchers discovered that when two people are engaged in a story, both brains response patterns are shared across a remarkable number of regions in an act of "neural coupling." Far from being a passive process, storytelling is a joint action, in which the speaker *literally* tries to get us on the same wavelength. This explains how great orators can rouse entire nations into committing acts of incredible violence or great love.

We've long known that storytelling is an incredibly powerful, primal medium through which we connect as a species, but the extraordinary fact that our brains are hard-wired to understand each other in this way has huge implications for the manner in which we deliver information.

Have you ever wondered *how* suspense thrillers and horror movies work? Or *why*, when you watch someone running away from a demented killer, your heart actually starts to beat faster? When you see an action performed on someone else, whether they're in front of you or on a screen, the mirror neurons in your somatosensory cortex become active and you actually experience the other person's emotional and physical response *as if you were going through it yourself.*

Even when it comes to something as universal as empathy, our responses do vary. As a rule, women tend to experience a stronger emotional response than men, which may explain why action movies and horror films tend to appeal to men more than women. When a scene becomes too violent, men can simply "turn down" their empathy, whereas women may find it literally too painful to watch.

CASE STUDY Casino Royale

While it's true that storytelling is a universal communicator, there are, of course, differences in the ways in which we respond to particular elements within a given plot. Allow me to give you an example.

In a study investigating our neural reactions to films, neuroscientist Professor Ohme set out to compare the brain activity of women and men in response to the famous Bond film *Casino Royale*.[11,12] If you've seen the movie and if you're a woman, you may remember a witty verbal scene that takes place between Bond and his leading lady, Vesper, during a taxi ride. I say "if you're a woman" because, at this point in the film, most male viewers had practically switched off. So if you're reading this and you're a man, you probably have no idea what scene I'm talking about, whether you watched the movie or not.

Now, I hate to play into gender stereotypes, but it seems that at least when it comes to films, men really are more interested in visuals than verbals. So, if you're pitching to a full-blooded male audience, supply a bit of action—whether it's in the bedroom or the boxing ring.

Women, however, aren't immune to a bit of eye-candy. In fact, far from it. In another emotionally charged scene, Bond finds Vesper cowering and drenched on the shower floor, having just witnessed a brutal murder. Now, if you are a woman, your attention levels would have spiked as you watched Bond undo his tie and start sucking Vesper's fingers (yes, it's fabulously sexy). You'd have been rapt as she started talking, but, as the shot panned out, your attention would have plummeted.

Why? Because of a toilet seat that comes into view on the left-hand side of the screen. If you're a guy you'd have probably never noticed—the toilet seat is down, so what's the problem? Here's the kicker: when asked to identify what specifically had turned them off, women were unable to articulate why it was they disliked this particular shot. Their brain scans told a different story: women had perceived the toilet peripherally and had responded to it at a subconscious level without even realizing that they'd seen it. No prizes for guessing what gender the director was.

MAKE THIS WORK FOR YOU

Target the right gender

The observations we have been exploring in this chapter have significant implications when it comes to creating visual media for specific audiences. If you're producing a video or a film targeted primarily at women, you may expect a far higher level of attention if you follow a verbal, visually pleasant sequence. If, however, your audience is male, action-rich visual sequences are more likely to be a hit.

Since the vast majority of our mental operations occur beneath the level of our conscious awareness, our ability to monitor subconscious reactions to media can yield huge insights and benefits to anyone seeking to engage with their audience at a deeper, more viscerally compelling level.

SELLING A FANTASY

We all want to feel happier, sexier, richer and, as a species, we have always searched for ways in which to enhance our physical and psychological states—be it via the shaman in the nearby village or the psychiatrist who prescribes our pills.

For millennia, anyone who had the power to successfully manipulate our emotions held the keys to our wallets, too. You need only look as far as the number of religious institutions that demanded (and in many cases, still demand) tithing in return for an exalted promise of eternal bliss to realize that this "fantasy" script, and our need for it, is as old as the hills.

Among the myriad institutions that employ this tactic, the advertising industry is particularly well versed in it. In fact, you may have noticed an ad or two promising to make you slimmer or wealthier and wondered how some companies can get away with it. Beyond asserting the patently ridiculous ("eat this burger 20 times a day and you'll lose lots of weight"), I think that if you genuinely have a fantastic product/service to offer, there's nothing wrong with employing the lure of fantasy to engage with and tantalize your audience. After all, a bit of titillation can brighten anyone's day.

In some cases, playing to our fantasies can actually result in surprisingly witty, effective ads. (My personal favorite is the recent run of Lynx deodorant commercial, in which a fairly lanky, metrosexual guy sprays on some Lynx and gets mobbed by literally hundreds of beautiful, scantily clad women.)

Playing out our wildest dreams isn't the only way in which ads and videos can influence our behaviors—humor works just as well. While anyone will tell you that comedy sells, what you may not know is that it can also boost your credibility. In one particular study, a group of participants were asked to view and rate either a funny or non-funny version of a public service announcement.[13] Of the people who took part, those who had seen the funny version not only enjoyed a welcome mood boost but also rated the announcement as more credible. Although they later found it harder to remember the content of the ad, the group that had seen the funny version actually showed the greatest attitude change in the long run.

It's precisely this ability to divert our attention *away* from intellectually engaging with a brand that may hold the key to humor's success as a persuasion agent.[14] So what happens when you mix a bit of fantasy with some humor?

CASE STUDY Allstate Insurance

If you're reading this in the USA, you may be familiar with the year long advertising campaign that Allstate Insurance ran in 2010. Starring actor Dean Winters, these commercials followed a narrative in which Mayhem was personified as a mischievous devil, hell bent on wreaking havoc on the innocent. The ads ran like a series of episodes and, in each, Mayhem would come in a different guise—a "deer in your headlights," a fallen tree in a windstorm, a teenage driver. Whatever the scenario, the core message was always this: if you want to be protected against all kinds of Mayhem, buy Allstate Insurance. The message worked. This hugely memorable, sticky campaign relied on a few fundamental principles to succeed.

- **Loss aversion** It played on our fear that we'd lose our car, house and peace of mind (more on this principle in Chapter 14)

- **Storytelling** It used the age-old narrative form to get its viewers to buy into the story and put themselves in the protagonist's shoes

- **Unexpected** The concept that mayhem could take on an embodied, Machiavellian form was unusual enough to be memorable.

MAKE THIS WORK FOR YOU

Role-play

While the use of comedy (and tragedy) can make your video memorable and incentivise customers to act, it will only work if its message resonates with your target audience.

By finding out what your customers most want to experience when using your product/services, you can create a fantasy script with which they will identify. As we saw in Chapter 1, the before and after technique is a great way to achieve this—and you can use this technique here.

Showing your customers a character that's similar to them helps them empathize with that person. Then, when you move that character from an unpleasant state to a positive one, your viewers will mirror that transition, associate the positive state with your product and be more compelled to purchase it. A word of warning, though—if you promise something that you simply cannot deliver, you risk hurting and alienating your customers—so make sure you can come through on any claims.

11 YOUR COLORS

> *Colors alter the meanings of the objects or situations with which they are associated and color preferences can predict consumers' behavior.*
>
> DR. MUBEEN ASLAM, MARKETING[1]

What does the color orange signify to you? If you're reading this book in Europe or the USA, roadworks and traffic delays might spring to mind, but live in Asia and you'll most likely associate this color with spirituality and celebration. If you're Zambian, you probably don't consider orange to be a separate color at all.[2]

A single color can have a multitude of different and often contradictory meanings, which, to a large extent, depend on their cultural context. The popular media tend to portray color meanings in rather simplified terms, preferring ubiquitous general principles to the altogether more nuanced, complex reality.

As we shall see in a moment, the color red is an excellent example of this. Often cited as signifying sexuality, the meaning of red (and our psychological and physiological responses to it) can vary dramatically from one situation to the next, signifying sexual availability and attraction in one context and danger in another.

The ways in which we interpret and respond to colors depends on a range of variables, including our cultural norms (in China, red is seen as lucky), learned associations ("Coca-Cola red" and "IBM blue")[3] and universally innate responses (the four F's: freeze, fight, flight and ... sex). While some researchers have argued that our emotional responses to color have a biological, evolutionary origin,[4] even when we do find biological tendencies these can sometimes be in conflict with acquired societal norms,[5] resulting in cultural differences and a bunch of "rules" that simply can't be generalized to everyone.

Suffice it to say that color psychology is a tricky field and one that is peppered with conflicting evidence. While I have endeavoured to collate and distill the best of the research here, you should take the information in the following pages with a pinch of salt. Allow this chapter to broaden your understanding of color and culture and inform the design decisions you make, but also know that our tastes and preferences change and there is no substitute for testing your website and branding on your actual target market. When in doubt, test, test and test again.

Since our online interactions occur almost entirely via visual media (images, videos, text), it is vital that you understand which visual factors yield the greatest influence—and color is one of the most powerful and instantaneous ways of conveying meaning. When applied correctly, the appropriate use of color can influence your visitors towards positive outcomes, such as perceiving you as more trustworthy, valuable and authoritative.

When it comes to cultural differences in aesthetics, again color plays a major role. It has long been claimed that colors can have a powerful effect on people's moods and behaviors, but to date most studies investigating these effects remain closely guarded secrets, held under lock and key by the marketing and advertising companies that commission them. There is new research, however, that is making its way into the academic domain and it is this that I would like to present to you over the following pages.

The way in which we react to color can be strongly influenced by our cultural background.[6] For instance, the color that one nation considers sacred may have an entirely different connotation elsewhere and, as such, the meaning (and, hence, persuasiveness) of a color depends greatly on its historical context.

To give you an example, in Western Judeo-Christian cultures, the palette of gold, red, white and blue/purple traditionally denoted opulence, power and authority.[7] Why? These colors were originally derived from rare, precious pigments, so were expensive to acquire. Hence, over time, they came to signify wealth and high standing.

Beyond specific colors, a culture's overall preferences regarding color combinations can also vary dramatically. Just look at the difference between India, with its love of highly saturated, bright mélanges of colors, and the Nordic countries, which favor a more muted palate, and you'll see a veritable jigsaw of cultural color preferences begin to emerge.

Whatever our backgrounds and wherever we're from, we tend to assume that our experiences, beliefs and societal constructs are "normal." As such, we often forget that we live in a tiny microcosm in which culturally relative rules apply.

Beyond our bubble lies an entirely different world and, if we are to succeed in reaching out to a global audience, we have to start taking a much broader look at the cultural quirks that define and influence us, such as all the elements that influence our perceptions of color—see below.

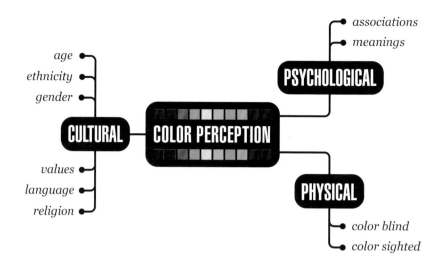

COLOR AND VALUE

Color can also be used to influence people's perceptions of a product's price and quality.[8] For instance, in the UK, the use of pink in products tends to be perceived as average-priced and young-looking, whereas neutral colors are perceived as expensive, "boring and dull" and "for a mature person."[9]

While our tastes do change with the latest trends, dark colors seem to enjoy a continuing association with value and richness, so are often used for expensive products to denote sophistication and quality.[10]

As we shall see throughout this chapter, choosing the right colors to represent you online via your website, branding, favicon (the icon that appears next to your URL), logo, etc. should depend not only on the message you wish to convey but also on the market that you're trying to reach.

Research shows that a brand's color can actually influence purchasing behaviors and, if used correctly, can even increase sales. A few decades ago, psychologist Carlton Wagner decided to put this theory to the test. He advised the American hot dog restaurant Wienerschnitzel to include a little orange in the color of its buildings. He believed that adding orange to the brand's image would convey the message that the chain sold inexpensive hot dogs, thereby attracting more customers and boosting hot dog sales—and he was right. After this slight change in color, Wienerschnitzel reported a 7 percent increase in sales.[11]

Color consultant James Mandle enjoyed a similar success when he advised Ty-D-Bol to change the colors on its toilet cleanser packaging from light blue and green to bright white letters on a dark background. Believing that the new bold color scheme would convey cleanliness and strength, as opposed to the original "wimpy" bottle design, Mandle's decision was vindicated when, over the next 18 months, the sales of Ty-D-Bol jumped a whopping 40 percent.[12]

PHYSIOLOGICAL EFFECTS OF COLOR

Color influences both human behavior and human physiology. Even though differences remain, there are values that transcend national frontiers.

THOMAS MADDEN, KELLY HEWITT, AND
MARTIN ROTH, MARKETING[13]

Colors can carry specific meanings that have important, real-world implications for psychological functioning. In fact, research has shown that when we look at certain colors that hold a specific meaning for us (for instance, I associate yellow with holidays in Southern Spain), the mere perception of that color can elicit thoughts, emotions and behaviors consistent with that meaning (I feel a surge of warmth as I think of Mum's home cooking and cocktails with Dad on the terrace).

In an online context, the persuasive power of color can be used to subconsciously prime and influence people's behaviors and motivations.[14] This has huge implications when you apply such knowledge to design, especially when you are representing your brand and business in a global marketplace.[15]

Beyond your brand and identity, colors can also retain strong associations with particular categories of products. For instance, in the USA, silver is evocative of dairy foods, pink is associated with Barbie dolls and cosmetics, while blue relates to a range of categories, from financial services to health foods and desserts.[16] While it is possible to launch mould-breaking products by bucking the trend, these successes tend to be few and far between. Instead, research suggests that, when it comes to buying high-involvement products, we tend to follow subjective norms.[17] So, if you are selling your products online, check out what colors and branding the rest of your market is using (especially the market leaders) and follow suit. In e-commerce, social conformity can really pay off.

With regard to branding, color can communicate your identity as an organization. For instance, in the USA, blue branding identifies a company as responsible and solid and is the color of choice for financial services[18]—you need only look through the websites of the Fortune 100 companies to see a distinctive preference for muted, grey-blue color schemes.

As well as conveying particular meanings, colors can also determine the way in which people interact with a website and can even influence the amount and type of information that your visitors later recall.[19] Since one of the first things you'll notice about a website is its color, it is crucial that you can identify and use the colors likely to elicit the most positive response from your visitors. While brighter, more saturated colors generally make us feel happier and more excited,[20] these may not be the colors or responses that lead to increased sales online, as we shall see in a moment.

Certain colors (and combinations of colors) affect us on a physiological level. As we discussed earlier, fast-food chains have traditionally used red and yellow branding and interiors to stimulate appetite and increase the speed at which they turn around their customers. Financial institutions, on the other hand, often use the color blue to promote a sense of security and calm and, indeed, research shows that websites with a blue color scheme tend to be perceived as more credible and trustworthy.[21, 22] In fact, banks are more likely to use blue or grey as the main color in their logos and design than orange,[23] which is reflective of the Western view that blue is seen as calming, whereas orange is considered cheap.

Certain colors can even increase our attention to detail by stimulating our arousal systems and looking at colors that make us feel energetic, active and lively can increase our subjective feelings of trust.[24] As a basic rule of thumb, when it comes to design, the higher a color's saturation, the higher the level of excitement (whether good or bad) it elicits. Let's try a little experiment to see how this translates online. Of the two websites below, which would you instinctively prefer to buy from? Why?

My guess is that, like most people, the yellow website would probably have you running for the hills, whereas the white one might capture your curiosity long enough for you to investigate the site a bit further.

You'll notice that while both sites use highly saturated, bright colors, the second site uses them very sparingly and then only in the high-res sliding product photo. The fact that the second website uses these colors within a wider context of a white background creates both an atmosphere of calm (a precursor to trust) and a focal point for the viewer's gaze.

Our dislike for the first, yellow website may not be down to subjective preferences, either. Research has found e-commerce sites that use yellow color schemes tend to be disliked by the majority of us, evoking a sense of distrust regardless of our cultural backgrounds.[25]

Source: http://www.cdiscount.com

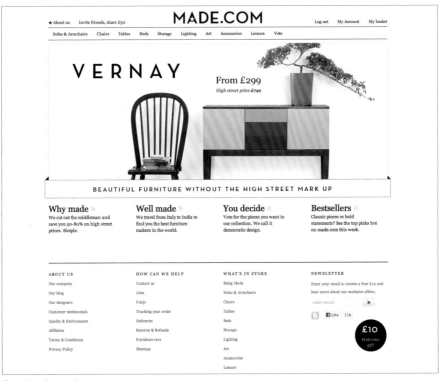

Source: http://www.made.com

BRIGHTNESS, SATURATION AND HUE

Psychologist Hans Eysenck identified a heirachy of preferences that humans express when it comes to colors, regardless of our gender and ethnicity. It is:

- blue
- red
- green
- violet
- orange
- yellow

In the last 70 years, this ranking has remained the same.[26]

While this provides a general rule of thumb, when it comes to advertisements, it's not just a color's hue that we respond to, but also the saturation. Psychologists Valdez and Mehrabian found evidence for "strong and highly predictable relationships" between a color's brightness and saturation and their effects on people's emotional reactions.[27] They found that people experienced the greatest pleasure from seeing bright, saturated colors and the stronger a color's saturation, the greater the response in terms of physiological arousal.

If you call to mind any Coca-Cola ads, old or new, the first thing you're likely to remember is the vibrant red of the brand, followed by any associations you may have with the product. One of the reasons that Coke's branding is so successful is precisely because of its bright, highly saturated colors. Once Coca-Cola became a hit in the USA (where red is associated with passion, excitement and sex, among other things),[28] the brand could then cross borders to forge new associations in cultures where red has traditionally held different meanings. If you remember Chapter 5, about glocalization, it's important to note that, while people around the world now recognize the red of the Coca-Cola logo, the peripheral branding (such as its websites, promotional materials and merchandise) have been adapted to suit the specific cultures of its local markets.

Valdez and Mehrabian's findings also provide support for the different color groupings traditionally used by designers—that is, warmer colors (red, orange, pink) induce greater levels of activity than cooler colors. Overall, they found that people's favorite hues are in the blue spectrum (blue, blue-green, green, red-purple, purple and purple-blue) and the least-liked hues are yellow and green-yellow, with the color red being rated in between. Interestingly, people said that they experienced submissive feelings in response to red-purple colors and felt more dominant in response to yellow and green-yellow. They also found that women were more sensitive to saturation and brightness than men, possibly because some women are tetrachromats (they have four types of color-perceiving cones in their retinas instead of three, meaning that they can perceive up to 100 million colors. Yikes).

When it comes to websites, French researcher, Jean-Eric Pelet has found that higher levels of brightness and saturation increase our intention to buy and improve our memory of the websites' information.[29] While we have to be careful about applying culture-specific findings to other demographics, such research highlights that, far beyond serving a purely aesthetic role, color can actually influence our attitudes, behaviors, memories and emotions.

With regard to products, common sense might dictate that bright, colorful packaging would attract more attention than a muted palette. Although there is certainly evidence to support this,[30] psychologists have also found that a society's preference for colors and packaging can depend on their level of masculinity and femininity (as defined by Hostede[31]—see Chapter 5). For instance, in one study, researchers found that women's deodorants were better received in masculine cultures when they were packaged with soft, low-contrast, harmonious colors, whereas women from feminine societies preferred packaging that used brighter, more contrasting colors.[32]

E-COMMERCE SITES AND COLOR

 Color sells ... and the right colors sell better.
COLOR MARKETING GROUP[33]

Think of your favorite drink. What springs to mind first? Its name or its color? Research shows that our brains store objects according to their color[34] and, when it comes to brands, we're no different. Colors are the first thing we'll remember about an item, followed by its graphics, numbers and, eventually, words.[35] That means, if you want your brand to be memorable online, making the right color choice is absolutely crucial.

While certain sectors do follow trends (for instance, "eco" products are usually green), in a crowded marketplace it's sometimes the brand that goes against the grain that stands out from the crowd (for instance, in the USA's cell phone market, Sprint owns yellow, AT&T blue and T-Mobile pink). In fact, research shows that color is one of the most prominent marketing tools used worldwide to create, maintain and evolve brand images in the minds of customers.[36] In the

USA, the impact of color is taken so seriously that it is even recognized in law. The Lanham Act actually legislates against "colorable imitation" and protects product colors as trademarks.[37]

To the extent that colors have been shown to elicit emotional and psychological responses,[38] you can see why so much of the research exploring this area has been conducted covertly by the big global players. Whoever possesses a thorough understanding of the real and specific effects of colors on consumers has the strategic advantage of being able to create a brand that speaks to its consumers at a very real emotional level.

Studies have consistently shown that trust is the most important factor for e-commerce success[39] and, since our first impressions tend to be rapid and long-lasting,[40] it is vital that you make those first few seconds count.

While it can be particularly challenging to build up your customers' trust online, there are subconscious cues you can use to effortlessly boost the perceived trustworthiness of your website, brand and business. One study found e-commerce sites that use pale, unsaturated colors (such as light blue, cream and grey) are perceived as more trustworthy, benevolent, competent and predictable[41] than their more colorful counterparts (for more information, see Chapter 19).

Besides being aesthetically more attractive, e-commerce sites that use a subdued color palette effectively provide their customers with a soothing, relaxing environment in which to interact comfortably. The use of vivid, highly saturated colors is generally seen as promotional and aggressive when applied to e-commerce sites, so lowers the perceived trustworthiness of the online vendor.

Color has been shown to influence the navigation, readability and memorization of information from a website[42] and it should go without saying that any information you do present should be clearly legible, both in terms of the font that you use and the level of contrast between the text and its background (you get the best readability by using colors with a greater luminance contrast ratio[43]). If you're looking for specific color pairings, blue text on a yellow background performs the best for readability (despite being aesthetically questionable), whereas purple letters on a red background perform the worst.[44]

The bottom line is, the more easily your visitors can understand you, the more likely they are to generalize this sense of "clarity" to your brand and business as a whole, thus increasing their level of trust in you as a vendor.

While you *can* use color for your text and backgrounds, in my experience, most people prefer to read dark text on a light, neutral page, probably as it is the format to which we are most accustomed. (In fact, some research has even found that, for the Times New Roman font, black text on a white background is

COMMUNICATE PERSUASIVELY

actually less legible than green on yellow, but switch the font to Arial and this green and yellow combination is much worse.)[45]

At this point, it is worth remembering that you have no control over the device, resolution, system, browser and individual computer settings that your visitors will be using when they view your website. While you can track some of these variables through tools such as Google Analytics, it is still difficult (and expensive) to cater for all eventualities. So, when you design your website, make sure that you research the browser, resolution, and device that the majority of your paying market will be using and tailor your site's design (and color palette) accordingly.

Incidentally, if you are using your website to sell merchandise directly, make sure you understand and adhere to the social norms for color that exist within your target market (more of this later in the chapter). Not only will this boost your website's ratings for its aesthetic quality but it can also actually increase your customer's intention to purchase.[46] To put it bluntly, if people like the look of your website, they're more likely to buy from you. This is why it is so important to get to know your market and then give them what they want, how they want it—especially if their preferences are subconscious.

If you run a global business, make sure that you do your homework *before* launching your website. Research shows that you can increase customer loyalty and website "stickiness" simply by reflecting the design and content preferences of your target market.[47]

This is especially important when it comes to selecting the color scheme for your website. The colors that *we* consider normal and appropriate may be perceived as utterly distasteful (and offensive) by members of other cultures. To give you an example, consider the embarrassment United Airlines must have felt after its concierges wore white carnations on Pacific flight routes,[48] un-aware that white symbolises death and mourning in certain Pacific cultures. The concierges and their seemingly innocuous flowers probably caused quite some confusion and offense to native travellers returning home.

INDIVIDUAL DIFFERENCES

Have you ever wondered why senior citizens tend to wear light-colored clothes? There is a reason, and it's not just cultural—as we get older, colors start to appear darker, making lighter colors look more appealing.[49] As children, we are much more open and experimental in our preferences, favoring secondary colors[50] and special effects, such as glitter and metallics,[51] over muted tones.

In fact, research indicates that many of our adult preferences may be learned (which may account for the vast cultural differences that exist),[52] since babies consistently stare longer at long-wavelength colors, such as red and yellow, than short-wavelength hues.[53]

Even the color blue—the "universal favorite"—is subject to age differences, with 13–34 year-olds preferring darker shades and those over 35 preferring a lighter, sky blue.[54]

So, if your demographic falls into a particular age group, make sure that their color preferences inform your branding and website designs, as the hue and brightness of the colors you choose can influence how well you're received.

Age isn't the only individual variable that affects our tastes—personality can also make a big difference—it should come as no surprise that extroverts prefer bright colors to the lighter, more subdued tones preferred by their introvert peers.[55] Even your social status can influence your color choices and, when it comes to advertising, primary colors tend to appeal to blue-collar audiences, while "upscale" demographics gravitate more towards pastel shades.[56]

THE MEANING OF COLOR

Assuming a narrow Western perspective of colors as "universal" and applying it to alien markets has often led to cultural faux pas.

DR. MUBEEN ASLAM, MARKETING [57]

One of the most important (but least-cited) facts that can have a huge impact on a color's meaning is its context—both in terms of culture and design. There is a paucity of well-referenced, evidence-based information on this subject, especially with regard to its use in an online context, which is why, in the following pages, you'll find a useful, concise and thoroughly researched examination of colors and their meanings.

While certain colors have a universal appeal (most probably due to their evolutionary importance to our race), countries and cultures do differ greatly in terms of the meanings they assign to particular colors. For instance, if you turned up wearing black to a funeral in the UK or Thailand, you would be considered appropriately dressed, but wear black to a Hindu funeral and, beyond turning a few heads, you'd also be the only mourner wearing black in a sea of white!

In the following pages we'll explore psychological research pertaining to each of the primary colors, as well as green and black (this selection of colors is governed by the research available). Although this content is by no means exhaustive, it should give you a good, evidence-based grounding in the psychological and physiological effects of color, which you can then use to inform your design choices online.

For specific color meanings by country, you'll find a comprehensive list hosted within the resources section of my website (thewebpsychologist.com/resources).

Red

 That woman is red hot …

Know what I mean? Your subconscious does. Red has long been associated universally with sexuality, lust and appetite and there is a wealth of research that shows we are biologically primed to respond to red in a powerful, visceral way.

It can raise your heart rate and make you hungry[58] and, if you're in a sports team (all things being equal), wearing red can even help you win[59] (sorry, Man United, your secret's out). In fact, in competitive situations we naturally perceive red as "danger"[60] and research has found that simply viewing the color red in an achievement context, such as taking an IQ test, can elicit avoidance behaviors in the viewer—we'll dodge the hard questions![61] (Strangely, red can also make time pass more slowly and red objects seem heavier than objects in other colors.)[62]

When it comes to sex, studies have shown that red leads men to view women as more attractive and more sexually desirable[63] and I'm sure we can all recall a story or two about the eponymous "woman in red." This seductive, mysterious figure crops up time and again in our films and novels: the Grimms' *Little Red Riding Hood,*[64] a tale of bestiality and repressed sexual urges; Number Six, the dangerously seductive Cylon at the center of TV cult classic *Battlestar Gallactica*;[65] and the elusive woman in the red dress who distracts Neo in that famous scene during the *Matrix*,[66] to name but a few.

While these characters are set in very different times, each carries with her the same undercurrents of sexuality and danger and reflects an archetype that has long been emblazoned on the Western psyche.

Culturally, of course, women across the globe have been beautifying themselves with various pink and red shades of lipstick for nearly 12,000 years and, every Valentine's Day, we send millions of red cards and flowers to the objects of our affection—except, that is, if you're in Saudi Arabia. Where, every year, red is banned from florists and gift shops ahead of the holiday, in the belief that Valentine's Day "encourages immoral relations between unmarried men and women."[67]

They may be right as red signifies sexual availability and is often used to encourage attraction (think Amsterdam's famous red light district). In fact, in one study, psychologists found that just wearing a red T-shirt was enough to give men a (subconscious) signal that the woman wearing it was more open to sexual advances.[68] In our primate cousins, females often display redness during estrus, which signals to the males that they are ready to mate.[69]

Although red is undeniably an arousing color, some psychologists believe it may actually be the *saturation* of intense reds that makes them responsible for these effects, as opposed to the hue itself.[70] The fact that we find vivid reds so provocative may explain their ubiquitous use for warning signals such as stop signs and traffic lights and, although every color is subject to cultural nuances, red is considered by most to mean "hot," "active," "vibrant" and "emotional."[71] In fact, in China, the combination of red with black has such positive emotional connotations that it is the most common color scheme for wedding invitations.

Just how much of the red effect comes down to nature and how much to nurture remains to be seen, but there is one thing of which we can be certain: the color red is a powerful, visceral cue that exerts great influence in both humans and other species. So, if you're going to use it online, do your research first and make sure it will elicit the response you want or you could end up in hot water.

Blue

 I'm feeling so blue …

If you've heard it before, you'll know that when someone says they're feeling blue they don't mean they've got light bouncing off them at a wavelength of 450 nanometers! The ways in which we use colors to express our emotions reveal a deep psychological connection between the two and research is now discovering that factors such as a color's saturation and brightness can have strong and consistent effects on our emotions.[72]

Blue is one of those rare colors that seem to have a universal appeal. Generally viewed as calming, reassuring, pleasant and relaxing,[73] blue is the color that is most often associated with trust, security and wealth,[74] which, as we saw earlier, may explain its ubiquitous popularity among corporate entities (such as banks and law firms), especially in the USA.

It may also explain why, with the exception of Pinterest, three of the top social media platforms (Facebook, Twitter and LinkedIn) all have blue logos. However popular it may be, though, the color blue is not immune to demographic factors such as ethnicity, gender and age. Research suggests that, in some countries (East Asia), blue is actually perceived as cold and evil![75]

The idea that blue might be a more or less universally attractive color stems back to some fascinating research conducted in the 1970s, when two American psychologists set out to discover the color and number preferences of a group of young students.[76]

The method was simple: they asked the students to name their favorite color and pick out their preferred number from 0 to 9. Intriguingly, the group showed a collective preference for the color blue and the number seven. Since dubbed the "blue-7" effect, this odd phenomenon points towards a psychological bias in relation to both numbers and colors.

In terms of cultural differences, blue represents a variety of things, including purity in India, death in Iran and warmth in the Netherlands.[77] Research comparing the effects of red versus blue on our perception and decision-making has found that we evaluate products more favorably when they are presented on a blue background.[78]

Surprisingly, we're also more likely to buy products displayed in a blue environment than a red one.[79] In fact, blue is anathema to red in many regards, stimulating our creativity,[80] suppressing our appetite,[81] and even lowering our blood pressure.[82]

That is, unless you're a Western woman of a certain milieu, for whom the robin's egg blue of Tiffany's famous little boxes will actually *increase* your heart rate by a good 20 percent.[83] No, I'm not kidding!

Blue can influence our sense of time and, when used as the main color on a website, it can even create the illusion of increased connection speeds, simply by inducing a state of relaxation in its users.[84] Blue is also the standard color for hyperlinks, which became the subject of debate when Google decided to test 40 different shades of blue (from greenish blue to blueish blue) on its users, to see which would attract more click-throughs. It turned out that blueish blue was the clear winner. Who knew?!

Blue can also make an object seem lighter (it has the opposite effect to the color red), and it is the most popular color choice when it comes to clothes (think jeans).[85] Light blue has even been found to improve cognitive performance,[86] and the discovery of a new, blue-sensitive photoreceptor that projects to the emotional centers of the brain supports what great artists have intuited for years: that blue is an evocative, emotionally resonant color.

Intriguingly, blue seems to be a firm favorite for other species, too, including bumblebees, moths and robins[87] (goodness knows how they figured that one out).

Our tendency to favor blue may come from our physical environment and its association with expanses of sea and sky. This pancultural preference does have its limits, though, and these limits are often context-dependent. For instance, while you might enjoy looking at a beautiful blue lake, you'd be hard pressed to prefer it to the normal color for an apple. You get my point.

Yellow

 Sunshine yellow... Yellow-bellied...

Contrary to its opposite—blue—the color yellow is universally active and exciting and, like red, can have an arousing, stimulating effect on its viewer. It is generally considered to be a warm, happy hue[88] and shares a pleasant association with brightness and the sun.[89] However, it is a fickle color and can also elicit a sense of wariness,[90] possibly because it so often signifies danger in nature (think wasps, snakes).

It may be for this reason that yellow is the least liked hue, despite its positive associations with spirituality in East Asian cultures. To the human eye, yellow often appears brighter than white,[91] which explains why we tend to use it to attract attention, whether on road signs or online.

Green

 Green with envy... She has green fingers... He gave me the green light...

Green, then, is one of those colors that can have diverse psychological effects according to its tone. Although it is primarily associated with nature (and is therefore considered quite relaxing),[92] in the USA darker greens also represent status and wealth,[93] while pea green tends to have a rather unpleasant association with nausea.[94] When it comes to pancultural meanings, green is often clustered together with white and blue—as "gentle," "peaceful" and "calming"—and, in some places (such as the USA, Hong Kong and Brazil), consumers also associate green with "beautiful."[95] As you'll see from the color charts on my website, green can also convey unique meanings depending on its cultural context.

Black

 As black as night...

As in this phrase, black is commonly associated with darkness, sophistication and death in the West and is also used to denote wealth, prosperity and sophistication ("*in the black*", "*black tie event*").

In terms of design, black is often used to convey formality and seriousness in Western, white-collar demographics,[96] and is closely related to brown, with its meaning of "stale" and "sad" across certain cultures.[97]

Intriguingly, research has discovered a link between malevolence and black uniforms in sports, so teams that wear black to compete are more prone to display aggressive behaviors than those dressed in white.[98]

12 YOUR SOCIAL MEDIA

> *It takes many good deeds to build a good reputation, and only one bad one to lose it.*
>
> BENJAMIN FRANKLIN, A FOUNDING FATHER OF THE USA

Everyone's talking about it. All of the Fortune 500 companies use it (or have a policy in place to deal with it). B2B marketers collectively spend millions of dollars on it every year. Yes, social media is now the most popular source of online activity in the world,[1] reaching 1.2 billion users globally. And yet 30 percent of these companies aren't even bothering to track the impact of it on sales.[2]

To what does social media owe its phenomenal success? Yes, it does satisfy our deep-seated desire for communication, but, more than that, social media also serves as a tool with which to measure the intimacy and influence index of our relationships. As any digital native will tell you, it is this that is key to many a modern adult's sense of self-esteem.

WORD OF MOUTH

> *Word of mouth (WOM) is the most important and effective communications channel.*
>
> ED KELLER, CEO, KELLER FAY GROUP[3]

Imagine you've just bought a super-fast broadband service from a major provider. The engineer's come round, installed it, checked it and everything seems to be doing just fine. All in all, a good experience.

Then it stops working. You go online (with your smartphone—how else?!) and spend ten minutes just trying to find a helpline number. Eventually, when you do find one, it's an 0844-bleed-me-dry abomination, but, left with no other choice, you dial it anyway, only to be put on hold for 15 minutes.

When you finally get through, the preprogrammed advice they give you doesn't work. Yes, you've switched it off and back on again. Yes, you've checked the cables and, no, the fuse hasn't blown. They tell you they'll send out an engineer on a workday in a week's time between 9 a.m. and 4 p.m. You get off the phone fuming, broke and sans Internet.

Frustrated, you take the only recourse available to you—you tweet furiously into the twittersphere about your harrowing customer they-call-it-service-for-a-reason experience in the hope that someone will hear.

At this point, one of two things can happen: said provider can respond to your desperate tweet and offer to send someone out to help, or that provider can ignore you. No prizes for guessing which response will restore your faith in the company and which will lead to a loss of business.

It's incredible what a massive, positive impact a business can have on the experience (and retention rate) of its customers by simply issuing a quick 140-character response to someone in distress. It shows that the company cares enough to listen and, more importantly, *hear* what's being said about it and its services. A swift response engages and calms customers, nipping small problems in the bud before they have the chance to snowball out of control.

If you are in any doubt as to the sheer power of social media, consider the fact that the reputations of entire businesses have been built and destroyed in no more than 140 characters, in an action not unlike a digital Archimedes' lever. Although the exact figure may fluctuate, around 19 percent of microblogs such as Twitter mention brands and 20 percent of these actually mention brand sentiment.[4] If you're not already listening to what people are saying about you, start now—and join the conversation.

It is no coincidence that social media's proliferation comes at a time in which the world is limping through a global recession and humanity's trust in corporatism is at an all-time low.

The very existence of social media has enabled many of us to revert back to a pre-industrial system of *reputational* capital, in which we rely on trusted, filtered sources of information to help us make informed choices on whom to endow our business and loyalty. Of course, this system is far from perfect and trust can sometimes be misplaced, but the fact that this system exists at all has forced many companies out from their PR closets to face up to and engage directly with their customers again. Social media has made businesses accountable.

This is perhaps one of the reasons that large businesses were so slow to embrace it as a new channel and may explain why a good 44 percent of companies track their employees' social-media activities both in and out of the office.[5]

Like it or not, social media is here to stay.

GLOBAL TRENDS

Until relatively recently, the world of social media has been driven by the prolif-eration of English-speaking, US-based sites. Not any more. With Internet access becoming a global reality, websites that are based in the USA and Europe are now attracting audiences beyond their native markets. The geographic footprint of these sites is beginning to evolve. The majority of LinkedIn users, for exam-ple, now come from outside the USA—a large proportion of them from Western Europe. In Russia, the networking site VKontakte (ranked seventh worldwide) draws 43 percent of its traffic from outside Russia,[6] a trend that is likely to con-tinue as we gain greater access to an increasingly more global web. (For a breakdown of which social networks are prevalent in which countries, check out alexa.com/topsites/countries.)[7]

With regard to age, it may surprise you to know that today's fastest-growing social media audience is composed of users over the age of 55.[8] In 2011, social networking reached at least 93 percent of online users aged 55 and older (in North America and Latin America alone) and it is predicted that any small dif-ferences in social media use may disappear completely as social networking continues to become more integrated into other online activities, such as online video viewing.[9]

BRANDS ARE GOING SOCIAL

In more recent years, social media has seen a massive surge in users from around the globe. Initially regarded (and decried) by many as simply a stomping ground for the hyper-social, the self-promoting and the young, it has taken sev-eral years for social media to emerge into its new, mature identity—as a channel for (potentially) meaningful communication and engagement.

This transformation has occurred so swiftly and completely that many (if not most of us) would now admit that social media occupies an important, if not central, part of our daily lives. So much so, that in a poll of young workers and university students, 56 percent said that they would refuse to work for a com-pany that banned access to social media (or, failing that, they'd join and find some way around corporate policy) and 24 percent said access to social media would be a deciding factor in accepting a job.[10]

If you care about your clients, social media is what will enable you to get noticed and sustainably increase your reputation, client base and profit. Among the multitude of platforms in existence, there are four major players that by now you can most probably name backwards in your sleep. Just in case you've missed them, they are as follows: Facebook, Twitter, YouTube and Pinterest.

Research[11] shows that larger companies now consider the first three of these platforms to be the cornerstones of their social media strategies, with digital, marketing and PR departments leading the growth in use of these within businesses. While everybody has something to say about how to "work" social media (the last time I checked LinkedIn there were well over 1 million results for the search term "social media"), very few large companies have got anywhere near a grip on the matter.

Despite this, research shows social media can yield a return on investment and, in 2011, a study by the National Restaurant Association discovered that consumers who used social media and related apps (including Twitter, foursquare, Urbanspoon, Facebook and more), not only dined out more but were also more likely to become repeat customers.[12] This is all well and good when it comes to social activities such as dining, but convincing blue chip companies to get on board is an altogether different matter.

It seems that social media is a force that, having gathered momentum in the early adopting digital and tech industries, is now still being led kicking and screaming into the corporate world. According to a recent survey by Weber Shandwick and Forbes Insights, 84 percent of senior executives believe that their brand's sociability actually falls short of world-class standards,[13] which means these businesses know there's a problem but may be ill-equipped to deal with it.

That being said, with all the social media hype we're exposed to it's easy to get carried away and think that if you only spent more time on platform X or Y, you'd triple your conversions. While this *can* happen, there is evidence to suggest that SEO still makes a huge impact on lead generation, with 57 percent of B2B and 41 percent of B2C businesses stating that SEO has a larger impact than social media and pay-per-click.[14]

However, if brands are closing around 55 percent of deals taken from social media leads alone (41 percent from Facebook, 21 percent from LinkedIn and 20 percent from Twitter), it's a case of striking a balance and engineering a digital strategy that will holistically bring you into greater profit online.

Risk-taking

One of the main reasons that businesses cite for not adopting social media is lack of controllability. Historically, large organizations (such as big business, political institutions and governments) have been known to go to great lengths to protect their reputations and conceal their mistakes, but, as we have witnessed, the advent and viral proliferation of social media across the world has led to a fundamental reversal in the way in which we communicate as a species.

No longer do *all* our communication channels dance to the tune of news outlets and TV operators. No longer do we have to rely on heavily vetted, spun-out spiels from authorities-on-high. We can now tune in to the many millions of voices of our many millions of fellow humans. Social media has arguably made journalists of us all.

While this transformation is in itself extraordinarily exciting, it unquestionably brings with it a host of new challenges—finding reliable news sources, filtering out the noise and establishing truth being not least among many concerns. However, social media does provide us with a direct route—straight from the horse's mouth to the listener. It doesn't take a genius to see how this could be useful. You need only look as far as the uprisings in the Middle East and the rush by government officials to ban Twitter to understand the scale of this cataclysmic shift. We are witnessing a revolution.

Social media has transformed the way in which we communicate on a global level. While it is still possible to manipulate the online landscape and bury unsavoury stories (search for "reputation management companies" to witness first-hand the demand that exists for this kind of service), nonetheless, this online (r)evolution means that big businesses are no longer untouchable.

Still not convinced? Here's a heart-warming story about how one unhappy customer brought a powerful company to account using nothing more than a video camera, his YouTube account and a sense of humor.

In the spring of 2008, Sons of Maxwell were traveling to Nebraska for a one-week tour and my Taylor guitar was witnessed being thrown by United Airlines baggage handlers in Chicago. I discovered later that the $3500 guitar was severely damaged. They didn't deny the experience occurred but for nine months the various people I communicated with put the responsibility for dealing with the damage on everyone other than themselves and finally said they would do nothing to compensate me for my loss. So I promised the last person to finally say no to compensation (Ms. Irlweg) that I would write and produce three songs about my experience with United Airlines and make videos for each to be viewed online by anyone in the world.

The consequence? The "United Breaks Guitars" video went viral and attracted over 11 million views. Under mounting pressure, United offered to pay to repair the guitar and gave Carroll flight vouchers by way of compensation.

MONETIZATION

One of the common criticisms surrounding social media is the difficulty of monetizing it. Personally, I believe this is one of its greatest strengths—the fact that social media requires effort and commitment from its users means that those who are willing to invest their time can reap dividends from their efforts—and I don't just mean financially.

The atomization of communities (meaning that communities are becoming more fragmented, for which the Internet is often blamed) has, among many, created a strong need for a sense of reconnection and belonging. Social media, when used with the intent of opening a conversation or for sharing information, has become a cure-all for this sense of isolation and, as such, if used by brands to reach out to its customers, can create a profound and lasting impact on the longevity and success of the business-client relationship and, indeed, the success of the business itself.

Essentially this shift in power—from the faceless, anonymous corporate to the social world of gossip and word of mouth—means that, for the first time in decades, smaller businesses can now play competitively alongside the big boys.

Until relatively recently, large businesses held the money and the power to control huge sections of the market, across all major industries. Certain wealthy, less scrupulous businesses could pay PR companies and marketing agencies to spin stories and influence customers while neglecting their needs and well-being, all the while preventing smaller competitors from entering the market. In this respect, social media has ushered in a new era and it's mostly smaller companies that have led the stampede.

In a study by Social Media Examiner,[15] 85 percent of marketers polled said that social media marketing had generated more business exposure for their companies, with 69 percent citing that it had increased their online traffic. A full 40 percent said that social media had improved their sales and the top five tools cited were Facebook, Twitter, LinkedIn, YouTube and blogs. While the majority of marketers polled (59 percent) were putting in a good six hours or more of social media time every week, in my experience, simply spending half an hour a day can have a dramatic impact on customer engagement and sales. As we shall see later (in Chapter 18), there are several strategies you can adopt to monetize social media and increase your profit online.

The magic number—150

You may not have heard of Dunbar's number,[16] but, according to this psychologist, almost no one has more than 150 friends (by which I mean actual, meaningful friendships)—whether in real life or online.

If you consider for a moment the frenzy that ensued when Myspace first launched, with everyone attempting to outstrip the next user's numbers of fans (commonly using friend-adding software and bots to automate the process), you may think this magic number is hard to believe. The fact is, though, after the initial Myspace rush, having had enough time to comfortably assimilate social media into our everyday lives, we're now starting to witness a swing in the opposite direction. You can see this in action through the relatively recent trend of "unfriending" that is spreading across platforms such as Facebook.

While in the context of social media this pattern may be relatively new, it should not be surprising. It is simply an expression of an ancient desire to connect in a *meaningful* way. From smoke signals (with the advent of fire) to satellites, we've been figuring out how to exploit technology for social gains ever since communication first started, often with surprising results.

There was uproar when the first letter was sent. Suddenly, women had the freedom to communicate with anyone who was literate, including anyone who was not her husband (this had unforeseen consequences in the realm of infidelity and the notion of women's rights). Then the telephone arrived on the scene. Originally used for transmitting serious information, people laughed when it was suggested that, in the future, there would be a phone in every household. The story repeated itself for the wireless radio, television, computer, cell phone ... You get the picture.

Beyond our social imperative, the fact that our natural ability to connect is limited to around 150 connections serves to highlight why it is vital that your business connects with your customers on a deeper level. Especially if you wish to establish a loyal, long-term client base.

Social media can help you to do this, but certain rules of engagement apply. In the next few pages we'll take a look at three of the major social media platforms in use today (Facebook, Twitter and YouTube) and explore how you can use each to increase your reputation, profit and client base online.

Facebook, in a nutshell

A firm favorite among marketers, Facebook boasts over 800 million active users worldwide, half of whom log on to the platform every single day.[17] With each user sharing valuable details about their private lives, it's easy to see why this particular platform would attract more attention than the others—it's a veritable goldmine of information. Not only does it provide one of the largest repositories of demographic information in the world (it's the fourth largest web property after Google, Microsoft and Yahoo! sites)[18] but, with a mean half-life of 3.2 hours for every link posted,[19] Facebook is also somwhat of a holy grail: it offers the perfect combination of insight, airtime and a massive market.

Although it has global reach, Facebook's rule does not extend to *every* corner of the world. There are seven markets in which it has a smaller audience than other social networks: Brazil, China, Japan, Poland, Russia, South Korea and Vietnam.[20]

Having received some flak for privacy issues and what some see as the erosion of personal rights, Facebook's power still lies not only in its inherent value as a social hub but also in its role as a passport to other platforms. This singular feat means that those who wish to access other services can only do so via their Facebook accounts. Besides being utterly Machiavellian, this strategy means that even if you choose to leave Facebook, it's not without the significant pain of losing out on other vital services.

In my opinion, this kind of strategy can only work so long before it backfires. As with any system, Facebook's success is subject to a lifecycle, which, sooner or later, will end, but that time is not yet upon us. So, with word of mouth and customer engagement the *plats du jour*, it's important that you understand how to use them as tools of influence.

Brand: Corona Light Beer
URL: facebook.com/CoronaLight

In October 2011, Pereira & O'Dell (the digital agency of record for Corona Light, Corona Extra and the Victoria beer brands) set out to make Corona Light the "Most liked light Beer" on Facebook. In a digital campaign that spanned social media, digital out-of-home and search marketing, Corona placed Facebook at the center of its efforts and from November 8 to December 6 gave its fans the opportunity to snatch their moments of fame on a 150-foot (45-meter) digital billboard in Manhattan's Times Square. Intrigued? Here's what they did.

HOW THEY DID IT

First, Corona encouraged people to "Like" their Corona Light Facebook page. Having done so, you were then granted access to the Times Square app, which you could use to upload a high res photo of yourself. Once uploaded, your photo would be featured in glittering lights on a gargantuan billboard in Times Square for all to see. Fabulous.

In a quote from Anup Shah (brand manager for Corona and Corona Light), he explained how this campaign was "a great way to reward fans for being brand ambassadors."[21] Psychologically, it was a beautifully conceived marketing strategy—one that owed its success to several key principles.

Social validation

We all crave validation and admiration from our peers (apparently we all want our "five minutes of fame") and we are hard-wired to "develop and preserve meaningful social relationships, and to maintain a favorable self-concept."[22] If applied intelligently, this strong, subconscious incentive can fuel our actions to engage with anything that promises to deliver this goal (in this case, the simple act of "Liking" a Facebook page). What better way to achieve validation than to witness your face hovering like a giant portrait over the thousands of people walking through one of the

▶

most iconic locations in the world? The lure of fame, it turns out, has a very wide appeal—during the Corona campaign, everyone from pets and music bands to brides uploaded their photos for the chance to be featured on the billboard.[23]

Reciprocity

Social psychologists and marketers alike have long known about this principle: that if someone gives us something, we will want to give them something back. Our success as a species has depended on our ability to form and maintain social groups, so it is no surprise that we have evolved to value reciprocal exchanges at a very deep level.

In the case of Corona Light, several reciprocal exchanges took place: Corona got loads of new fans, viral promotion, word-of-mouth buzz (where fans bragged to all their friends that their face was on a billboard in Times Square), valuable demographic information (fans' data, interests, locations) and longer-term advocacy from those who went on to invest emotionally in the brand after this "special" experience.

In comparison, I think the fans got a bit of a bum deal—a few minutes of fame and a nice picture to put on their wall about that one time when they were on a billboard in Times Square.

Social proof and word of mouth

When a group of people start behaving in a certain way and that number reaches critical mass, an odd phenomenon takes place: herd instinct kicks in and vast swathes of a population can be influenced into adopting a particular behavior. In an online context, the critical mass needed to kick-start a revolution needn't even start from one geographic location. In Corona's case, people from all over the world could take part, spreading the campaign to all corners of the globe and allowing social proof to act on a global scale. In fact, during the run of the campaign, the number of "Likes" increased by over 6,000 percent, reaching close to 200,000 "Likes" in a single month and extending Corona's reach to millions of other Facebook users across the world.

Of course, once people had "Liked" Corona Light's Facebook page, Corona could then use the data collected to tailor future communications to its target demographic, thus forging a more personal connection with its fan base. As outlined in a statement from Jasmine Summerset (strategy supervisor at Pereira & O'Dell), "The long-term strategy is to have this program help us build a base of consumers we can re-engage through-out the year, thus developing long-term relationships and dialogue."[24]

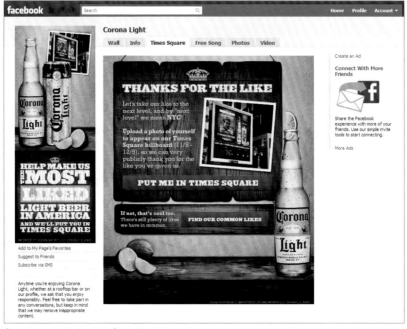

Source: http://www.facebook.com/CoronaLight

MAKE THIS WORK FOR YOU

Ten steps to Facebook success

1 Target the right audience Different social media platforms attract different crowds, so find out where your customers like to hang out before you invest in a particular channel. For instance, in the USA, Facebook tends to attract a predominantly female audience aged between 18 and 34,[25] so, if you're selling high-end gadgets aimed at older men, Facebook may not be your best bet. To find out who's using which platforms, check out Quantcast.

2 Social validation As we've just seen, people will go to great (and little) lengths to obtain the admiration of their peers. Once you know whom you're targeting, find out their preferences by using a service such as Preference Tool.[26] You can then use this information to create campaigns that will validate your fans in a way that's most meaningful to them.

3   **Reciprocity** This is a cornerstone of social exchange. If you want your customers to "Like" you, give them something to like you for. It doesn't have to be much, but, whatever you do give them, make sure it fulfills their actual needs and they'll be more willing to give you something back.

4   **Social proof—a game of numbers** "Like" campaigns and fan pages need people in order to work. This builds on the previous point: if you can find a common denominator of needs within your audience (such as Corona's five minutes of fame), you'll appeal to a much wider demographic and gain a much larger following as a result.

5   **Integrate your channels** Make it easy for your customers to find your Facebook page by linking to it from your website and other channels. Include a Facebook link in all your brand communications (newsletters, Twitter homepage, LinkedIn company page), and make the link more prominent if you're driving a particular Facebook campaign. The easier it is for people to find and "Like" you, the more fans you'll attract.

6   **Become an invaluable resource** Convert new customers by providing real value to your Facebook fans. As we shall see shortly in the case study of Dell, it has a great track record of successfully using social media to turn a profit and, when it comes to Facebook, it's just as engaged. By providing social media resources to small businesses (facebook.com/dellsocialmedia), Dell has created a Facebook page that not only attracts a lot of traffic but also sparks conversations and gets people talking about the brand and, with reputational capital, come customers.

7   **Support existing fan pages** If you're lucky enough to have dedicated, passionate customers who have created their own fan pages for your business, reward them for their support. When two Coke afficionados set up a fan page for their favorite brand, Coca-Cola thanked them with a free tour of their facility in Atlanta. Keen to maximize their success, Coke's marketing team encouraged the guys to make their own video about the story of their fan page (facebook.

bitly.com/coke_facebook_video), creating a storm of free PR around the brand and sending out a clear message that loyal fans would be rewarded.

8 **Special offers** Offering unique vouchers to your Facebook fans is a great way of attracting new customers and rewarding existing ones. You can also use them to build your database, by requiring customers to submit their name and email address in order to "activate" their coupon. It doesn't have to cost you much—even something as simple as free shipping can work well.

9 **Competitions** In a similar vein, running Facebook-only competitions can also raise your profile and reputation. If you want to innovate a product or get feedback, asking people to comment on your wall for the chance to win free products/services is a great way of achieving this. Make sure any competitions you do run are transparent, with terms and conditions clearly explained to avoid misunderstandings.

10 **Run a local event** Whether your business is large or small, running a free event in your local community is one of the most powerful ways of building relationships. Social media doesn't work in a vacuum and, with a media-rich platform like Facebook, providing an event about which people can post videos, share photos and tell stories is a great way of kick-starting your fan page and promoting yourself on Facebook.

Twitter, in a nutshell

This is my personal favorite. With a jaw-dropping 500+ million users worldwide[27] and tweets that reach as far away as the International Space Station (across 17 different languages),[28] this quirky platform enjoys global popularity. If you're an avid Twitter user and feel like you just can't get enough, be warned: recent research has found that Twitter is harder to resist than cigarettes and alcohol[29]— and I don't think they've found a cure.

While Twitter may seem like a natural habitat for navel-gazing social media luvvies, it is fast gaining traction as a key outlet for news dissemination and citizen journalism throughout the world. Nowhere is this more evident than in the uprisings we've witnessed in recent years, documented and enabled by entire populations taking to Twitter.

In the absence of representative reporting through traditional media channels, we seem to be taking information into our own hands and using Twitter as a broadcasting platform from which to share our stories with the world. When the US Airways plane landed in the Hudson River in 2009, it was a Twitter user, Janis Krums, who broke the news. Broadcasting his story a full 20 minutes before official channels picked it up, he used his phone to document and photograph the event and his images went on to be reposted worldwide by citizens and journalists alike. It just so happened that he was in the right place at the right time and, with Twitter to hand, he was able to share this incredible event in real time.

In terms of social rules and etiquette, Twitter seems to be the only self-policing ecosystem in which trolling (the neanderthalic art of inciting anger online) can expect to be met with 140 characters of unanimous condemnation.

Nevertheless, Twitter remains a polarized environment in which both the mundane and the incisively intelligent coexist side by side. When Beyoncé broke the news that she was pregnant on MTV's Video Music Awards, Twitter recorded a massive surge of 8,868 Tweets per second[30]—enough to raise an eyebrow perhaps, but not earth-shattering stuff. Yet, when the tsunami hit Japan, record numbers of people used Twitter to mount huge humanitarian efforts and share vital information, saving countless lives in the process. When you look at the bigger picture, you get an idea as to the scope and power of this medium at its best.

Social media is not simply a tool for communication, though. Harnessed correctly, it can also be used as an accurate predictor of real-world trends and behaviors. In one experiment, two psychologists used the chatter from Twitter to accurately forecast box office revenues for films.[31] Having developed a simple model that focused on the rate of tweets specific to particular topics, they found that this Twitter-based model outperformed existing market-based predictors.

While this holds incredible promise for trend forecasting across industries, you don't need a sophisticated model to be able to use this yourself. In 2011, the year of the Arab Spring, #egypt rose to become the most-used hashtag on Twitter, providing an insight into the focus of millions of people worldwide and facilitating the coordination and live reporting of events where other channels failed. Twitter's power as a platform for the people's voice is reflected in the fact that governments (from countries such as Saudi Arabia and Egypt) have repeatedly tried to block it. When Twitter looked as though it was starting to bow under foreign pressure, announcing that it might start censoring tweets from users in certain countries, the collective response from the Twitterverse was #sh*t.

It would seem that while many of us are heralding social media as the dawn of a new era, not everyone is happy with the state of things. You need only look at the vitriol that Twitter has attracted from some corners of the press to see the threat that it poses to traditional, one-directional forms of newscasting. It is clear that Twitter is only as useful as the information its users choose to share and its greatest assets are also its greatest liabilities. Yes, we can access any information online, but checking the validity of the information contained within a tweet can be tricky and rumours spread like wildfire. Moreover, the speed with which we now expect to communicate via Twitter means that customers expect their brands to respond to them instantaneously and failing to do so can have devastating results.

CASE STUDY Dell

Brand: Dell
URL: twitter.com/delloutlet

 The web was an ideal place for us to connect directly with customers. Social media brought that and something more—a way to listen, learn and engage with customers, with a clear emphasis on the engage part of the equation.
       LIONEL MENCHACA, CHIEF BLOGGER AT DELL[32]   ▶

Connect and respond

In an article for the Huffington Post[33] dated December 8, 2009 (when the world was in the grip of recession), Manish Mehta, the vice president of social media and community at Dell, indicated that Dell had generated nearly $7 million in revenue through Twitter (@DellOutlet) in the USA alone. Since entering the world of social media in 2006, Dell had seen its global community (aggregated across various social media channels) grow to over 3.5 million people—a striking testament to the power of simply "connecting and responding to customers."[34]

It's an impressive feat, but one that relies on the implementation of a few fundamental principles to succeed. Simply put, social media is the digitalization of real-life social interactions. The same rules that govern our offline relationships also drive the way in which we relate online— and our adherence to these rules can determine our online success.

As we have already seen, our desire to form relationships is based around the yearning to feel loved and valued, to experience a sense of belonging. It is on these principles that the most successful businesses base their social media behaviors and it is for these same, universal reasons that they attract and retain large, engaged customer communities.

Think of a secure relationship you have enjoyed at some point in your life. What were the elements that made it so special? Beyond chemical attraction, it's likely that the relationship was based on trust, mutual respect and understanding, along with a desire to support one another and a sense of feeling loved.

As a business, just imagine the loyalty and commitment you would enjoy from your clients if you genuinely made them feel special and loved. Once you've created a product or service that your clients need, the key to establishing a strong, loyal and engaged client base is to make them feel valued. You can do this simply by talking with them.

According to Mehta at Dell, "That's how every company can achieve success using social media—by facilitating the conversation. No strategy necessary."[35]

Ten steps to Twitter success

1 Have a clear, personal identity If you are using a platform (such as HootSuite) that allows employees to tweet from a single business account, make sure you have an agreed policy in place as to the tone, content, frequency and response rate of your tweets. Many companies would rather avoid social media completely than have their employees speak on their behalf (at the risk of misrepresenting the business), but if you have a strong, explicit set of guidelines in place, trusting your staff to do the right thing can go a long way to building their commitment to you and fostering a personal side to your business online. If you're using automated ad-bots, don't (I'm surprised that people still do this). Using software that automatically adds and follows people is tantamount to spamming—the direct antithesis of what Twitter is for. If you're looking to build a real, lasting client base, relate as you would in the real world— personally.

2 Find the best way to engage with your followers/peers Twitter is unique in the fact that it has generated a culture in which its users naturally connect directly to others, whether they're the CEO of a multinational or your mate who lives down the road. It's the closest thing to a non-hierarchical social structure and, as such, it has enormous potential for enabling direct communication between you and your clients. Be open, ask for feedback, engage in conversation and, if you receive a complaint, reply honestly and quickly—this will show that you're listening and you care.

3 Become valuable—create unique, meaningful content One of the best ways to become influential within a community is to create content that your followers will find useful. Not only will this increase your reputation as a leader in your field, but it will engender trust in your audience and direct valuable traffic to your website, thus increasing conversions and your rankings in search results.

4 Curate your links As well as generating your own content, show your social side by linking out selectively to other people's content. By engaging with your community in this way (and keeping it as

▶

congruent with your online identity as possible), you're showing your followers that you are secure, interested in others and actively seeking to connect.

5 **Follow people selectively** In the case of who you follow, it really is a question of quality, not quantity. Just imagine how you would be perceived if you went around telling people you had 3,000 real-life "friends"—they would think you were a complete fake. Well, the same applies here. The people you follow say a lot about who you are and, arguably, about your values and integrity, so choose wisely. Follow:

 - past and current clients
 - people within your industry and adjacent industries, as appropriate
 - contacts, friends
 - good sources of information
 - people you find interesting, depending on your business (this will be different if you are a consultant versus if you're working for a large organization).

6 **Want more retweets? Use verbs** Twitter updates that include verbs (for example, "click," "register," "download," "read," "vote," "grab," "receive" and "claim") are 2 percent more likely to be shared than the average tweet.[36] So, if you want your tweets to reach more people (and drive more traffic to your website at the same time), include calls to action that refer people to your landing pages, where you can then ask them to take further action. Incidentally, when asked what makes them retweet other people's tweets, 92 percent of people surveyed answered "interesting content," 84 percent said "humor," 66 percent said it was due to a "personal connection," 21 percent responded "celebrity status," 32 percent did so due to offered incentives and 26 percent did so on being requested to "Please RT!"[37]

7 **Have a real conversation (don't just broadcast)** To really reap the rewards of Twitter, openness and reciprocity are key. If someone has made the effort to reach out to you, take the time to respond authentically. This doesn't mean you should stop linking to news or articles (indeed, this is a key element I work hard to include in my Twitter activity), but it does mean that, in most cases, people want more from you than just a newsfeed. So, include your opinion and invite your followers to respond with theirs.

8 **Develop a listening (research) strategy** As well as using Twitter to converse with people, you can use it as a platform to monitor trends and listen to what your customers and competitors are saying about you. You can do this by searching hashtags (#) for keywords that are specific to your industry and you can monitor click-through rates and retweets (RT) via platforms like bit.ly or su.pr. This will help you determine the reach of your broadcast and links. It can also be a very powerful (and, better yet, free) way of increasing value to your business, both in terms of its reputation and the level of care and relationship that your customers will enjoy.

9 **Connect, converse, convert** Twitter is a two-way conversation and people will judge you on the overall way in which you contribute to that conversation. To get the most out of Twitter, adopt an holistic strategy of connecting with your peers and customers and conversing with them in a way that is personal and adds value. Over time, this will foster a trusting relationship between you, creating a natural environment for conversion. Only then should you soft-sell your services or products to your customers and, when you do, these services should be carefully tailored to the needs of your followers.

10 **Be real—and own up to your mistakes** Psychologically, we trust and like people whom we consider similar to ourselves—and, as humans, we're all beautifully flawed and make mistakes. So, if you've messed up, own up. Far from tarnishing your reputation, admitting fallibility will show your customers that you are real and that you're brave enough to take ownership of (and make good) your mistakes. For the cynics among you, research shows that supportive, trusting relationships (in which you can admit your fallibility) promote psychological safety[38]—and, if your customers feel safe with you, they are more likely to trust you with their business.

YouTube, in a nutshell

Ah, YouTube. That innocent place we all visit for a spot of light entertainment … only to get sucked into a black hole of kitty videos and childish pranks before being unceremoniously spat out three hours later, with no idea how we got there or how to reclaim those hours of our life.

As a species, we watch over 500 years of YouTube videos via Facebook every day and tweet around 700 videos per minute.[39] With over 100 million of us taking social actions (such as "Likes," "Shares," "Comments") on YouTube each week, it's safe to say that this is one of the most influential social media platforms out there.

It's also one of the most lucrative, with YouTube monetizing over 3 billion video views per week globally. As more and more of us start to access YouTube via our mobile devices, video may be the best medium with which to get your brand into the hands, hearts and minds of one of the largest audiences out there. It's a truly global one, too: at the time of writing, YouTube is available in 39 countries, 54 languages and counting, plus it's one of those rare platforms where humor and music really do have universal appeal. Brands are increasingly turning to YouTube to not only drive revenue from ads but also attract attention through clever marketing campaigns in the hope that they'll go viral.

CASE STUDY Evian babies

Brand: Evian[40]
Platforms: YouTube, Twitter

COMMUNICATE PERSUASIVELY

HOW THEY DID IT

Teaser videos

Two weeks before the launch of the "Evian Roller Babies" video, the company behind the campaign (Euro RSCG[41] created it, Unruly[42] seeded it) launched two teaser videos to get people talking and create a sense of excitement around the imminent release. One of the teaser videos was the "Baby Moonwalk," and the other was the "Baby Break Dance." Both were carefully designed to hark back to the previous, hugely successful "Evian Water Babies" campaign, which, in turn, was designed to further reinforce the brand's image and social media presence.

Twitter

Once the "Evian Roller Babies" video launched, Unruly pushed the video through its own Twitter channels, members of the Twitterati (prominent Twitter users) and a number of Twitter-related websites and apps. The result? This entertaining little video got picked up and retweeted so fast that, in November 2009, it was declared the world's most viewed online advertisement in the *Guinness Book of Records* and resulted in over 61 million views (official and unofficial) worldwide. It received over 54,000 comments and tweets and attracted over 440,000 Facebook fans.[43] The campaign's success was such that it even extended to *other* Evian content, creating a halo effect around sister products and subsequent "making of" videos.

Suffice to say, it was a roaring success.

Tracking

One of the common gripes about corporate social media use is the difficulty with which its reputational and economic impact can be measured. This is especially true when fans start ripping, mixing and re-uploading original campaign content to their own media channels. Putting aside copyright issues (which, in my opinion, are antiquated and in need of serious revision), this kind of user engagement actually has clear advantages: users who identify strongly enough with a given campaign are more likely to become advocates and will disperse the campaign through their own networks, reaching a far greater audience than if the video were disseminated through official channels alone.

▶

In some cases, when the remix of the original is good enough, such tampering by fans can send a campaign viral and multiply its audience beyond imagination. That is exactly what happened to Cadbury's 2007 "Gorilla" video (in which a Gorilla drums along to Phil Collins' song "In the Air Tonight") when it was remixed by a fan to Bonnie Tyler's song "Total Eclipse of the Heart" and uploaded to YouTube.[44]The video became so popular that, in August 2008, Cadbury picked up the remix, created an HD version of it and broadcast it in the UK as a "Gorilla's Anniversary Edition."[45]

While it is tricky to measure social media's true impact, it's not impossible. In the case of Unruly's campaign, it solved this problem by ingeniously tracking the video's audiovisual fingerprint. With the fingerprint secured, unruly used software to track potential video matches across 30 billion web pages. The results were impressive. Unruly identified over 2,000 individual uploads of the video across hundreds of video-sharing platforms and found that 27.3 million views (44 percent of total views) had been generated by videos uploaded by users to unofficial channels.

By implementing a little bit of technology, this case study shows how it *is* possible to monitor a campaign's reach in real time, enabling us to measure the full impact of a video campaign on a global scale.

MAKE THIS WORK FOR YOU

Ten steps to YouTube success

1 Brand identity Establish a memorable, personable, clear identity and tone for your brand's online persona.

2 Consistency Design your campaign to be consistent with that persona.

3 Teaser content Create teaser content designed specifically to raise brand awareness and create anticipation.

4 Lead time Release teaser content relatively close to the actual campaign launch. Two to four weeks prior should give you enough time to generate buzz and keep your fans interested (leave too much time between teaser content and the campaign launch and they'll lose interest).

5 Stickiness Make sure any videos you create are sticky and memorable. The most successful viral ads tend to have several things in common: they're usually provocative, funny, outrageous or frightening—and they keep us guessing as to whether they're "real" or not.[46] (One of my personal favorites is the surfing sheep video created by Cornwall-based British clothing manufacturer, Finisterre.)[47]

6 Video tracking If you have the budget, extract a video fingerprint (before launch) to enable you to employ video tracking.

7 Link tracking Use a URL shortener, such as StumbleUpon (su.pr, which is free) to shorten any links that you send out from your campaign. This will help generate extra traffic and enable you to track click-through rates.

8 Video launch Launch the video through your official channel and seed it through your relevant social media platforms (Twitter, Facebook, Pinterest, foursquare and others). Make sure you tailor your communications from each social media platform to suit each audience—a personal touch goes a long way and will make fans feel valued and unique.

9 Engagement Encourage your fans to remix and re-upload campaign content to increase levels of engagement and ensure the widest reach.

10 Reward your viewers Reward any great remixes by featuring them or applauding them publicly in your official blogs.

OTHER USES FOR SOCIAL MEDIA

Researching your customers

Brand: IKEA

Platform: www.theshare-space.com

In 2011, Swedish design giant Ikea launched "Share Space," a new online social space for its customers to "inspire and be inspired" the IKEA way. The website encourages IKEA customers to upload pictures of the spaces they have transformed using IKEA products, which can then be tagged and made searchable to users visiting the site. Essentially, it's a user-generated compendium of designed interiors that allows you to save rooms and items to your wish list for subsequent purchase.

By developing this online sharing space, IKEA succeeded in not only increasing its user engagement but also creating a platform through which to keep track of its customers' needs, current trends and commentary.

Using peer feedback and incentives like "Pick of the Week" (where one lucky member's photo submission is selected and praised in the official blog), "Share Space" essentially provides a centralized, target-specific hub for its members. By exploiting our psychological needs for inclusion and validation (and promising to satisfy these desires via a public, in-group platform), "Share Space" plays a central role in IKEA's wider-reaching (to coin my own term) socio-digital strategy.

How you can research your customers

To engage with and research what your customers are saying about you, you can either create a dedicated forum or website for your customer community or you can use tools such as Twtpoll.com (to track Twitter sentiment) and SurveyMonkey or SurveyGizmo (to drive people to a survey page to collect information).

To aggregate information from across all digital channels, your best bet is to use a premium service such as Repskan, which provides a more detailed, sophisticated level of analysis.

By monitoring your level of influence across different platforms and sectors, it provides a much more accurate picture of your digital presence than you might get from more basic ratio-based platforms. If you send out newsletters to your clients, you can also use tools such as Constant Contact, ExactTarget or MailChimp to include polls and surveys in your e-newsletter.

Customer retention

CASE STUDY Comcast

Brand: Comcast
Platform: Twitter

As Benjamin Franklin is quoted as saying, "It takes many good deeds to build a good reputation, and only one bad one to lose it." So it is with social media. At a time in which the prevailing sentiment is one of distrust in authority and institutions, the growing need for integrity and honesty (both socially and in business) is something that many of us are now placing firmly at the center of our business identities and, by extension, our socio-digital strategies.

It can cost three to five times more to acquire a *new* customer than to retain an *existing* one, so any small investment in engaging and listening to our current client base is a worthwhile endeavour. To give you a real-world example, consider the story of Comcast's Frank Eliason, director of digital care.

When he noticed that customers were tweeting their comments and complaints about Comcast, he decided to get involved. He converted a one-way stream of complaints into a personal two-way conversation, offering suggestions and solutions to customers' problems, thus transforming negative online chatter into an opportunity to create brand advocates. Research shows that "a good recovery can turn angry, frustrated customers into loyal ones"[48] and a good relationship between a business and its customers can actually remove the difference in behavioral intentions between customers who have been compensated for a lack of service and those who have not received compensation at all.[49]

Plainly put, if you care about your clients, they will care more about you. If you think back to Maslow's hierarchy of needs (in Chapter 7), our

▶

psychological desire to feel valued is of central importance to our sense of well-being. Once our basic needs have been met, it is with this higher ideal that we approach our lives and relationships. So, if you can meet your clients' needs at this level, you will both benefit from the relationship.

Frank Eliason had an innate understanding of this and, by taking a risk and talking directly with disgruntled customers, he created advocates who went on to tell others about their positive experience, thus promoting the brand. While he has since passed the mantle over to Bill Gerth (@comcastcares), this story goes to show that a little time and effort can return a lot of value—both to your customers and to your business.

Lead generation

CASE STUDY Scientific American MIND

Brand: Scientific American MIND
Platform: www.scientificamerican.com/sciamind

One of my favorite publications (to which I regularly subscribe) is *Scientific American Mind* (SciAm MIND). I realized while writing this section of the book that it implements a great lead-generation strategy when it comes to social media. As well as maintaining active, interesting streams on Twitter (@sciammind), Facebook (facebook.com/ScientificAmericanMind) and its parent's (*Scientific American*) YouTube channel (youtube.com/sciamerican), it also posts regular podcasts (www.scientificamerican.com/podcast/podcasts.cfm?type=60-second-mind), and articles on its website to generate interest and serve as a point of reference for insights into the workings of the mind.

SciAm MIND's ongoing activity and use of cross-referencing across these platforms serves to direct valuable traffic towards its website, whereupon users can access articles and extracts of the published articles. Having first proven its worth by offering valuable materials for free, SciAM MIND then soft-sells its website visitors a paid-for subscription to gain access to the full publication. Who could resist?

PART 3

SELL WITH INTEGRITY

Professor Robert Cialdini's

6 principles of influence

and how to use them online

We rely on cognitive shortcuts - known as heuristics - to guide our behaviours and the decisions we make on a daily basis. Understand how they work for greater influence online.

RECIPROCITY

give and take

An obligation to give
an obligation to receive
an obligation to repay

Start the exchange:
- be proactive
- give something away
- make concessions

CONSISTENCY

commitment

We act in a way that
is consistent with our
values and identity

Get a commitment:
- identify clients' traits
- activate self-concept
- make your request

Did you know...

prices ending in are called charm prices because they

NUMBER **9**

sell more?

SUBCONSCIOUSLY

When visitors arrive at your website they will **scan for cues** on what it's about, **if it's secure** and whether or not they **can trust you**

SOCIAL PROOF	LIKING	AUTHORITY	SCARCITY
herd instinct	*similarities*	*expert appeal*	*in short supply*

We naturally look to other people for cues on how to behave

We conform when:
- the group is strong
- physically close to us
- has many members

We prefer to comply with people whom we actually like

Boost your likeability:
- highlight similarities
- genuine compliments
- be trustworthy

We are rewarded for behaving in accordance with authority figures

Make this work for you:
- show you're the expert
- back up with evidence
- be inspiring

We tend to value that which is in scarce supply

Use it online:
- have flash sales
- include a countdown
- show limited stock

What stops us buying online?

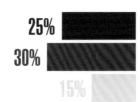

- 25% **lack of customer service**
- 30% **privacy / security**
- 15% **no real salesperson**

What information do we trust?

- 70% **consumer reviews**
- 90% **earned media**

13 INFLUENCE: AN INTRODUCTION

> **"** *Who shall set a limit to the influence of a human being?*
> RALPH WALDO EMERSON, POET, ESSAYIST, AND LECTURER, THE
> CONDUCT OF LIFE, *"POWER" (1860)*

- You have a great product.
- You have a clear business strategy.
- You even have a beautifully designed website.

Now what?

Now, you sell—but not to just anybody and certainly not just by launching your website and hoping for the best.

If you've been reading this book in order, you'll already be armed with a good understanding of who your target market is and how best to communicate with them. This alone will go a long way to creating a rapport and engagement with your audience—factors that are essential to increasing your influence online—but there is one final step. To really see results, you need to learn and apply the principles of direct, automatic influence.

In the following pages we'll take a look at the theory behind these persuasion principles, how and why they work and when to use which ones. By the end of this chapter, you'll have the building blocks you need to wield influence online.

THE ART OF PERSUASION

Psychologists define persuasion as "the process through which the attitudes and behaviors of an agent are intentionally conveyed in a certain direction by another agent without coercion."[1] To put that in plain English, persuasion is the art of shaping someone's attitudes and behaviors.

In an online context, it's about designing an environment that will persuade your users to behave a certain way. Persuasion techniques can be used to encourage people to sign your petition, rate your products, comment on your blog, purchase your new service, subscribe to a newsletter—in fact, any symbolic or physical action that you wish your users to make can, potentially, be influenced by persuasion.

When visitors arrive at your website, they will literally (and most of the time, subconsciously) scan the page for cues as to what the website's about and how they should interact with it.[2] By engineering this virtual space in such a way that only *some* actions and resources are available, you can reduce the possible actions your user can take to encourage favorable outcomes.

To give a simple example, if your primary goal is to build an email database of subscribers, you can construct your website so that users can only access your newsletter by submitting their email address. In this particular case, by designing your website around this reciprocal email-for-access exchange, you are sending a clear signal to new visitors that this is the action they should take.

MAKE THIS WORK FOR YOU

Clean and simple

- **Give us a clue** What cues are you providing to your website visitors? Identify three actions that you wish visitors to take and provide clear calls to action. For instance, "Sign up to our newsletter for special discounts!," "Try it [service/product] for free!," "Like us on Facebook!"

- **Fair exchange** Make sure you use the principle of reciprocity to ensure a fair sense of value exchange. Requesting a user's name and email address in return for access to valuable information is usually seen as a fair trade.

COMPLIANCE

"Compliance" refers to the act of requesting something from someone and getting the desired response. Whether this request is overt (being asked to babysit for a friend) or covert (seeing a laundry detergent ad that claims to "wash whiter" in the hope that you'll switch brands), when it comes to compliance, the person being targeted will *know* that they're being impelled to respond in a certain way.

Disrupt then reframe

Of course, with the growing popularity of influence literature and an ever-increasing public awareness of how persuasion tactics work, it can be tricky to use such techniques effectively. This has not escaped the notice of the academic world, where researchers are now unearthing new, powerful mechanisms that can work on even the most jaded of audiences.

Perhaps the most intriguing and effective technique to be discovered is the one known as "disrupt then reframe." This particular process works by intentionally disrupting someone's resistance to an attempt to influence by reframing the request or message so that the target is more susceptible to it.

Allow me to give you an example. In one study, two psychologists named Davis and Knowles[3] went from door to door trying to sell holiday cards for three dollars apiece. In order to test which elements (or combination of elements) were the most persuasive, they introduced a disruptive component in their sales pitch, telling their targets that the cards were worth "300 pennies" (as opposed to three dollars). Alongside this simple "disrupt" condition, they also included a reframing component, saying that the cards were "a bargain."

The experiment yielded fascinating results. The process worked—but *only* when targets were approached with the "disrupt then reframe" sales pitch. In being told that the cards were "300 pennies ... that's three dollars. It's a bargain," the targets' natural thought process of "I am being solicited" was disrupted by the uncommon wording of the request. This created room for the reframe. By disrupting their targets' resistance processes and catching them off guard, this simple technique ultimately resulted in a significant increase in the levels of compliance and sales.

MAKE THIS WORK FOR YOU

Cause disruption

- **Catch them off-guard** How can you disrupt your visitors' natural anti-soliciting defence mechanisms? Take a look at your website and those of your direct competitors and identify the common sales pitch ("Try it now for only $4.99 a month!").

- **Reframe it** Once you've identified your soliciting pitch, find a way to reframe it so as to stand out from your competitors and catch your clients off-guard. For example, instead of saying "Try it now for only $4.99 a month!," you could experiment with "Try it now, for less than a bucket of beans! For only $4.99 a month, it's an amazing bargain."

Fear then relief

Interestingly, the sequence in which we experience emotions prior to receiving a request can also influence whether or not we comply. In a field study set in Poland, two psychologists took to the streets to test just that.[4]

They placed a card that resembled a parking ticket on the doors or under the windscreen wipers of illegally parked cars. While the cards placed on the car doors were simple advertisements designed to elicit relief in the car owners, those placed beneath the wipers were either fake parking tickets (to elicit fear) or advertisements (fear then relief).

Of the drivers whose cars had been targeted, which do you think were the ones most likely to comply with a subsequent request?

If you guessed the advertisement group, you'd be right. The psychologists found that the drivers who experienced fear then relief were more likely to comply with a subsequent request than fellow participants who had either not experienced any fear or continued to be anxious after the event.

The researchers concluded that this seemingly mindless acquiescence was a result of the subjects' fear response, in which their attention would have been diverted to assess and manage the threat (the potential parking ticket) they were facing.

Anchor points

When it comes to asking people for favors in the real world, salespeople know only too well that the key to success often lies in the delivery and content of the initial request. Using a technique called "anchoring," a salesperson will deliberately manipulate your decision-making process simply by providing you with the "anchor" of an unattractive initial request.

In this context, any subsequent (and less outlandish) requests will appear more acceptable than the first, resulting in a higher probability that you'll "compromise" and comply with the second. Of course this doesn't work all the time, and if you get it wrong and ask for something completely ridiculous, you risk getting dismissed out of hand.[5]

Innate interesting-ness

Research exploring the psychology of decision-making shows that we are motivated to achieve our goals in the most rewarding, effective way possible and our responses to a request will usually stem from the way we *feel* about it.[6]

For example, one group of psychologists found that when it comes to complying with a public request, such as being asked to donate a prize to the school raffle, we tend to act from the need to avoid feelings of fear and shame. When it comes to responding to a favor in private, however, we may act from the need to alleviate feelings of guilt or pity.[7]

In terms of positive motivations, research has shown that we are more inclined to comply with requests that we find interesting in and of themselves. This would suggest that the kick we get from performing an exciting or stimulating task can be rewarding enough to ensure compliance.[8]

So, how does this work online? Well, the team over at Silverman Research[9] (an employee research company) decided to test just this—on one of the most boring tasks known to humankind: the employee survey. I'm the first to admit that these time-consuming, bureaucracy-serving forms fill me with sense of dread, but what if they could be made interesting? Exciting, even? That's the challenge the Silverman Research team took on when it launched "Opinion Space,"[10]—a project it helped build in collaboration with computer scientists at the University of California, Berkeley.

Designed to enable its client, Unilever, to collate and analyze richer, more accurate data from its international assignees (IAs), the Silverman team decided to break away from the traditional tick box format and, instead, created a fantastically innovative solution to the problem.

They developed an interactive, visually compelling online survey that allowed employees to give feedback, while seeing where they were in relation to their peers. The employees were asked to write a comment in response to the question, "How could Unilever improve its IA policies?" Using algorithms to interpret this data, the answers given by each respondent created a unique data point that was then represented visually by a glowing white dot, so the employee could see his or her placement relative to the other dots within the employee galaxy (see below). They could then click on the dots of their (anonymous) colleagues to read and rate their comments, resulting in a survey unlike any other.

The outcome? Unilever was delighted with the resulting data and the project went on to win two industry awards.[11] It just goes to show, if you can make this, the most mundane of activities, exciting enough to elicit high levels of quality compliance, you can do it for your own online business.

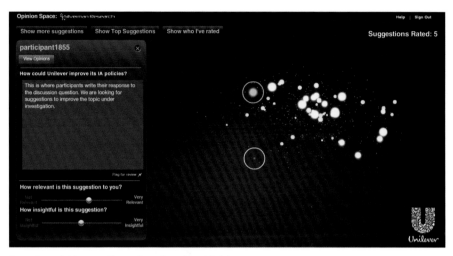

Source: Screenshot from www.SilvermanResearch.com/home/clients/

MAKE THIS WORK FOR YOU

Real-time fun

- **And ... action** What actions are you trying to get your users to take? If it's something simple and mundane like gathering a name and someone's email address, you may wish to revert to the principle of reciprocity (as mentioned earlier, that's when they give you their email address in exchange for access to valuable information on your website).

- **Make it interesting** If you're looking to collect richer data, such as getting users to take a poll on your website or during an online webinar, you can make the task more interesting by using a system that visualises real-time results. Not only does this increase the innate interestingness of the task itself but it also panders to our fundamental interest in how we match up to our peers. For website polls, you can use simple software like SurveyMonkey[12] to get real-time results, or to poll attendees during live webinars, you can use platforms such as InstantPresenter[13] to invigorate your data collection.

14 PRINCIPLES OF ONLINE INFLUENCE

> ❝ *The ever accelerating pace and information crush of modern life will make this particular form of unthinking compliance more and more prevalent in the future.*
>
> ROBERT CIALDINI, SOCIAL PSYCHOLOGIST[1]

THE POWER OF AUTOMATIC INFLUENCE

Social psychologist Robert Cialdini dedicated his entire career to exploring and uncovering the mechanisms of influence. Below, we'll take a look at how these principles work and how you can use them online.

COGNITIVE SHORTCUTS

As sophisticated mammals, we have evolved to streamline our attention so that, at any given time, we can focus on the information that is most important to us. Right now, as you read this paragraph, you'll probably be vaguely aware of your surroundings, conscious of these words in front of you and aware of the fact that you're reading this text in a book or on a screen. It's unlikely that you'll have given a second thought to the feeling in your left elbow or the pace of your breathing as you read. This is because most of our behaviors are automatic—we tune out the majority of the sensory input we receive and run on autopilot, to the point that we don't even realize we're doing it.

Our ability to function effectively in our environment results from the ability to learn and use cognitive shortcuts, which we rely on to guide our behaviors and the decisions we make on a daily basis. In our increasingly complex, fast-paced world, these shortcuts are vital in helping us to navigate more efficiently—which they do, most of the time—but there are situations in which running on autopilot can also get us into trouble.

Take stereotyping, for example. We all do it to a certain extent, and in some cases, it's very useful. For instance, a child only has to learn how to open *one* door before it can stereotype that action across *all* doors. The child learns the action once and is subsequently equipped for most door-opening situations. Where we trip up is when these stereotypes don't work (the child tries to pull open a sliding door) or when they are used against us (child locks often work on this principle).

Financially, we use rules of thumb to discern value—or, to quote a popular adage, "you get what you pay for." Over time, we build up a set of general rules about the world based on our previous experiences until, eventually, these heuristics become automatic.

A friend of mine once told me a story about an artist she knew, who couldn't seem to shift many pieces of her work. The paintings themselves were beautiful—visually compelling and skillfully executed. They attracted a lot of attention from the people who passed her shop, but no one was buying them and she couldn't understand why. So she went to a successful marketing consultant, who advised her to add an extra couple of zeros to the sale price of her tableau— just for one week—to see if this would make a difference. The artist reluctantly agreed—and the paintings started selling, fast.

What happened? By marketing her paintings at what she thought was a fair price, the artist was, in fact, putting customers off—*they* considered her low prices to be impossibly cheap, which in their minds indicated a product of poor quality. In bumping up the sale price, the artist's customers automatically interpreted this higher price as a reflection of a superior product and they were quite willing to pay double or triple for a beautiful painting that now appeared much more valuable.

This is a powerful example of the price–value heuristic at work, but it must be noted that in this and other successful cases, the products themselves do not necessarily have to be of high quality in order for this tactic to work. Rather, the issue tends to be that the value of the product is not reflected in its market price.

People do sometimes price items extortionately in the hope of making a sale (I remember visiting several shops in Saint Juan Les Pins where this seemed to be the norm), but, in the long term, unless you are selling to incredibly gullible punters, this strategy will almost always backfire if you use it to peddle trash.

If the price is right

- **Don't undersell yourself** If you are offering a good-quality product or service, consider your pricing structure carefully as this will influence your customers' perception of its value. If you're not sure what your pricing should be, check how your competitors are pricing comparable products. Alternatively, give yourself discreet timeframes in which to experiment sequentially with your price for one particular product (you may choose to do this via an A/B split test) so that you can directly monitor the effect of pricing on the number of items sold.

- **Stand out from the crowd** People often think that by slashing their prices they'll attract the lion's share of the custom and will out-sell their competitors. This does not always work. A smart solution is to add real value to your products or services (offer something your competitors don't) and reflect this in the price.

RECIPROCITY

We are human because our ancestors learned to share their food and their skills in an honored network of obligation.

RICHARD LEAKEY, PALAOEANTHROPOLOGIST[2]

Reciprocity is a form of cooperation between two or more people that involves the exchange of something valued by the parties involved. This could be material goods, assistance and services, advice, contacts, help or opportunities.[3] Whatever it is, the idea is that we will always try to repay in kind what another person has given to us. It is an effective influencing strategy and research has shown that it is more effective than those based on simple rewards.

Where does reciprocity come from? Psychologists have theorized that it relies on a universally shared and strongly held feeling of future obligation, where the success of the exchange depends on your confidence that, in giving something of value away, it will not be lost but repaid to you in the future by something of equal or greater value. It is, if you like, a form of indebtedness that humans will almost always strive to repay, even when the expectation of repayment is tacit, vague or undefined.

You don't even have to be altruistic for reciprocity to work—in fact, reciprocal systems can thrive even when everyone involved is looking out for their own best interests. You need only look as far as LinkedIn to see reciprocity in action: people who receive testimonials from happy customers or associates will usually respond in kind without even being asked. Why? Because we somehow feel compelled to do so. Even if we don't feel utterly obliged, we know that it's just not good business to be seen to break this unspoken rule, so fundamental is it to our social success.

If you consider reciprocity in the context of our ancestors, by sharing their knowledge, tools and assistance in this way, each individual increased his or her chances of survival. It has been argued (from an evolutionary perspective) that this very rule formed the foundation to the success and proliferation of human culture and society.[4]

How it works

Social psychologist Robert Cialdini said, "There is an obligation to give, an obligation to receive, and an obligation to repay."[5] Society tends to shun and ostracize people who violate this rule, so, in most situations, you can expect reciprocity to work. It's easy to implement, too. To invoke this behavior, simply give your target audience a gift. I must add at this point that, while it is possible to set this principle in motion even with a low-grade "gift," integrity *does* matter and, if you value your reputation and the satisfaction of your customers (which the most successful online businesses do), you should only give away something that your clients will actually value. There are several ways you can do this.

MAKE THIS WORK FOR YOU

Give and take

- **Surprise your clients** This works best when face-to-face with a client or online when you are in a live webinar or Skype meeting. If you surprise your clients by offering them a free gift and then making a request, the fact that they aren't expecting it (and are momentarily disarmed by your offer) can increase your influence and their compliance.

- **Write free articles** By writing articles and offering information or advice to your readers, not only will you be giving them something of

▶

value for free but you will also be building your reputation and establishing yourself as a credible authority in your field.

- **Run a free webinar** Get people to interact with you and hear your voice for a greater personal connection, then offer your products as further training in an up-sell at the end of the webinar.

- **Give away a free e-book or PDF** This doesn't have to be a novel, but, by giving away a downloadable "how to" guide or advice booklet, you're setting yourself above the competition in both quality and content—and your customers will thank you for it.

- **Offer special benefits to subscribers** If you want to up the ante, you can reserve some of your free articles, webinars or e-booklets for your dedicated subscribers. By establishing a tiered reciprocity system, you're identifying levels of value. Giving a free teaser to those who don't subscribe will encourage them to sign up (reciprocity) and, once they have signed up, the fact that they can now access more quality resources will reinforce the system of reciprocity so they are in a position of wanting to commit to you.

- **Make concessions** When we are seen to make a concession, the other party will feel indebted and obliged to reciprocate in kind. If you want to sell an item at a particular price, come in above your asking price ("anchoring") and allow yourself to concede at an acceptable level (compromise). More often than not, your financial concession will be reciprocated by a purchase.

- **Compromise** Building on the previous point, reciprocal or mutual concession is a powerful way of creating a system of reciprocity. By showing that you are willing to compromise, your client is likely to reciprocate in kind so that a mutually beneficial outcome is achieved. This is especially useful in negotiations.

- **Reject and retreat** Again, based on the principle of concession, this particular tactic can work well if you use it during an online conversation (via instant messaging, email, a forum, Skype or Live Chat). It can be particularly effective if you are requesting clients to take actions that they may consider to be costly, such as providing customer feedback or donating time or money to the charitable wing of your organization.

First, make a large request of someone—a request that they will likely decline, such as "Could you volunteer to write ten articles for our guest editorial post?" Then, once this request has been rejected, retreat from it and ask for the action that you actually want—"OK, maybe you could just write one post for our website?" By positioning the second request as a compromise, you are more likely to get a positive response to it.

CONSISTENCY

Psychologists have long known that people have a strong, unconscious motivation to boost their own self-perception. Numerous studies have documented what is known as "consistency"—the process of acting in a way that is congruent with our post actions, commitments and beliefs (in short, with our self-image).[6] While we all vary in our preference for consistency, as a technique it can be very influential when it comes to compliance, especially with individuals who are highly motivated to be self-consistent (yes, there are tests that can measure this).[7] Understand this principle and the motivations behind it and you will be able to design effective strategies for selling your products and services.

The foot in the door technique

If you have a background in marketing, this technique will be old hat to you and there's a reason for that: when it comes to compliance, this is one of the most influential techniques out there. The foot in the door technique begins by asking a target to comply with a small request that they're unlikely to refuse (such as donating $2 a month to a children's charity). Once they have said yes to this request, you can then ask them to comply with a second, larger request that is related to the first (in this case, asking the target to increase their donation to $5 a month).

The remarkable efficacy of this technique stems from the fact that it exploits our deep-seated desire to maintain a consistent, positive self-concept. When we make a decision to act charitably, we subconsciously, internally, ascribe this "charitable" trait to our own sense of identity so that, later, if we refuse to increase our donation, we feel as though we are somehow acting inconsistently with our sense of who we are.

This is one of the reasons that getting people to provide customer feedback or comment on a blog post is so effective—once new visitors have taken such an action that identifies them as "active" members of your website, they are more likely to take actions consistent with that new identity in the future.

MAKE THIS WORK FOR YOU

Keep it consistent

- **Identify useful customer traits** Identify a few key actions that you would like your visitors to take (for example, becoming an active member of your forum, providing customer feedback). Once you have listed them, consider which customer trait(s) would be conducive to eliciting these actions (getting your customers to see themselves as "thought leaders," for instance).

- **Design a two-step strategy** When you have identified your key customer trait(s), you can use this to design a two-step foot in the door strategy to activate the appropriate self-concept in your clients. For example, if you are a microbrewery selling fabulous local ale and you think your business could use some word-of-mouth advertising, the desirable customer action could be getting clients to contribute high-quality testimonials or reviews of your product. If the appropriate trait you wish your clients to internalize is "expert," your two-step strategy might look something like this.

  1 Ask your customers to complete a quick poll using their *expert* opinion (in this case, the way you phrase this request is vital—include the word "expert"). Send them an email thanking them for their valued feedback.

  2 Two weeks later, ask these same clients to contribute a more detailed testimonial or *expert* review by first thanking them for their previous, valuable contribution.

  By instilling in your customers the sense that they are *experts* in microbrewed beer, they are then more likely to use this identity to inform future actions—including telling their friends about their *expert* find. You get the picture.

Commitment

Not only do we strive to be internally consistent but we also strive to behave consistently with our past commitments—especially when those commitments were made actively.[8] In a fascinating study, psychologists asked two groups of participants whether they would participate in an AIDS awareness project.[9] To show their support, the first group was asked to proactively opt in by ticking two boxes, whereas the second group could simply leave the two boxes unticked to show their support. Those participants who had ticked the boxes were more likely to show up to volunteer, even weeks after the survey had taken place. Furthermore, those who were more active were also more likely to attribute their decisions to internal traits and attitudes than their passive peers.

Going public

There is also evidence to suggest that commitments we make publicly are more enduring (and effective in securing compliance) than the ones we make in private.[10] Allow me to give you an example.

Imagine that you are standing in an electrical appliances shop during the sales and you want to buy a fridge. A sales rep comes up to you and asks if she can be of any assistance. Clocking your sense of indecision, she offers you an unbelievably good price on one of the top fridges in the range. Keen to get a good deal, you talk with the rep a while longer before deciding that this really is a great opportunity, one you'd be foolish to miss. She goes away to fetch the relevant forms for you to sign, leaving you to think about your decision. It really is a great price and just look at all those fantastic features! Yes, this fridge is an absolute find.

The assistant returns with the papers and, as you're about to sign, she informs you that the internal tray and the automatic digital thermostat are extra components that you have to pay for separately. Oh, and if you also want the de-icing functionality in the freezer, that will cost extra, too. Standing there on the shop floor, pen in hand and having publicly made the commitment to buy, you feel too uncomfortable to walk away now, so, reluctantly you sign on the dotted line—and pay a whopping surcharge for the privilege.

Known in the industry as the low-ball technique, the secret to this strategy's success is precisely the public nature of the commitment made.[11] However, collectivist cultures (such as Poland and Japan) tend to prize interdependence more highly than individual self-concept (and the pursuit of related goals) and, as such, people who belong to these cultures are likely to be less receptive to such techniques than their individualist neighbors (such as the UK). Therefore it is important, as always, to have an accurate understanding of who your target demographic is and to choose your strategies accordingly.

MAKE THIS WORK FOR YOU

Ask for commitment

- **Go public** If you are selling a product/service and you're releasing it in beta or offering a free trial period, get your customers to commit to you publicly. With the range of social media the web has to offer, this couldn't be easier. If you are happy getting people to commit fairly passively, ask them to "Like," "Stumble," "Digg" or "Google+" your product.

- **Get active** For a more active commitment, you can use the Tweet To Unlock[12] platform to get users to engage more interactively in order to access your content. Tweet To Unlock requires you to send out a public tweet about the product in question in order for you to gain access and most people will tend to personalize the tweet before they send it so that it is congruent with their Twitter profile/persona. It's the perfect example of twenty-first century public commitment.

SOCIAL PROOF AND CONFORMITY

Colloquially referred to as "herd instinct," social proof is the changing of one's own behavior to conform to the behavioral code of the group. It can be a powerful way of influencing the behaviors of large swathes of people, and it's one of the reasons that religious organizations and cults are so successful.

Back in the 1950s, two psychologists, Deutsch and Gerard, theorized that conformity arises from two very different types of motivations.[13] The first, *informational conformity*, is our human desire to behave "correctly" according to an accurate perception of reality. The second type of motivation, *normative conformity,* is our desire to gain social acceptance and approval from those around us. Both of these goals serve a third, deeper motive: the impulse to protect our self-esteem and maintain our self-concept.[14]

It is this sense of self-concept that can also motivate us to *consciously* select the groups (and resulting social norms) to which we wish to belong. In this case, conforming to group norms can be a result of a rational process connected to our sense of identity.[15] For instance, I consider myself an insatiably curious type of character and my self-concept is that of an individual with a diverse range of interests. I also happen to be an avid reader of *Monocle* online and enjoy not only the sense of community I feel with other readers whose traits reflect many of my own but also the intellectual association that this in-group membership affords me.

The pioneer of persuasion psychology, Cialdini, showed that we look to other people for cues on how we should behave.[16] This effect is especially noticeable when we're faced with a crisis or an ambiguous situation and, in day-to-day life, where people automatically defer to "experts" or authority figures (this is known as *judgemental heuristics*). This deference to authority stops short, however, when people are emotionally involved in a situation. In such an event, we tend to pay closer attention to the actual content of the information being given, overriding the judgemental heuristic with a controlled response. Beyond looking to figures of authority for cues on how to behave, we also look at the social norms at play within our environment to inform our understanding of, and responses to, social situations.[17]

The way in which we respond to other people's beliefs often relies on our perception of how widely held those beliefs actually are.[18] You may have seen this principle in action in groups of people where one member expresses a view that strongly contradicts the opinion of the collective. In this scenario, as long as the dissident's self-concept is not immediately under threat, that person will minimize the opposing message so as to avoid being ostracized by the group.[19]

So, for example, if you are a member of the neighbourhood committee and you are deciding what to do with the kid who keeps spraying your street with graffiti, you will weigh up the amount of shared support for reporting this kid to the police before voicing your own, opposing, opinion (that this kid needs all the help he can get and should be offered support, not punishment). If you're the only one on the Board to take this view, you will either decide to back down (it's not worth the arguments that will follow) or, if your opinion is based on a fundamental, identity-level belief that justice is not best served by punishment, you'll stand up to the other committee members and speak out.

It is important to note that, while conformity may exert enough pressure to coerce individuals into publically adopting the group's social norms, these may not reflect the individual's own, privately held views (which may remain dissident). The key here is that most of us would rather be accepted into a group than go it alone and it's this that is behind the terrifying force of peer pressure.

In the 1980s, psychologist Bibb Latané[20] developed the social impact theory to explore and explain this phenomenon in greater detail. He theorized that our likelihood to conform to a group's norms is influenced by three main factors:

- the group's strength
- its physical proximity to us
- the number of members within it

Strong, immediate, large groups will have a much larger influence on the individual's level of conformity than a group that is weak, physically absent (far away) and small.

Since that time, Latané's original framework has evolved into the dynamic social impact theory (DSIT), which states that "the tendency for people to be more influenced by nearby rather than far away people gives rise to local patterns of consensus in attitudes, values, practices, identities, and meanings that can be interpreted as subcultures."[21]

It's not just offline that you'll find this kind of clustering. While our geographic proximity to others can influence our beliefs and attitudes in the real world, online, you'll find that these natural clusters of people appear across every social network imaginable. All the more reason, then, to identify which types of customers you'll find at which social network hangouts.

Cultural differences

As established earlier, the need to belong is a powerful one and aligning ourselves to the social norms of our wider group is one way to meet this need. When it comes to conformity, though, not all cultures are born equal.

Evidence suggests that when asked to comply with a request, people from collectivist cultures (such as India or China) are more likely to rely on the actions of their peers to inform their decisions than those from a more individualistic country (such as the UK), for whom this effect is much reduced.[22,23]

This difference in behaviors may result from the cultural lens through which we look, which affects how we attach meaning to the concepts of conformity and non-conformity.[24] For example, in individualist cultures we tend to see *non-conformity* as a good thing, and often associate "uniqueness" with positive traits such as originality, independence and freedom. In East Asian cultures, however, *conformity* is admired as a positive trait, as it connotes harmony and a sense of connectedness. Indeed, there is a tendency for East Asian communities to perceive anything that strays from the social norm as "deviant," to the extent that some will go to great lengths just to fit in.

It is this impulse to conform that many people believe to be behind the rapidly growing demand for luxury goods in collectivist countries such as China and Japan.[25] While there are, of course, other factors at play (such as the rise of the super-rich[26] and the middle classes), if you're from a culture in which the social imperative is to fit in, chances are you will literally scrimp and save to keep up with the Joneses.

The difference in motivation between people from collectivist versus individualist cultures can be beautifully observed in one simple experiment. East Asian and American participants were asked to choose either a green or an orange pen from an assortment of five pens to take home as a gift. The selection was always a mix of two colors and, because there were five pens in total, there was always one color that was more common than the other.

In keeping with the theories of cultural conformity, the experimenters found that East Asian participants consistently preferred pens of the "common" majority color, whereas Americans favored the "uncommon" minority.[27] This divergence of attitudes towards commonality has implications for online businesses, especially if you're selling items to a diverse, global market. It provides support for the necessity of glocalized websites and web content. It also underlines the pivotal role that accurate cultural knowledge can play in the success of your business, both on- and offline.

Conversion

The ability to convert someone from one viewpoint to another is a covetable skill. Luckily for us, it is one that can be learned. Research has found that people who hold *moderately* opposing attitudes to that of the group are susceptible to adopting the consensus position. Not only that, but they will tend to process the message in such a way as to interpret the numerical size of the group as evidence for an objective consensus. In plain terms, when we change an initial, moderately opposing position to conform to that of the wider group, we believe we are doing so in the face of rational, reasonable evidence.[28]

A nice example of conformity at work is the ubiquitous five-star rating system. Despite everything being available to us at the click of a button or swipe of a finger, when it comes to buying goods online (especially the expensive, electrical kind) many of us spend hours just trawling through review sites to find the definitive answer on what to buy from where.

Some people do seem to *enjoy* this type of "gathering" behavior, but, in general, most of us find it a painful experience. It sucks up a lot of time and effort for very little reward (I have to say, the longest I can muster is around 15 minutes).

That's why, when something comes along that can do the hard work for us, we storm the gate and practically swear our allegiance at the click of a button. Amazon's rating system demonstrates this beautifully. Not only do these handy, user-contributed reviews solve our research needs (providing a one-stop shop— no more buyer's remorse, no more time lost to interminable research), but they have also been shown to increase the level of satisfaction we actually experience when purchasing such a reviewed item.[29]

Priming

If you've read around the topic of influence, you may well have come across the bizarre psychological effects of priming. It happens largely beneath our conscious awareness and is a process whereby you can increase someone's sensitivity to a particular stimulus by exposing them to it beforehand.

For example, if I were to give you a list of words to read that included the word "canister," and I later asked you to complete a word beginning with "can____," the fact that I had primed you earlier would increase the probability that you would complete the word "can" by saying "canister." It's a simple but powerful effect—one that can profoundly influence our decision-making processes.[30]

My favorite example of priming can be found in the research conducted by Bargh and his colleagues.[31] In a simple, but ingenious experiment, the psychologists tested the behavioral effects of subconsciously priming students with particular words. Here's what they did.

When a new participant arrived at the designated waiting area, an experimenter greeted them and showed them into the testing room, where they were told they'd be taking part in two short studies to do with language ability.

Before commencing the test, they were informed that it would take around five minutes to complete and, once they had finished, they should go into the hallway to find the experimenter, who would be in another room, waiting to give the student the second part of the study.

Once the student had agreed to take part, he or she was given an envelope that contained one of three forms of a "scrambled sentence test," in which the student had to use five jumbled words that were listed to construct a grammatically correct four-word sentence, as quickly as possible. So, if one of the items read "he it hides finds instantly," the student could reconstruct the sentence to read "he finds it instantly."

This experiment had a catch, however. Although the students didn't realize it at the time, the words in the scrambled sentences weren't random and the real test actually extended beyond the word lists. First, depending on the group to which the students had been assigned, they either received a test containing words intended to prime for rudeness, politeness or neither. Students in the "rudeness" condition were given words such as "aggressively," "intrude" and "brazen," while students in the "politeness" condition were exposed to words such as "patiently," "sensitively" and "courteous." Second, once each student had finished the test and went to find the experimenter, a hidden confederate discreetly monitored each student's behavior.

This is where it gets interesting. The psychologists had set up a fake scenario in which, when the participant turned the corner, he or she would see the experimenter talking with another participant (actually a stooge) and the real test was to see how long each student would wait before interrupting the experimenter. The results were astonishing. Students who had been primed with words related to rudeness interrupted the experimenter more quickly and more frequently than the students who had been primed with words related to politeness.

MAKE THIS WORK FOR YOU

Conform and convert

- **Cultural conformity** Why is this important online? Well, if your target audience is based in a collectivist culture and you wish to influence them into taking a particular action, your strategy will have to take into account current trends and the propensity of your audience to follow the lead of their peers. In short, it is a question of getting enough key people to behave in a certain way so as to activate the principle of social proof. Reach critical mass and the converts will come.

- **Rate it** Encourage your customers to rate your products. If you already offer good products and a reliable customer service, this can attract new customers and boost your sales.

- **Steer the group** The principle of social proof highlights the power of the group over the individual. If you run an online forum, Twitter feed or LinkedIn group, you will probably have witnessed this principle in action: people who post to comment threads on a regular basis will tend to respond to "deviant" comments from out-group members with surprising ferocity. Within most groups there tend to be a few key members who exert more influence over their peers than others (for more

▶

information, see "Authority," later in this chapter) and you can use this to your advantage by interacting more actively with these key people in order to influence the perception and behaviors of the wider group.

- **Damage control** You can also use this principle to influence the way in which your business is perceived when things go wrong. When it comes to making mistakes and upsetting your customers, which is something that happens to the best of us, respond to the crisis by reaching out to the groups to which your customers belong. By showing the majority of your customers that you care and are doing everything you can to rectify the problem, you can, in effect, use social proof to protect your integrity and reputational capital.

- **Get to know your clientele** If, as research suggests, we are motivated to maintain a positive self-concept, you can take advantage of this fact by learning to see your customers the way that they see themselves. Invest some time in gathering information about who your consumers believe themselves to be. You can do this by using any number of tools, from the fantastic Whit.li[32] (a platform that enables you to create a portable psychosocial identity for consumers), to the personality profiling platform Preference Tool.[33] By using this demographic information to create a richer, psychologically optimized website, you can create a more personalized online experience for your customers—one that is congruent with their positive self-concepts and identities.

- **Convert the fence sitters** You already have a loyal client base and interact with them via social media on a regular basis, but what about the fencesitters? Those people on the fringes of your customer base who are not quite yet within the fold? If they are active within particular social networks, you can encourage existing group members to persuade fencesitters to convert. How? By providing incentives to the wider group (such as special member offers and benefits) and letting the principles of normative conformity work their magic. Those potential customers who are within the group but have not quite yet bought into your products/service are more likely to be converted by the attitudes of fellow group members. So, by encouraging positive attitudes towards your brand in the majority of your customer community, you will, in effect, be reaching out to (and converting) a much wider group.

- **Prime your visitors** While it isn't possible to brainwash people simply by beaming subliminal messages through their device (thankfully!), you can prime your website visitors to experience certain states and heighten the likelihood that they will remember you more positively. Write down a list of positive words that you wish your brand to be associated with (for example, happy, good, expert, positive, smile, relationship, support, friendly). Embed these words in prominent parts of your website (such as on your homepage and in your headings), where they are likely to be read by the most people. This will subconsciously set the tone for your brand and, if you subsequently ask your customers for feedback, they are more likely to remember and write about you positively.

The chameleon effect

Have you ever seen a young couple flirting with one another on their first date? If you have, chances are you'll have witnessed a beautiful example of behavioral mimicry in action. When two people are in rapport, they tend to subconsciously mirror each other's body language, gestures, facial expressions and even vocal characteristics.[34] While this is a natural phenomenon that happens automatically, it can also be used to artificially engineer a sense of connection with someone. In fact, studies have shown that interacting with someone who gently mimics our behavior will increase our sense of affinity for that person.[35] Good salespeople are particularly proficient in this art.

Whether or not we are consciously aware of it, this chameleon effect is at its strongest when we are in a social mindset or situation. This has interesting implications for the use of behavioral mimicry in social media and may go a long way in explaining why Skype and face-to-face computer interactions are so much more powerful and persuasive than their less interactive, textual counterparts.

In fact, research carried out by Dunbar and his colleagues at Oxford University,[36] found that media channels actually follow a satisfaction hierarchy. Unsurprisingly, real-world face-to-face conversations trump Skype, which, in turn, is considered more satisfying than interactions via phone, text, email and social media platforms.

Given our long-standing proclivity for social connection, it makes perfect sense that we would prefer any form of interaction that places us in the same physical space as the person with whom we're engaging. Until holodecks become a reality, there simply isn't a substitute for being able to see, respond to and laugh with someone in real time. Incidentally, Dunbar and his colleagues even found that emails that included a symbol for laughter, such as a smiley face or LOL, were viewed more favorably than those which didn't.

MAKE THIS WORK FOR YOU

Establish rapport

- **Use humor** When you're interacting with potential clients, a little humor can go a long way. While it may not be appropriate in all situations (use your discretion), you can create a greater sense of rapport with your visitors by showing some emotion and using emoticons or other symbols to express yourself. As always, be aware of cultural norms and sensitivities here.

- **Mirror your clients** Many businesses now use Skype, webinars and video to communicate with their customers. If you're in a live, face-to-face interaction with someone, notice and subtly mirror back the pace at which they are speaking, the gestures they are using and any salient facial expressions they may exhibit. (A note of caution—if you feel uncomfortable mirroring, practice with your friends first until you have the balance right. The last thing you want to do is offend clients because they think you're mocking them.)

- **Matching** If you're using a one-way communication medium in which your clients can only see you (videos or webinars), do your research first and match any major characteristics that your demographic expresses. For example, if you're presenting to a board of CEOs from New York who dress sharply and speak quickly, where appropriate, match their clothes and mirror their language to establish a sense of rapport. If you want to know more about body language, there's one book that you simply must read: *What Every BODY Is Saying*, by Joe Navarro (HarperCollins, 2008).

LIKING

We've all experienced cases where we've been happier to do a favor for some-one we like than for someone we're dubious about and there is a huge amount of research to back up this feeling.[37] We also tend to like the same things as our social group (it goes back to our sense of belonging), and if you want to see this in dramatic action, just visit the next sci-fi convention in your area. When it comes to succeeding online, it stands to reason that if you can show how like-able you are (for example, by giving people a way to link their friends into a shared "Like"), you can increase the level of connection your customers will feel with you.

Before we dive in, let's take a look at where this particular impulse originates. Having evolved to be social, our desire to be liked stems from a deep motivation to create meaningful relationships with those around us and this is the driving force behind many of the behaviors we see online today. It's the psychological cornerstone on which Facebook has built its monumental success (we all want to feel connected), it's the power behind the "Like" button (if we "Like" the things that our friends "Like" they'll approve of us) and it's one of the key reasons that so many user-generated videos go viral (if we discover and share valuable con-tent, our peers will like us more and we'll gain social status). Most of the time these behaviors, which seem so natural to us, operate below our conscious awareness, which makes harnessing them a powerful tool.

When it comes to getting people to like you, there are several factors that can have a dramatic impact. Unsurprisingly, a key one is physical attractiveness. How attractive you are has been shown to influence people's responses to all sorts of things, from the probability that you'll get asked your age at a bar,[38] to earning more tips on your shift.[39]

In the online world, however, leveraging the principle of "liking" requires a bit more skill. Sure, we can all slap an attractive photo of happy customers on our landing page and hope that people will like the image enough to stick around, but haven't we all become a bit jaded and wary of this kind of contrived beautification?

Well, possibly—but you can turn this to your advantage. While we may treat online information with a certain degree of scepticism, our fundamental desire to connect and the principles that underpin our social behaviors remain the same. If you can increase your business' level of perceived trustworthiness while including content that showcases how likeable you are, you can leverage the principle of "liking" to increase your engagement and conversions online.

Strangers and the law of attraction

So, at a time when the majority of businesses depend on a robust digital strategy to attract new online customers (most of whom will have never even heard of you), how can you use these psychological principles to attract *strangers*?

As we saw earlier, in order to make sense of our world quickly and effortlessly, we rely on cognitive shortcuts called heuristics to help us make decisions. As a rule of thumb, when it comes to existing relationships, the more we like someone, the more likely we are to want to help them out or comply with their requests. This heuristic works well in existing relationships, but what's interesting is that we automatically use this same principle when faced with a *stranger's* request.[40]

When it comes to interacting with people we've never met before, our subconscious picks up on situational cues, activating heuristics that inform the way we respond to these strangers—either as an acquaintance or friend.[41]

Of these cues, one of the most important is the style in which we communicate with this other person. Think back to the last conversation you had with a friend—did you talk about a common topic, taking it in turns to speak or was the interaction altogether more one-directional? The exact communication style does of course depend on the individual and relationship in question, but, typically, what you find is that communication between friends tends to be a two-way affair. Meet with a stranger, however, and you're more likely to encounter a monologue. Psychologists who studied this pattern found that the simple act of a person engaging a stranger in trivial conversation—"Hi, how are you today?"—created enough rapport to increase that person's compliance with a future request by the stranger.[42] They also discovered that, even in the absence of any verbal interaction, by simply being exposed to a stranger for a short amount of time, the level of compliance to that stranger's request increased substantially.

This has fascinating implications for the use of online video and personalized content for increasing conversions on your website. If by the mere fact of being exposed to someone we can be led to like that person more (as in my Christopher Hitchens experience, recounted in Chapter 10), it makes perfect sense to take advantage of this by increasing the reach of your online presence. Add to this the fact that just by watching a favorite TV show we can experience the same sense of belonging we get from a real interpersonal interaction and video begins to look like a potent tool for persuasion (for more information see Chapter 10).

There are many platforms with which you can do this (such as the various social media channels we explored in Chapter 12), but, regardless of the platform you choose, the best results will come from promoting yourself as genuinely as possible. This does not mean talking to your clients the way you would talk to your friends down at the bar after a hard day's work, but it does mean presenting yourself from a position of integrity and authenticity.

This is the antithesis of the pre-approved, consistent-with-the-company-tone-of-voice corporate speak that some well-meaning but woefully mistaken businesses demand of their employees. It doesn't work and, what's more, your customers will be savvy enough to smell a rat and reject this fabricated persona in favor of a competitor's more genuine approach.

Similarity

Another factor that can improve compliance is perceived similarity. As with physical attractiveness, similarity is another element that we use on a subconscious level to identify potential friends, partners, and allies. We are more likely to comply with someone's request if we believe that they are similar to ourselves.

The intriguing thing here is that these similarities don't need to be particularly deep in order to be influential—something as cosmetic as a shared fingerprint type or birthday can be sufficient to elicit greater compliance.

When you're applying this to an online context, however, remember that you have to take into account your customer demographic. Most of the participants who take part in "liking" and "similarity" studies tend to be female. So, if, as some research suggests, women are more relationship-orientated than men,[43] you could reasonably expect to elicit stronger compliance levels with these techniques if you are working with a predominantly female user group.

Ingratiation

Another neat little tactic that you can add to your arsenal is ingratiation—the act of trying to become more attractive or likeable to your target. It may not sound like much, but even something as subtle as remembering someone's name can pack a punch.[44] I'll wager it doesn't stop there either. When people remember other information about us, such as our favorite food or our passion for a particular hobby, we feel special, that the other person cares.

Typically, the person being flattered will view the flatterer with a more positive regard than other onlookers[45]—most probably due to the fact that we all secretly like a boost to our self-esteem and will interpret such flattery as genuine in order to serve this goal. At this point, the flatterer can ask his target anything he wants and is likely to be met with greater compliance for his troubles.

Whether this effect comes down to a sense of indebtedness (the target who is receiving the flattery feels duty bound to reciprocate) or is due to a greater sense of affinity with the flatterer is unclear, but the bottom line is that it tends to work. Of course, the more genuine you are, the better.

Get your visitors to like you and it's half the battle won.

MAKE THIS WORK FOR YOU

Trust me, I'm like you

- **The power of chit-chat** You now know that, when it comes to strangers, we're more likely to comply with a request if we enter into a light dialogue first. Use this to your advantage by genuinely engaging with your visitors on a personal level—via social media, instant messaging or Live Chat. By simply including niceties in your communication with them (and you can do this via email, too), you're showing that you're interested and the nature of your relationship is two-way. Your customers will subconsciously pick up on these cues and then run the same heuristic program as for their friends, resulting in greater compliance to your requests.

- **Trust + likeability = conversions** Improve your business' level of perceived trustworthiness (see Chapter 19) to maximize the positive impact of likeability cues. You can do this by using universally likeable content, such as a video of one of your naturally attractive employees having a two-way conversation with a happy client.

- **Similarity** Whether or not your audience is predominantly female, you can use the principle of similarity to establish rapport and trust with your visitors. For example, if you know that your demographic mainly comprises international 30-something professionals, reflect this back in the design of your website and various communications. You can mirror their physical characteristics by using photos of similar-looking people and you can mirror their language and interests in your social media communications.

AUTHORITY

> *Individuals are frequently rewarded for behaving in accordance with the opinions, advice, and directives of authority figures.*
>
> ROBERT CIALDINI AND NOAH GOLDSTEIN,
> SOCIAL PSYCHOLOGISTS[46]

As we've already seen, authority (and even the *illusion* of authority) can be a powerful way of making your message more persuasive. I don't know about you, but if I'm visiting a gynaecologist (or, if you're a man, a urologist for a prostate check) for the first time, he or she had better be sure to have all the relevant certificates and diplomas on the wall before I take a single step into the examination room. It's not just a few select situations like this in which we look for reassurance but also in everyday life—from purchasing a new family car based on its NCAP safety rating to choosing a five-star resort for that special getaway. Whatever the situation, we automatically seek clues as to other people's levels of authority. That's why this principle is such an influential one—especially when it comes to online business, where legitimacy can be a lot harder to ascertain.

Soft tactics vs. hard tactics

When it comes to wielding influence from a position of authority, the strategies people use tend to fall into one of two main categories: soft tactics and hard tactics.

Soft tactics are strategies that are either *inspirational* or *consultative* in nature.[47] The influence from this kind of strategy stems from elements within the person who is doing the influencing (such as integrity, credibility and charisma).[48]

Inspirational tactics include the use of rational persuasion and personal/inspirational appeal to create compliance. In this kind of scenario, the receiver of the request is often given leeway when deciding whether or not to comply.

To put it into context, let me ask you to think back through your own experiences for a moment. Can you remember a time when a boss, teacher or parent asked you to do something by appealing to your values, ideals and aspirations?[49] Well, whether or not they were aware of it at the time, they were employing soft tactics to get you to comply and usually, it works.

When it comes to the online world, this is one of the most widely used tactics—from charity websites that appeal to our sense of fairness for donations (playing to our values) to sites that sell luxury cars with the promise of fulfilling our lifelong dreams of success (aspirations).

Consultative tactics call for the active involvement of members (or co-creators) in a particular task or endeavour. This can include planning an activity, strategy or change where you need the support and assistance of a team or group.[50] They work because they instil a sense of shared ownership in the participants, so are often very effective at getting the best level of performance and cooperation from a group of people. YouTube, Pinterest and LinkedIn are all platforms the success of which relies on their members' willingness to co-create and share valuable content.

One of the greatest upsides to using soft tactics is that they encourage a sense of shared ownership and the people being asked to comply tend to feel they are being valued for their contributions.

Hard tactics are an altogether different kettle of fish. Comprising what psychologists call *pressure* or *legitimating* tactics, hard influence gains compliance through assertiveness and force, which can sometimes lead to strained or damaged relationships. This strategy works due to social structures that exist external to the influencer (such as your job title within your organization).[51]

Typical *pressure* tactics can involve things like demands, threats, frequent checking or persistent reminders.[52] While they may serve in an offline management environment, I would advise you not to use such tactics online.

Legitimating tactics, however, are slightly different.These depend on the hierarchical structure of a social group in order to work and you *can* use these online to dramatic effect. In this scenario, if the person making the request is in a position of authority, he or she can use that status as leverage to get his or her own way. While they do rely on power differentials to work, such techniques need not be explicit to generate results.

Consider the way in which we (in the West) tend to attach a high social status to doctors and lawyers. In terms of their contributions to society, who's to say that they are more valuable than the people who grow our food, build our houses or teach our children? The point is, most of the time, we adopt cultural cues that form our view of the world and of the people within it to whom we should defer.

On websites and in commercials, people use all sorts of authority figures to compel us to take action—from the woman in the white lab coat trying to sell us "scientifically proven" beauty products to the athlete who endorses a miracle weightloss pill. Like it or not, using authority figures to get people to buy products works.

MAKE THIS WORK FOR YOU

Expert appeal

- **You're the expert** Show that you're an expert in your field by writing well-researched, informative blogs on your specialist subject. By building an archive and providing your users with a free resource, you will increase your reputation and engender more trust from your visitors.

- **Soft tactics** In terms of getting users to take certain actions on your website, a soft tactic could involve using rational persuasion to enlighten them as to the benefits of your service/product over those of your competitors. In this case, including some statistics or evidence to support your position can do a lot to encourage people to try your services for the first time or sign up to your newsletter.

- **Personal appeal** Using personal appeal can also work wonders. If you are well known within your industry for writing inspiring articles, delivering juicy webinars or giving captivating talks, you can use your inspirational appeal to influence the behaviors of others. Do this by personally asking people to take action—a simple photo accompanied by a personal note with your actual signature at the bottom can add significant weight to your requests.

SCARCITY

The rising success and proliferation of websites that "gamify" real-life shopping by providing group discounts and "flash sales" to their members (such as Groupon,[53] Achica,[54] Gilt[55] and Dalani[56]) have also influenced the way in which we operate online. No longer content with the drudgery of browsing through online shops to find overpriced items that we'll have to wait days to receive, more and more of us are turning to the high-adrenalin sport of shopping at gamified stores.

It's not just e-commerce websites that are at it—scarcity has long been used in the advertising world to fuel our desires, inflate a product's value and, ultimately, drive sales.[57] You need only look as far as Apple devotees to see this principle in action. In fact, when it comes to particularly innovative, customised products, scarcity is the magic ingredient that makes this particular cocktail of characteristics irresistible to those consumers who consider themselves "unique."[58]

Whether it's a scarcity of products ("limited edition," "while stocks last") or a scarcity of time ("sale ends today"), this is a powerful principle that works well both on- and offline. It's the single most compelling factor behind online auction websites such as eBay and, if you need convincing, go and see for yourself where the fiercest bidding wars take place. They're almost always on the products that have the highest number of "watchers" and a rapidly approaching deadline.

Other websites, like Net-a-porter,[59] the luxury online fashion outlet, owe their success to not only the designer items they sell but also the fact that they only ever order in a certain amount of stock. Then, once it's gone, it's gone.

The effectiveness of this strategy was demonstrated delightfully by a bunch of psychologists and some cookie jars.[60] Pretending that they were running a consumer products survey, Worchel and colleagues offered students a chocolate chip cookie from one of two jars. The first jar was full of cookies, whereas the second contained only a few. Even though the cookies were absolutely identical, the students reported that the cookies from the second, emptier jar were more desirable, delicious and expensive than the cookies from the first. If such a simple device can have such extraordinary effects, it's no wonder that smarter businesses are using scarcity to boost their sales online.

MAKE THIS WORK FOR YOU

In short supply

- **Use a countdown** If you're promoting a product, tickets to an event or a special discount on a particular service, embed a simple countdown timer on your website to activate your visitors' sense of scarcity. For best results, limit the offer to a short amount of time (such as one day or a week) and increase the impact of this principle by making it clear that there is only a limited stock. Scarcity of time combined with a scarcity of products can be a potent formula for sale success.

- **Limit your stock** While I'm not advocating the deliberate mismanagement of stock, flagging up items that are in low supply can be a good way of encouraging people to buy an item before they "miss out." If you're selling limited edition prints or other such products, keep track of how many items you have left and you can even include "sold" signs next to current batches that have now fully sold out.

15 BUILDING REPUTATIONAL CAPITAL

> *More than image, a firm's reputation is a form of capital often neglected in the boardroom and overlooked in conventional analysis of financial statements.*
>
> KEVIN JACKSON, AUTHOR[1]

THE STORY OF DOMINO'S PIZZA

Domino's Pizza actively monitor social media channels to track its customers' comments about its pizzas—and a good job, too. In 2009 the company quickly realized that people were very unhappy with the poor quality of their food. Instead of spinning a story, as other companies might have done, Domino's decided to listen to its critics and, using their feedback, created new pizza recipes to turn the pizza experience around.

Here's the genius part. To communicate this transformation, Domino's launched an integrated online campaign called the "Pizza Turnaround," which included a documentary-style video where it showed company officials reacting to the original criticisms. By showing that it cared enough to listen to and act on its customers' concerns, Dominos saw an immediate impact. In the first quarter of 2010, its sales in the USA were up 14.3 percent year-on-year—the biggest ever jump in sales in the fast-food industry.[2]

It's not just the big companies that can benefit from a bit of customer engagement and word of mouth. According to Nielsen's "Global trust in advertising and brand messages report,"[3] 92 percent of us say we trust "earned media," such as personal recommendations from our friends and family, more than any other kind of advertising. Online consumer reviews come a close second, with 70 percent of us trusting the brand information we find there—which should come as no surprise, given that we're all a bit partial to social proof.

If you're looking to pitch via mobile devices, however, it's a different story. Here, only a third of us around the world trust video or banner ads and, while this figure does seem to be on the rise, it's not worth blowing your budget on these kinds of ads just yet. It's interesting to note that, while our trust in online advertising seems to be increasing (perhaps due to younger demographics?), our confidence in traditional paid media, such as TV, magazines and newspapers, is on the decline, though still significant enough for companies to warrant huge spends in this area.

WORD OF MOUTH

Ask any marketer and they'll tell you that when it comes to increasing your sales, you can't beat word of mouth referrals. Not only does it appeal to businesses because it appears more credible but also it doesn't cost much to acquire new customers in this way.

One study[4] investigating strategies for generating electronic referrals (e-referrals), found that offering the referrer and referee the same size of incentive led to the highest increase in referrals. The second highest increase came from offering the referrer more than the referee.

Whereas pre-Internet referrals usually happened organically via conversations between friends and acquaintances, online word of mouth referrals have a far larger reach. These e-referrals can take the form of emails, blog comments, tweets and instant messages and can spread virally among strangers if the product or service at the center of that referral is relevant and persuasive enough.

In one of the largest research studies to date, Facebook's data team decided to explore the phenomenon of word of mouth referrals head on by examining how information spreads through a social network.[5] Until recently, the leading theory was that the Internet encourages us to cluster into self-validating in-groups of "people like us." This idea—that similarity breeds connection[6]—is instrumental in the way in which we form our social networks, both on- and offline. From this you could reasonably expect to see online groups seeking out, sharing and consuming the same kinds of information with each other across social platforms, but what the researchers actually found, was something quite different.

By observing how 253 million Facebook users interacted with the 75 million links they shared, the team discovered that people's *weakest* ties were actually the most influential. In fact, you're ten times more likely to share a link that one of your weak ties has posted than one posted by a close friend.

Why? Because the people you know less well are more likely to share novel information with you. Compare this to links and information that you and your group normally share (which, due to your similar interests you're already likely to have seen) and you'll see why our weak ties are collectively responsible for the majority of information spread.[7]

We're novelty-seeking Internet users, so those weak ties provide us with an indispensable source of new information.

MAKE THIS WORK FOR YOU

Automatic word of mouth

- **Tell a friend** You can leverage this phenomenon by using "tell a friend" calls to action on your website or requiring your customers to "tweet this link" to unlock the product they're wishing to download. Using such a lock can be a very powerful way of sending your blog, website or campaign viral and yet you can download the code for a small amount at websites like CodeCanyon.[8] *Enforced* word of mouth referrals may not appeal to all of your visitors, but they will certainly capture some and help spread the word about your business and its services.

CAN I TRUST YOU?

As we shall see in Chapter 19, one of the biggest barriers to acquiring new customers online is persuading them that they can trust you. Knowing which websites and sources you can rely on is already a tricky task, but it's one that is made even harder by the sheer volume of sites that are out there.

While we do have filters to help us choose which information to tune in to, such as circles of friends, trusted news sources and established blogs, we're a curious bunch and will still stumble across new websites for which we have little frame of reference. How can we tell if the information on that fabulous new tech website is credible? How can your users know to trust yours?

In general, when we're looking for information we can depend on, we tend to trust people we *believe* to be credible. As we saw earlier in Chapter 14, the mere *appearance* of credibility can have a massive influence on whether we trust someone or not. When we are trying to assess someone's credibility online, though, we tend to be more influenced by the source credits of the institution (such as the website) than by the creators themselves.[9] So, how can you increase your credibility online?

Psychologists consider credibility to be a perceived quality, one that can be summarised as follows:

Trustworthiness + Expertise = Credibility

In the real world, we tend to rely on markers such as character, competence, influence and sociability to assess whether someone is credible or not. Whilst we like to think of ourselves as reasonable and fair-minded, psychologists have found a profound bias in the way that we assign credibility. We tend to consider members of our "in-group" (our circle of friends, work team, family) as more credible than people from "out-groups" (people outside of our social circles).[10]

What's more, when we're online, we apply these same principles to virtual agents or avatars, even though they're entirely inanimate projections.[11] This alone has huge implications when it comes to boosting your website's credibility. It means that if you can identify some of your visitors' characteristics, such as the way that they look, dress, speak and gesture, you can use this information to create an avatar that mirrors these traits, thus creating a sense of familiarity and, by extension, credibility. It will also save your visitors the time and effort it would take them to seek out peripheral credibility cues, such as links to official partner websites and testimonials.

Keep it credible

- **Overall credibility** Increase your website's overall credibility by incorporating design elements such as a balanced layout and cool color tones.[12] While the effects of color are subject to cultural differences, this is something you can leverage by analyzing your target demographic to isolate and use the elements that increase perceived credibility for that particular market.

- **Source credibility** Boost your website's source credibility by including links to other reputable websites and highlighting any institutional credentials or quality rating awards you might have.[13] For example, if you're a Zagat-rated restaurant, make sure that you show this award in your header or sidebar—somewhere that's easy for new visitors to see.

- **Collaborate** Team up with other credible sources in your field. If you work in collaboration with other businesses in your industry, form a guild and support one another by publicizing your group on your website. You can do this by creating a badge or logo that each business within the group will add to its profile or website. You can even set up a collaborative blog or LinkedIn group to add credibility across platforms.

- **Association** Identify industry-leading websites and write for them. Show your potential customers that you know your field so well you're writing guest posts for the heavyweights. If you're a designer, write a guest post for *Mashable* or *Smashing Magazine*. By associating yourself with a well-respected online institution, you will not only increase your own personal credibility but you'll also be broadcasting your expertise to an entirely new audience of potential customers.

- **Show you're legit** If you run a non-profit, governmental or educational website, make sure you obtain the relevant URL suffix to reassure users of your legitimacy (such as .org, .gov and .edu or .ac).[14]

- **Testimonials** Collect and showcase real testimonials from satisfied customers on your website. By doing so, you'll be showing new clients that you can deliver and that others trust you. When it comes to credibility, a little bit of social proof can go a long, long way.

▶

- **Framing** If you are developing a website that curates articles and content from experts within your industry, make sure you showcase the most well-known among them on the homepage of your website to "frame" the experience and expectations of your users. If they are new to your website and see that you work with writers they respect and trust, its reputation will benefit by association.

- **Vested interests** Avoid including links to businesses with which you have commercial relationships. If, for example, you run an online healthshop and your sponsored links are from pharmaceutical companies, your potential customers will see these as vested interests and will be less likely to buy from you.[15]

FOCUS ON CONTENT

In one study[16] investigating the importance of content versus design on a website's credibility, some interesting findings emerged. Users visiting a website to research information or products were more likely to pay attention to the website's content than to the way in which it was presented. In this category, the accuracy, usefulness, clarity and focus of a website's information was most important, along with the writing tone, privacy and customer service. In contrast, regular visitors whose visits were less short-lived, were more likely to notice the design, readability, functionality and perceived security of the website. While it's impossible for your website to appeal to everyone, nonetheless, you can increase your website's success by making sure that you stick to the following rules.

MAKE THIS WORK FOR YOU

Clean and clear

- **Clarity** Whatever industry you are in, make sure you use clear, concise, spellchecked language on your website. Avoid lengthy reels of text at all costs. Where necessary, supply dropdown boxes if extra information is required.

- **Tone** The writing style of your website should reflect your business and the expectations of your customers. For example, if you are a corporate bank that provides services to high net worth individuals, your tone should reflect your clients' concern for privacy, discretion and security.

- **Easy to read** While the design of your website will depend largely on its function and purpose, it should nevertheless be easy to read, navigate and search through. Your clients should be able to find what they're looking for in as little time and with as few clicks as possible.

16 INCREASE YOUR SALES

> *" E-commerce sites, even at the functional and graphic design stage, should consider elements that make it possible to increase the potential for participation, engagement, interaction, and fun.*
>
> MICHELLE BONERA, PROFESSOR OF ECONOMICS AND
> BUSINESS MANAGEMENT[1]

With more of us going online to purchase products and services, it is more vital than ever to make sure you are using all the available tools to capture, convert and capitalize on your audience. Unlike real-world shops where you can physically interact with the products, when it comes to e-shopping you are restricted to 2D representations, which means that you have to rely on images, information and videos of your products to make a sale.[2]

As we saw earlier, your ability to build trust online is crucial and your success (or failure) will depend largely on the way in which you present your products and services to your customers.[3] This crucial factor, along with clear navigation and easy order fulfillment, will contribute to your consumer's overall experience and will influence whether they end up buying from you or from somebody else.

ALL WORK AND NO PLAY ...

It's not just good usability and the use of trust cues that will boost your website's sales. With greater numbers of us turning to e-commerce for sheer recreation, our purchasing behaviors are becoming increasingly influenced by the playfulness of the sites that we visit, with factors such as security and usefulness following behind.[4] I for one have lost track of the times I've wiled away an evening in the comforting glow of my laptop, happily grazing from one website to the next in search of beautiful ephemera and it appears that I'm not alone. Research from the field of business economics shows that we not only prefer *fun* websites but also those of us who visit these sites will probably make a purchase.[5] Apparently playfulness makes for great ROI.

How does this fun factor actually influence our purchasing behaviors? It may come down to the neurochemistry of reward. Research has found that the dopaminergic reward system in our brains gets activated for a wide range of things, from drugs[6] and money[7] to beautiful faces[8] and sports cars.[9] With the increasing gamification of our online experience (we even use the terms #win and #fail in our Twitter conversations), it's no surprise that websites are increasingly using reward incentives to get us to buy—whether it's a limited time sale or the chance to win a Lamborghini.

In fact, the popularity of online social play has given rise to new revenue streams for those brands with deep enough pockets. In the summer of 2011, social game manufacturer Zynga paired up with Unilever to create a virtual "LUX Fantastical Manor" for "FarmVille" players in China. For one month only, players were able to interact with Shu Qi, the brand's ambassador, and make their farms more attractive by purchasing virtual beauty items with their virtual currency. Yes, it sounds bonkers, but in countries where social play is popular (China, India and Mexico are the most avid gamers, followed by Argentina, USA and Brazil),[10] it makes sense to use social play as a means through which to build rapport with your audience.

You don't have to be minted to leverage this phenomenon—even funny cartoons[11] give us a dopamine hit, which may explain why user-generated videos that make us laugh also tend to be the ones that go viral.

Designed with pleasure in mind, the power of successful websites rests in their ability to entice and influence their customers (and shopping behaviors) by simply providing an attractive, interactive play space for them to explore. Not only does this make the outlet's brand more memorable but it also creates a positive emotional association with the website. This means that customers are more likely to return to get another fix.

When it comes to clothes, most high street fashion outlets already provide a degree of interactivity on their websites and other retail sectors are starting to follow suit. It has become fairly common practice for businesses to embed videos of their products/services "in action" to highlight particular features or benefits to prospective customers and interactive 360° photographic views are becoming increasingly popular in the fashion and gadget world. In short, any functionality that emulates our offline shopping experience (minus the jostling crowds and screaming kids) is likely to increase the likelihood that people will enjoy your website and buy your product.

Some fashion e-retailers are taking this interactivity a step further, using third-party technology and applications such as Bodymetrics[12,13] to allow consumers to try on clothes virtually before buying them. Other than injecting the fun factor back into online shopping, platforms like these are also a powerful way for the brands that use them to gain free publicity and promotion. Think about it, every time a teenager virtually tries on an item and posts it to his or her entire social network, he or she is effectively marketing that brand (and the application) to hundreds of new potential customers. It's only a matter of time before we're all at it.

MAKE THIS WORK FOR YOU

Gamification

- **Make it fun** If you are selling merchandise, give your visitors an enjoyable experience that they'll remember. Not only will you put a smile on their faces but you'll also be increasing the likelihood that they'll come back for more, simply for the sheer pleasure of it. Adding a bit of comedy (appropriate to your market) can be a great way of boosting engagement.

- **Go interactive** Offer your visitors attractive features that will enhance their online experience with you (such as interactive videos, zoomable images and even short polls). If you're not sure what features to include, ask your clients directly. They will appreciate your desire to make their experience more enjoyable and their feedback will provide some great insights into what's in demand right now.

CUSTOMER SERVICE

Whether your online customers are shopping locally or visiting your website from the other side of the world, when it comes to communication, people universally want (and expect) a clear, continuous and useful interaction.[14] This includes everything from sales advice, return and payment policies, to FAQs, shipping and tax information and handling costs.

MAKE THIS WORK FOR YOU

People want to speak to a real human

- **Live Chat** Services in which clients have the option to text-chat immediately with companies are growing in popularity and are fast becoming the norm across e-commerce websites. There's a good reason for that. Instant, personal support is what we're used to in the offline world. By offering this to your online customers, too, you're giving them the chance to connect with you on a human level—great for boosting trust, satisfaction and emotional engagement.

- **Keep it personal** Not all instant messaging platforms are created equal. As we saw earlier, when it comes to dialogue-based systems, we consistently prefer to use platforms that allow us to see who we're talking to (such as Skype or Facebook IM), as the experience feels more personal and is easy to follow.[15]

MERCHANDISE

The easier it is for people to buy, the better. You can minimize the hassle factor for customers shopping at your site by following a few simple rules.

MAKE THIS WORK FOR YOU

Useful functions

- **View all** Your customers should have the option to view the full selection of merchandise within a category at a glance. A quick, comprehensive inspection of an expanded set of options will save your clients time and hassle, encouraging them to return to your site.

- **Filter** The option to filter search results by categories such as price, size and type of item is a great way of empowering your customers by making it quick and easy for them to find what they're looking for. If you provide services to which several keywords might apply, include a search box on your site and make sure you "tag" (label) your services accordingly.

- **Reliability cues** A good track record for reliable, trustworthy service is key to ensuring e-commerce success for your business.[16] While preferences for usability, privacy and customer service do vary depending on your demographic, it's good practice to maintain a high quality of service, which can be achieved by offering full refunds on returned items and free postage and packaging. If business is going particularly well, you can even offer a no quibble guarantee. Whatever options you choose to offer, make sure you clearly state your terms of service so that you give your clients the cues they'll need to trust your site.

Uniqueness

This is one of the easiest ways to reduce price competition and stand out from the crowd. Simply offer products, services or discounts that people desire but cannot get elsewhere. You can achieve this in several ways.

MAKE THIS WORK FOR YOU

Give them something special

- **Exclusivity** Offer exclusive private-label merchandise to your clients and limited run items. Whether you're a massive retailer with an established supply chain or a small boutique site that works with up-and-coming designers, this tactic can boost both your exclusivity and your bottom line.

- **Branded variants** Work with established retailers to offer special "branded variants" of their products that can only be bought from your shop or website. One of the biggest success stories for this strategy comes from (RED),[17] a campaign that was started by U2's Bono and Bobby Shriver in 2006 to raise funds in order to eliminate AIDS worldwide. By licensing the brand to partner companies such as Converse, Nike and GAP, (RED) was able to offer branded products that were unique to each company. This strategy worked so well that the brand is now global.

– **Bundles** Create complementary bundles of products that are available only separately elsewhere. You can do this by offering selected groups of items at special "discount prices" or collaborating with other local businesses that offer complimentary products or services. For example, I know a wine shop that adds value to its customers by offering complimentary recipe cards from local chefs with every bottle of wine it sells. The wine shop benefits from having a unique selling point, the customers gain culinary inspiration and the local chefs enjoy a boost in their reputation.

Multiple items

This is a quick, efficient way of making more sales and offering more value to your customers. By offering multiple item sales, you can effectively offer your clients a shopping experience tailored to their needs, while also reducing their shipping costs. Offering complementary merchandise also eliminates the hassle and time required to look for goods elsewhere, thus creating a more enjoyable shopping experience for your customers.

Amazon is the expert in this field. If you go online and click on any book, you'll be taken to a page that not only gives you the main information about said book but also provides you with a section titled "Frequently Bought Together," which sits neatly beneath. How nice—here, Amazon helpfully suggests not two, but three items that you can buy together and—oh, look—they're relevant to your tastes and interests. To make it even easier, Amazon even supplies you with the "Price For All Three" and a purchase button that reads "Add all three to Basket." They don't even need to offer an actual discount. Simply by offering you more of the stuff that you want means you'll be lucky not to come away with more than you bargained for.

Distribution

If you are selling physical products, make sure you offer your clients a clear selection of shipping options and rates, and maintain a reliable delivery service. When in doubt, under-promise on time, and over-deliver on efficiency.

If you are selling downloadable products, ensure you provide clear instructions to your customers on how the process works and make it as quick and easy as possible for them to download the item. Add value to your service by giving your clients the ability to return and re-download the item in case of accidental deletion and provide a dedicated contact email address or phone number for clients to access if they run into difficulty. A little help goes a long, long way.

INFORMATION

When it comes to parting with money, we all like a healthy dollop of information that we can rely on to inform our purchases. In fact, studies show that the higher the quality and extensiveness of information available to us, the better our buying decisions and overall purchase satisfaction.[18]

So, remember, one of the primary roles of an online shop is to provide clear price- and product-related information. By making it easy for your clients to find what they're looking for, you are implicitly showing that you care about their experience and their time, which, in turn, will engender in them a sense of trust and security.

MAKE THIS WORK FOR YOU

Be transparent

- **Price comparisons** It may seem counter-intuitive, but providing your clients with price comparisons across vendors for the products you are selling can add value and credibility to your website. Not only does this demonstrate transparency, which in turn will increase perceived trust and encourage customer loyalty, but it can also increase your customers' level of satisfaction in their purchase.[19] (You don't even have to be the cheapest on the market—stores like John Lewis and Marks & Spencer may not be the best for price, but, because they offer great *service*, people are prepared to pay more.)

- **Accurate product images** If you are using your website to sell products, make sure you use professional, large, high-quality images that are authentic in color—research shows that this conveys competence and it can boost visitors' level of trust in your website.[20] (Small images tend to set off people's alarm bells, repelling potential customers and losing business in the process.) In order to help your web pages load more quickly, you can include decent-size thumbnails that have a roll-over or lightbox functionality to allow customers to view an enlarged image (or "zoom").

Capture and use customer information

Everyone who shops online can be identified and their user journeys tracked. This means that not only can you record what your customers buy, but also what they inspected and for how long, giving you the opportunity to add value to their online shopping experience by offering special discounts tailored to include their preferred items. You can also use this data to identify your core market and refine your business offer accordingly.

Personalizing the shopping experience to your users' tastes will not only increase overall satisfaction with your service but also customer loyalty and, thus, your business' sustainability. Again, Amazon has this down to a fine art, with personalized recommendations awaiting every user under the guise of titles such as "More Items to Consider," "Related to Items You've Viewed," "Inspired by Your Wish List," "Your Browsing History" … and so on.

If Amazon is the master of this art, Google is the god. In order to reach more customers with targeted advertising, you may wish to consider using Google AdWords (which dominates this market). This services works by using cookies to remember and store unique identifier numbers for each user, which are then placed into specific demographic categories, such as biking enthusiast, outdoor sports, male, and so on. Based on these cookies, Google can then target you with ads directly related to your interests. This tailored approach results in you seeing a selection of ads that you're likely to find relevant. (As an aside, you can stop Google from doing this by clearing your browser's cookies, opting out of interest-based advertising or browsing in Incognito mode.)[21]

Another way in which you can collect customer information is by monitoring what people are saying about you across different social media platforms. While there are several free, rudimentary tools out there that claim to measure your online influence (such as ratio-based Klout),[22] if you want a truly representative sense of the public sentiment around your business, a more refined approach is required.

Services that differentiate between your brand's general, world influence and your sectorial influence, such as the aforementioned Repskan,[23] can provide accurate insights into what people are saying about you in the circles that count. For example, Warren Buffet's opinions generally carry a lot of weight, but when it comes to influence he clearly holds more sway in the finance sector than in the world of fashion. While his general influence score would give you a rough idea of his social standing, in order to glean any *useful* information you'd have to look more closely at the chatter in the financial sector.

The same principle applies to you. If you want an accurate read on who your customers are, what they think of you and what they want, tools that combine your sector-specific metrics with that of your general, world influence are likely to provide a good indicator as to whose feedback and commentary you should be paying attention to.

17 PRICING AND VALUE

Value represents a trade-off between quality and costs.

GILLIAN NAYLOR AND KIMBERLY FRANK,
PROFESSORS OF MARKETING AND ACCOUNTING[1]

THE CHARM OFFENSIVE

We've all done it. Gone out to the local shop for some basic supplies, only to return hours later with way more than just a few essentials. Those bright red letters that spell SALE are tricky to ignore at the best of times, but they're even harder to resist when combined with the charm offensive—and I don't just mean a sexy sales assistant.

While nobody knows exactly how it got started, the mythic power of "charm prices" (numbers ending in 9, 99, 98 and 95) has long been documented in the marketing world. Whether in 99 cent shops or the famous jewellery boutiques that line the Riviera, this psychological trick has been helping businesses to drive sales and attract new customers for years, and now research is uncovering exactly why we find these little numbers so hard to resist.

In 2003, two American researchers, Anderson and Simester, set out to put the charm of $9 to the test.[2] Would more people buy a particular dress if its price ended in the number 9, than if it ended in any other number? To find out, they teamed up with two national mail-order companies that sell women's clothing and played around with some digits.

They altered the price of four particular dresses and mailed out different versions of the catalogue to customers across the country. When the orders started coming in, the results confirmed what they had suspected all along. Each of the four dresses sold most when their price tags ended in a 9—even if that figure was *more expensive* than the other figures (see Table 17.1).

Table 17.1 The charm of $9

Price	Numbers sold
$74	15
$79	24
$84	12

Source: Adapted from Anderson, E.T. and Simester, D.I. (2003), p.94.

How could this be? Although there are several theories as to why this trick works (some say we associate 9 endings with sale items and discount pricing;[3] others say we round down the leftmost digit, making $79 look more appealing than $80),[4] the fact remains that pricing your products and services show that they end in a 9 does help to drive sales—even if the thing you're selling is a one-bedroom apartment in Hampstead for $799,000. In the absence of any innate, accurate sense of value, this is a technique that can work well anywhere, on- or offline.

MAKE THIS WORK FOR YOU

Persuasion by numbers

- **Dressed to the nines** Whatever you're selling, it pays to play with your pricing. If we do indeed associate 9 endings with discounts and your products or services fall within a mid to low price range for your industry, then converting your prices so they end in 9s can help increase your sales.

- **From zero to hero** However, if you're selling high-end products to an affluent demographic, you may wish to think twice before using this pricing strategy. Where 9 endings denote sales, 0 endings infer high quality, which is why, when used in the right context, price tags ending in 0 can give consumers subconscious cues as to the luxury standard of your merchandise. If this sounds like your market, you may want to avoid the use of 9 endings except for strict use in sales—the use of 9s at other times could damage the perceived quality and value of your brand.[5]

- **SALE + 9 = profit** Interestingly, Anderson and Simester also found that adding a "SALE" sign to a charm price can have an additive effect, actually boosting sales even further. For instance, an item marked "MSRP $88, SALE $79" will have a stronger effect than if it's simply marked "$79." So, if you want to influence your customers to buy more, use both techniques together.

LOSS AVERSION

 Losses loom larger than gains.

DANIEL KAHNEMAN AND AMOS TVERSKY,
BEHAVIORAL ECONOMISTS[6]

As we saw at the very beginning of this book, many of the things we enjoy (money, sports cars, attractive faces) give us pleasure by stimulating the reward (mesolimbic) system in the brain. So, if gaining something like money makes us feel good, then isn't parting with it going to hurt?

In a seminal piece of research conducted in the 1970s, behavioral economists Kahneman and Tversky famously stated that "losses loom larger than gains." The idea that we prefer avoiding losses to acquiring gains implies that we might value an item more acutely when asked to give it up than when we first acquire it. Think of something you own and love—it could be a beautiful watch, a trinket you bought on your honeymoon or that tatty jumper your grandmother knitted for you as a kid. Think of how much it cost you originally. Do you have a figure in mind? Now think of the price you'd accept if you had to sell it this instant.

Chances are the second figure is larger than the first. In fact, research has found that on average, we request *twice* the original price we paid for an item if asked to sell it later—meaning that, somewhere along the way, we've imbued it with extra value.

Referred to by behavioral economists as the *endowment effect*[7] or *status quo bias*,[8] the fact that we place a higher value on objects we already own (relative to objects we do not) has some serious implications for purchasing behaviors.

What happens when the thing that we're "losing" is money itself? We "lose" money every day, on purchases large and small, from essentials to luxuries. Whilst we may not experience the pain of loss physically, the fact that companies go to great lengths to disguise and delay customer payments suggests parting with money is, at the very least, *psychologically* painful.

This may explain why people tend to choose flat-rate payment plans for services such as health clubs and utility bills, even when switching to a pay-per-use tariff would save them money.[9] In fact, the popularity of alternative currencies such as loyalty points and frequent flyer miles may also stem from this phenomenon: by acting as a form of compensation, such systems help reduce the pain of payment.

How not to lose out

- **Love, Love, Love** This is easier said than done, but if you want more people to buy your products or services, offer them something they'll fall in love with. The endowment effect works because we become attached to what we own. Create a sense of longing and emotional attachment in your audience, and the pain of paying for your product will be dwarfed by the desire for the item itself. The classic and obvious example to cite here (again) is Apple, which has been so successful at engineering emotional attachment that the areas of the brain that light up when believers look at religious imagery, also light up when Apple fans view their favorite brand's logo and products.[10]

- **Don't lose out** If you are selling something that will save people money, frame it in terms of loss. Allow me to demonstrate. If I told you that by switching insurance providers you could save $300 a year, would you do it? Maybe. What if I told you that by staying with your current provider you were actually *losing* $300 every year? When it comes to a good sales pitch, we tend to respond most strongly to deals aimed at averting losses, so bear this in mind when you're structuring your message.

- **Status quo bias** When things are going smoothly, we don't like to rock the boat and this is especially true when it comes to money. For customers, parting with money is not the only part of a transaction that can be painful. "Pain" can mean anything from making a large, one-off downpayment on a new house to the hassle of having to purchase top-up credit for your phone. So, make it easier for your clients to part with their money by offering a variety of payment options. Monthly plans can be a great way of making a large price tag more palatable, as can "buy now pay later" policies.

ONLINE AUCTIONS

Since their infancy in the 1990s, online auction sites like eBay have gained so much in popularity and reach that this form of e-commerce now accounts for a sizeable chunk of online retail. Aside from the thrill of the chase and the excitement of pitting yourself against other bidders, the conditions involved in online auctions also make for some curious behaviors—as psychologists Ariely and Simonson discovered.[11]

They were investigating people's behaviors at online auctions, when they found that top bidders seemed to be acting differently from the rest. When in the lead, it appeared that the highest bidder would start thinking about the item in more concrete terms and, in imagining that this item would soon be theirs, would develop an attachment to it.

This "pseudo-endowment effect" (thinking that an item is yours before you've won it) was boosting their willingness to continue bidding. The longer they had been in the lead, the more likely they were to keep going in order to secure "their" item. By psychologically identifying themselves as the new owner while the auction was still live, the lead bidder was, in effect, making it more painful to "lose out"—which, in this case, would have meant being outbid.

While this selling style may not be suitable for all businesses, it does highlight the benefit of auctioning products to yield a higher return, especially when you consider that, at least online, consumers tend to under-search (and hence over-pay) for a range of widely available commodities. Add this to the fact that auction prices usually lead to higher winning bids and the use of auctions as a sales strategy becomes rather appealing—for both the consumer (the purchasing process is more exhilarating) and the vendor (who secures higher profits in the process).

MAKE THIS WORK FOR YOU

In it to win it

- **Auctioning emotions** We are less likely to give up items that we feel an emotional connection to.[12] Therefore, if you are selling your products via auction, you can increase their value by targeting customers who are likely to have a natural attraction to the items you're selling. To find out more about the personality traits of your customers and how this affects their online behaviors, check out the aforementioned Preference Tool[13]—a fantastic behavioral profiling platform created by researchers at Cambridge University. Using psychological tests, it sources data from social media platforms and collates the results from millions of users to improve understanding of human behavior. Plainly put, it helps you to discover what makes your customers tick.

▶

- **Risk-takers** Although online auctions can be a fun way of boosting sales, they won't appeal to everyone. Auctions are most likely to attract consumers with an affinity towards risk (high dopamine), but may alienate other potential buyers. If you want to use this technique, minimize *your* risk by employing it as an adjunct to your main sales strategy. For example, lots of mainstream businesses do this by posting their sale items on official eBay pages, attracting flocks of new customers while retaining their established client base.

DYNAMIC PRICING (PERILS AND POSSIBILITIES)

Dynamic pricing (when different vendors can set different prices for the same item) is a strategy that is widely, and successfully, used offline to increase profits. However, use it as part of your e-commerce strategy and you risk being met with outrage and cries of unfair pricing. Add to this the fact that we now consult more sources prior to purchase than ever before (in 2011, shoppers in the USA visited around ten different sources before they went on to buy,)[14] and you start to see the importance of fair and competitive pricing.

Although low-cost airlines frequently advertise different fares on less competitive routes[15] and seem to get away with it, you may remember the furor that Amazon caused over a decade ago when their customers found out they were being charged different amounts to purchase the same DVDs.

While Amazon claimed to be running a "limited test" to "measure what impact price has on a customers" purchasing patterns' (Patty Smith, Amazon spokeswoman),[16] many suspected that Amazon was using its buyers' profiles and browsing behaviors to personalize its prices (and inflate its profits) according to each person's means.

In fact, it was reported that when a visitor deleted the cookies on her computer identifying her as a frequent Amazon customer, the sale price that she was offered for a DVD dropped from $26.24 to $22.74[17]—a difference of nearly $4. Although Amazon didn't admit to any wrongdoing per se, it did issue a public apology and refunded all its customers who had paid the inflated prices.[18]

In economic circles, this kind of tactic is referred to as "first-degree price discrimination,"[19] and it basically does what is says on the box. By judging your willingness-to-pay, specialist software can directly tailor the offer you receive based on your purchasing history, thus discriminating in terms of the price you will pay. To be frank, when it comes to online purchases, I would feel betrayed if

I found out that I was paying more than the next person for an identical item, so would advise against using this particular strategy. It's one thing bidding in an auction and paying top dollar for something you really want, but to be duped into paying more than the next person simply because you exhibit different purchasing behaviors seems downright punitive.

That said, there is one notable exception in which dynamic pricing can yield positive returns online. How? By using the name your own price (NYOP) mechanism. In contrast to classic offline retail settings, NYOP relies on the *buyer* to make the initial offer, which can then be accepted or rejected by the seller, depending on whether it exceeds or falls short of a predetermined threshold price.

Essentially, this strategy follows similar rules to an auction, in which it is the vendor's prerogative to name a reserve price, which, once met, ensures a win for the highest bidder and a healthy profit for the vendor. If the buyer doesn't meet this threshold price, he or she can amend the offer in the following rounds until the item is secured. The only major difference between an auction and NYOP is in the fact that customers in the latter category are not in competition with one another.[20]

NYOP strategies in e-commerce don't just benefit the businessowner, however. The consumer wins, too. By opening up your products to flexible pricing, you're effectively reaching a wider market—customers who were previously priced out can get a look-in, giving good hagglers the opportunity to save more money than their less experienced peers.[21]

It's a strategy that worked really well for Radiohead when, in 2007, the band offered its latest album on a name-your-own-price basis direct to their fans, cutting out the middleman and the wildly expensive promotion that usually accompanies any major release. While this strategy didn't involve a threshold price, by asking the fans to pay whatever they deemed reasonable, the average album sold at $8 apiece, totalling around $10 million in profit over a single week. It exceeded the launch week sales of all three previous albums combined.[22]

MAKE THIS WORK FOR YOU

Name your price

If you're thinking of using this strategy for your business, here are just some of the benefits you can expect.

- **Sustain fewer losses** You (the vendor) can establish fixed threshold prices for every item you sell. This means that you'll always secure

▶

a minimum profit per item, helping you to sustain fewer losses in the long term (either through pricing your items too high for people to buy or so low that you don't break even).

- **New customers** By using low threshold prices, you'll attract low valuation customers and realize sales that you would have previously missed out on. Similarly, affluent customers will be attracted by higher threshold prices (as we saw earlier), which means that you'll extract a greater profit than if you simply use a fixed price.

- **Fair play** Because the final price is driven by what the consumer is willing to pay, the outcome is not perceived as unfair (even though dynamic pricing is in play). The fluid nature of the pricing also makes it harder for customers to use the final price as a cue with which to assign value to the item sold.

In order to offer your customers the right threshold price, you can either go for a completely flexible "Radiohead" approach or use an automated proxy system to segment your prospective buyers into value strands (based on their offer history). Either way, NYOP strategies can be a great way of increasing your sales and are worth considering if you want to boost your bottom line.

Price discrimination

Have you ever bought something online and reached the checkout, only to find a range of painfully expensive shipping options? Well, you may have inadvertently stumbled across one of the covert ways in which companies bolster their profits.

This neat, under-the-radar trick is a common price discrimination technique and works on the basis that we place different values on delivery times and methods. Those of us who value faster, secure deliveries will be more willing to pay a premium for a "better" service than our patient peers.

Known in the industry as quality-based price discrimination, the success of this strategy relies not only on the ability of the retailers to ship in bulk (thus driving down their own costs) but also on the psychological relationship we assign to price and value. Simply put, expensive-looking delivery methods will look more appealing to us than budget options, simply because we tend to equate price with value—even if the time difference for delivery is only a day or two. In fact, I recently put this to the test and deliberately chose the three to five days delivery option (which was free) and, guess what—the parcel arrived within two days. Surprise surprise.

Reduce your costs

- **Vary your options** Besides offering tiered delivery options, you can also increase your profits by offering other premium services, such as priority customer support. I know of several businesses that use this strategy successfully—their customers win by getting immediate attention and they win by making a profit on streamlining their support services.

- **Combine deliveries** At the risk of stating the obvious, another way to reduce your costs is to give clients the option to combine their purchases into one single delivery. Not only does this save you time and money, but it also reduces your customers' hassle factor and saves them a pretty penny in the process.

PRICE BUNDLES

When it comes to shopping, we all like to think that we're getting good value for money, but what happens when our perceptions of "good value" are way off? You'll no doubt be familiar with the concept of all-inclusive packages, from all-you-can-eat buffets to the special offers you find on Expedia. The enduring popularity of these kinds of "deals" stems from our preference for simple one-off payments over the less appealing option of making smaller, separate payments for the same stuff.

Far from weighing up our options in any rational way, research shows that, when it comes to certain things, we'd rather pay *more* money and pay it once than pay *less* money for the cheaper (but more stressful) option of dealing with separate charges.[23] Regardless of whether or not the inclusive price is actually better value, it seems that most of us are willing to pay a premium for peace of mind.

This strategy's success (and failure) lies in our expectations. Have you ever had the experience of booking yourself into a "stress-free," all-inclusive holiday package, only to turn up and find that you actually have to pay for a whole host of unexpected "extras?" Chances are you felt cheated and won't be using that company again.

You're not alone—first-time guests whose experiences fall short of their expectations typically rate the value of their package as much lower than people whose expectations were met. It's not the financial cost per se that is the issue here, but, rather, the transparency with which the transaction takes place. If you want to take advantage of this strategy in your business, there are several ways in which you can implement it online.

MAKE THIS WORK FOR YOU

Bundle up

- **Start with all-inclusive packages** No one wants to feel like they're losing out. If you start out by offering your customers a higher-priced, all-inclusive package with the option to downgrade (they can remove items/features for a lower price), you'll find that your clients will tend to go for the higher-priced package. Why? Well, having been offered all the bells and whistles as standard, they'll be reluctant to pay less and risk missing out.

- **Bundle for higher perceived value** Most of your customers will happily pay a peace of mind premium—it means less stress for them and more money for you. So, where possible, package your services into bundles to help generate a higher perceived value and customer satisfaction. Everybody wins.

- **Bundle transparency** Unless you're a multinational budget airline, when you sell services or products in price bundles, be transparent and show your customers exactly what they can expect (and what they're paying for). This will avoid any unwelcome surprises and help establish trust, leading to a sustainable customer relationship.

18 THE "BEHAVIOR CHAIN"

> *The success of many online services today depends on the company's ability to persuade users to take specific actions.*
>
> B. J. FOGG AND D. ECKLES, SOCIAL SCIENTISTS[1]

The "behavior chain"[2] is a technique developed by psychologists for understanding the "structure of persuasion over time."[3] With regard to websites and online services, the behavior chain is a three-phase strategy designed to achieve particular goals or "target behaviors." This could be getting someone to visit your website for the first time, then signing up for a trial subscription and, ultimately, gaining him or her as an active member of your online community.

Once a particular goal has been achieved, the user can then be taken through the next strategic step and so on until he or she eventually completes the chain by taking the full action desired by you, the website's owner.

When people use successful web services today, they are almost always guided through a predetermined behavior chain. Although first-time visitors usually learn about a service before visiting a website, the reverse is also prevalent—some websites are so well-designed, they attract new visitors before they even know what the website does (as we'll see in a moment with LinkedIn). To understand how this process works, we'll take a look at what the behavior chain involves and how it's been used (whether consciously or not) by various social networking sites to attract and sustain massive member communities.

PHASE 1: DISCOVERY

1 Target behavior: learn about the service

During this first phase of a behavior chain, the goal is to make potential users *aware* of your website. This can happen in any number of ways: via social media, through friends, emails, word of mouth, pay per click (PPC), links from other websites and other digital channels. While all of these routes can be effective at attracting new customers, I'm sure you'll have guessed by now that some routes are significantly more influential than others (personal recommendations are a firm favorite).

Beyond simple word of mouth recommendations, another factor that can heavily influence the success of Phase 1 is the users who are already at the level of true commitment (Phase 3—see later in this chapter). Users in Phase 3 are experienced and committed—they create, upload and share their own content with other members and, if this content is valuable, to both the existing community and to a Phase 1 newbie, it can act as a strong incentive for newcomers to take a step forward and sign up.

Here's where Pinterest comes in. Now one of the leading social media platforms in the world, it's a website that acts as an online pinboard, where its members (in Phases 2 or 3) can upload and "pin" their images according to themes (such as chipmunk, toaster or yacht, for example). While you can only upload your content if you're an invited member, you don't have to sign up to try it out. As a new user (Phase 1), you can come straight to the site, key in your search term and look through the thousands of images that Pinteresters have uploaded themselves. While you can "Like," tweet or embed an individual image or page, in order to comment, pin or "Like" the image *within* the Pinterest community, you have to become a member.

2 Target behavior: visit the website

Social filtering services, such as StumbleUpon, can influence people to visit a site for the first time based on the collective credibility of the community's recommendation.

In the case of a website like LinkedIn, the platform itself is designed in such a way as to encourage people to "find" it. How do they do it? When you sign up to LinkedIn, your profile is automatically optimized to appear in Google searches. This means that whenever someone Googles your name, your LinkedIn profile comes up as one of the top results, which, in turn, increases the likelihood that whoever's searching for you will navigate directly to LinkedIn and sign up themselves. The greater the number of people who sign up, the more often LinkedIn appears in Google searches—resulting in an almost exponential growth in LinkedIn adoption by new users. In this case, a new user will visit the website before gaining any prior knowledge about the service.

PHASE 2: SUPERFICIAL INVOLVEMENT

1 Target behavior: decide to try

In Phase 2, compliance is key. New users are encouraged to interact with the website so that they can "discover" a particular product or service that will fulfill their needs. The aim is to prime and engage users in such a way as to establish trust, so that they can move successfully to Phase 3, where they can then be influenced into adopting new, long-term behaviors (such as actively participating in forums and uploading user-generated content—actions that require commitment and loyalty).

While the order in which these steps are rolled out depends on the website in question, it's interesting to note that some of the most successful platforms enable people to sample their content for free *before* having to sign up to use it—YouTube, Spotify, Twitter and eBay all allow people to browse their content whether you're a member or not.

In the case of Wikipedia, any visitor can edit content without having to register, but the cost is that "If you save any edits, your IP address will be recorded publicly in this page's edit history."[4] This format does have its own issues and makes it difficult for the website owner to control the quality of the information being shared.

A word of caution here: if you try to engage with your users in a way that damages their trust in you during this crucial phase (for example, you get them to sign up to your newsletter and then you start spamming them) you risk losing them before you even get to the next phase.

Let's return to Pinterest to witness a very successful Phase 2 method in action. Although it's basically just a glorified bulletin board, some of the smarter businesses out there have been successfully exploiting this platform to prime users into trying their products and services. How? Simply by uploading a few of their product photos in among a board full of other related, but non-commercial images.

I'll give you an example. American food retailer Whole Foods[5] uses Pinterest to pin images of delicious-looking food, ingenious recycled products and fabulous food art—all ostensibly in the name of encouraging people to be environmentally responsible. The upshot of this is, of course, the free publicity they're generating in a previously untapped market of potential customers.

By becoming *the* place to find all your food-related inspirations, Whole Foods' Pinterest page not only pulls in a huge amount of traffic to its photoboard, but also, by extension, into its shops. It's priming new customers and getting them to mentally invest long before they even step foot into one of its stores.

In the case of Ideeli (a retail deal site), its use of Pinterest as a Phase 2 method worked so well that it increased its website traffic by 446 percent, resulting in a 500 percent increase in sales.[6] It's not just big brands that can benefit. With 21 percent of Pinterest users purchasing products they find on the site,[7] conversion rates seem to be particularly high for a platform that is ostensibly all about aesthetics.

2 Target behavior: get started

Once you have attracted new visitors to your website and they have decided to try out your services, the next step in the behavior chain is to encourage them to "get started" by taking a single action, such as creating a new account or signing up for a free trial. By offering a "free" service in exchange for a little information (notice the use of reciprocity), you are, in effect, securing your access to other, more persuasive means of communication, such as carefully crafted email updates and access to your users' social media profiles.

Whatever your thoughts on customer recruitment, this form of information exchange is fast becoming common practice. Websites are increasingly asking us to sign into their services with our Facebook, Twitter, or Google accounts, granting companies unprecedented levels of access to our information, in increasing levels of detail. Whilst this relationship may appear reciprocal, the information we're actually being asked to part with is usually a *lot* more valuable than a few free trials and downloadable e-books.

This aside, it is crucial that you obtain enough customer information to enable you to communicate persuasively with your clients. However, you do not want to make the signing up process so long or so detailed that you actually end up alienating more people than you sign up. As a general rule of thumb, the shorter and easier the process, the more people will do it.

There is a theme here, however, around value. In some cases, by asking your customers for a bit more information (as long as you tell them what this information will be used for), they may end up valuing your services more highly as a result. As always, it is worth A/B split testing your registration process to ensure that you strike the right balance between useful data collection and ease of registration. To see this "Get started" technique in action, let's revisit LinkedIn. LinkedIn uses three main strategies to persuade new visitors to start using its service.

- On its homepage, LinkedIn uses the principle of *social proof* to encourage you to sign up to its services: "Over 150 million professionals use LinkedIn to exchange information, ideas and opportunities." If everyone else is using it, it must be good. The three bullet points beneath this statement appeal to new visitors on a personal level, promising that, if you sign up, you'll be granted access to all the vital information, contacts and knowledge you need to "achieve your goals" and "control your professional identity online."[8]

- LinkedIn *leverages its existing members* to persuade new visitors to connect with "People You May Know." It also encourages you to import your contacts from different email accounts and then gives you the option to automatically invite anyone in your database who isn't already a member.

- Once you have successfully signed up, LinkedIn uses an incremental approach to influence its users to give up more of their information. Each time you sign in, if you haven't already completed your profile, LinkedIn will nudge you to add more data with a prompt like "Your profile is 75% complete—add your past experiences." By requesting that you complete one small action every time you log in and rewarding you with the positive reinforcement of seeing your "Profile Completeness" bar go up in stages towards 100 percent, LinkedIn has developed a highly successful behavior chain. This chain takes almost all new visitors and converts them into active members—many of whom go on to pay for a business account.

PHASE 3: TRUE COMMITMENT

This third and final phase is the stage at which content can go viral, attracting unprecedented numbers of new visitors.

Unlike the previous two phases, Phase 3 involves encouraging your users to develop new, long-term habits of interaction with your website. This can mean anything from getting members to comment regularly on blog posts and contribute to member forums to encouraging your users to create and share their own content with the rest of the community.

A word of warning, if you are using a strategy that sacrifices your credibility for the sake of compliance, you are likely to fail here. This means that the classic door in the face marketing technique—in which you first ask someone for something unreasonable, they refuse, then you ask them for the thing you actually want and, because you're seen to have "compromised," they agree to it—is a sure-fire way of losing valuable customers.

At this point, the fact that your customers are contributing user-generated content (UGC) and getting their friends involved in using your website is likely to attract new users into entering the behavior chain.

1 Target behavior: create value and content

The most useful form of UGC occurs when users contribute content that others will find valuable. Amazon has developed an entire e-commerce platform around this model. By encouraging users to rate and review the products they have bought, they and other online consumers will be more likely to buy from Amazon, as it's the place where they can use feedback to help them make "better" purchasing decisions (though, of course, this system is not immune to tampering and exploitation).

On LinkedIn, the platform extracts valuable content from its users by rewarding certain actions. These rewards can include recommending other people or services (reciprocity), floating the most commented on discussions to the top of a discussions board (social validation) and publically citing "top influencers" at the top of group dashboards, to mention but a few. By receiving this kind of positive feedback (even a simple "thank you" following a submission can work wonders), users are actively encouraged to create value and content for that platform. For those members who contribute, the fact that they've identified themselves (both publicly and subconsciously) as active members within the community means their longer-term commitment and engagement to the platform is pretty much in the bag.

2 Target behavior: involve others

The goal of most web services is to increase the size of its active community. This technique has become a classic among successful social media sites and, when it comes to attracting new clients to your business, this technique can be used to grow your ranks and your profits.

When Facebook started out, the *way* in which it involved others was one of the most significant contributing factors to its success. Instead of adopting a carpet bomb approach, Facebook grew its popularity incrementally, by focusing its efforts on one specific pre-existing college community at a time. From its auspicious beginnings in the dorms of Harvard University, Facebook was adopted college by college until it reached such a point that it became a student network of national proportions. Having started out as a students only network, when Facebook eventually opened its gates to the world, the hype surrounding it was so potent that the explosion in new users took the Internet world by storm.

With regard to attracting new visitors to your website or web service, there are several ways in which you can do this. Most social sites encourage their existing users to involve others in two ways:

- by inviting others to join and be their friends (Facebook), followers (Twitter), subscribers (YouTube) or connections (LinkedIn).
- by encouraging users to share content and links with their peers.

You can increase your probability of success by incorporating both of these techniques into your website strategy. By encouraging your users to create original content, which other members will comment on, rate and discuss, you are, in effect, killing two target behaviors with one stone—creating value and content, and involving others.

3 Target behavior: stay active and loyal

> *Understanding how or why a sense of loyalty develops in customers remains one of the crucial management issues of our day.*
> LAM ET AL., *ACADEMY OF MARKETING SCIENCE*[9]

Once you've attracted a community of members to your site, how do you go about making sure they stay active and loyal to you? With a swathe of competitors out there, it's vital that you know how to influence your users to commit to your service over all others. Inherent within this is the assumption that your service is actually useful and provides a solution to peoples' needs, but, once you have that, what do you do next to ensure that your users keep coming back?

Facebook does this via email alerts—depending on your saved preferences, you'll likely receive emails from Facebook every time a friend messages you or when you are invited to an event. If you're on Skype you'll get an alert when it's someone's birthday. On LinkedIn, you'll get digest emails from your groups or when one of your contacts updates his or her profile. Whichever alerts you receive, from whichever service, they will all have one thing in common: you will always have to click on the website link to access the key information. Not only does this keep you coming back for more, but also, once you *do* click through, you will often be met with other enticing content, such as updated messages and news feeds—all designed to stoke your curiosity and reel you further in.

Again, LinkedIn does this beautifully. Once you've completed your profile, you're encouraged to stay active and loyal through a seemingly endless stream of tasks: "Ask for recommendations," "Create your profile in another language," create new events, form groups, establish yourself as an expert in your field by answering relevant questions in the Q&A section of the website … the list goes on. In short, once you're committed, you can go as deep as the rabbit hole will take you.

HOW THEY DID IT

Phase 1: discovery
1 Learn

You learn about the service by seeing other people within your network "Like" it on Facebook, tweet about it or embed a Pinterest image on their websites. You start reading about Pinterest on your favorite blogs and news feeds and when you hear that even the United States Military[10] has created an account, you can't resist it any longer—you simply *have* to check it out.

2 Visit

Having succumbed to the hype, you decide to visit the website and have a look around. You're greeted by an interesting assortment of images, ranging from weird little crochet flowers to tattoos and Porsche 911s … but then something catches your eye. You see one of those they-shouldn't-be-so-cute-but-my-God-they're-adorable animal snaps that simply demands a click and …

Phase 2: superficial involvement
1 Try

… you're off. In one simple little action, you've taken that crucial step into the world of Pinterest and you're now engaged.

2 Get started

After realizing that you've actually whiled away a good hour in this weird and wonderful new world, you decide that, actually, you do quite like it and, against your better judgement and after an internal debate (how much can this *really* interfere with my work …?!) you decide to get involved and sign up. You take the next step and request an invite or, if you already have friends who are members, you ask them to invite you instead (after all, who doesn't want to belong to a private club?).

Phase 3: true commitment

1 Create value and content

When you receive your invite, you're so delighted to have become a member that you get right on it and start uploading your own content straight away.

2 Involve others

To show that you're now part of this "in-group," too, you begin to share your Pinterest photos with friends in your other networks, selecting the kinds of images you think they'll like and value.

3 Stay active and loyal

If you run your own business, you start uploading images of related content to your pinboard and intersperse it with photos of your products—after all, if people are visiting your board, why not engage in a bit of self-promotion? Some of your products attract a lot of attention and start driving traffic to your website, increasing your Google ranking and sales. From your Google Analytics dashboard you can see that Pinterest is one of your highest referrers of traffic.

Congratulations Pinterest. It has successfully taken you through the entire behavior chain and secured you as a valued Phase 3 member. What's more, your business has profited as a result.

MAKE THIS WORK FOR YOU

Chain reaction

Now that you know how other successful websites are using the behavior chain to attract, engage with and elicit commitment from new users, you can use this knowledge to inform how you structure your own website's user experience. You can do this not only in terms of its architecture but also in terms of the psychological motivations you can harness in order to achieve certain target behaviors.

▶

For instance, one-time actions like signing up may require a different motivation (reciprocity, say) than getting a user to contribute content over a period of time (which may require employing social validation or positive reinforcement, for example). By analyzing the actions you wish your users to take, then identifying and using the best psychological tools for the job, you can use this framework to map your website's own behavior chain and maximize your chances of success.

19 RISK, TRUST AND PRIVACY

> *A lack of trust and face-to-face interaction prevents many people from purchasing online.*
>
> PETER DE VRIES AND AD PRUYN,
> MARKETING PSYCHOLOGISTS[1]

WHAT STOPS PEOPLE FROM BUYING ONLINE?

It's a known fact that consumers require a greater level of trust and confidence when buying online than face to face.[2] When you're dealing with an unknown shop selling products of unknown quality, trust plays a major role in mitigating feelings of uncertainty and winning over new clients.[3] In the absence of any other information, we'll look to the brand's website for cues as to whether we can trust them or not.[4] In fact, when potential customers visit your site, the first thing they will do is subconsciously scan it for these cues.[5]

Contrary to what you might expect, when it comes to e-shopping, we tend to be more concerned by security and privacy issues than price. In one study, when asked what would prevent them from making an online purchase, around 30 percent of people reported privacy and security concerns, 25 percent cited a lack of customer service and only 9–15 percent said that the absence of their friends or a real salesperson would put them off.[6]

In short, the two main things that prevent people from shopping online are the absence of face-to-face interactions and the greater risk associated with online transactions.[7] Both of these elements contribute to a greater sense of uncertainty and fear, which is why we tend to seek greater assurance that our sensitive information will be protected when we shop online than we do in a physical shop.

Making your customers feel safe can be tricky. New visitors typically find it difficult to assess a website's level of privacy and security and they will initially look to your website's functionality and design (its "professional look and feel") and the reputation of your company to decide whether they can trust you or not.[8]

GENDER DIFFERENCES

As we saw earlier (see Chapter 6), the way in which your audience interacts with you can be strongly influenced by their gender. In general, men are less concerned about privacy than women (possibly because women are more skeptical of online information),[9] and they are also happier to part with more sensitive levels of personal information.[10,11]

Although women tend to perceive online purchasing as riskier than their male peers,[12] when it comes down to it we're all somewhat concerned about the security of our online transactions and credit card details.[13] That said, it's an easy issue to remedy. In studies where customers visited websites that used overt trust marks (such as security symbols), both genders seemed quite comfortable with online transactions in general.[14] Which would imply that while our concerns for online security may vary, these fears can be assuaged by the careful use of a few well-placed cues.

Indeed, research investigating gender difference in the effectiveness of such signals found that women place higher value on cues relating to security, information flow and functionality than men.[15] So if you're targeting a predominantly female audience, make sure you highlight that any information you do receive will be treated in utmost confidence and not passed on to any third parties.

TWO KINDS OF TRUST

When it comes to trust, psychologists make a distinction between two different types: cognitive and affective. *Cognitive* trust is knowledge-driven and, in this case, refers to your customers' confidence in the reliability and competence of your service.[16] When it comes to online shopping, this kind of trust stems from your customers' previous experiences with your shop, whether directly or through word of mouth.

Your clients will subconsciously use the information they have gathered about you to predict if they can rely on you to fulfill your obligations. If your shop or brand already has a strong reputation, the first interactions you may have with a new customer are vital in determining whether or not you live up to their expectations. It can mean the difference between winning new business and growing your online market, or losing a valuable client due to lack of preparation.

Affective, or emotional, trust is your clients' sense of feeling safe, valued and cared for.[17] Unlike its cognitive counterpart, this kind of trust tends to be based on direct, personal experience and will usually deepen over time as the relationship grows.

Interestingly, if your clients trust you emotionally, it can cloud their objectivity and grant you more trust than is actually warranted in reality. This effect can be further amplified if your clients believe that your actions are motivated out of an innate desire to help them.

If you think I'm painting a picture of the "stupid consumer," think again—and consider for a moment the socio-evolutionary context of this trait. As discussed earlier, one of the main reasons we're here today is because our ancestors were able to forge strong social connections and trust other members of their tribe thus enabling the survival of the group. Emotional trust was part of the glue holding these early human societies together, and it was this kind of trust that contributed towards our species becoming one of the most prolific on Earth.

MORE ON EMOTIONAL TRUST

❝ *Emotional exchanges are a critical and ongoing part of consumer-level service relationships and form the basis for trusting bonds.*
>
> DEVON JOHNSON AND KENT GRAYSON,
> PROFESSORS OF MARKETING[18]

Today, this kind of trust still holds sway and frequently trumps the more reasoned approach of our "rational brain." Allow me to give you an example.

Imagine you are looking for a bank to set up your new business account with. After browsing through a range of banks on a comparison website, you schedule an appointment with the top three and go into the first one for a chat. You sit down and the adviser gives you a spiel about the different rates and benefits you'll receive if you sign up to the bank's business account today. The rates are competitive, the adviser is knowledgeable and it seems like a good deal. You leave feeling confident and go to your second appointment with bank number two.

This time, an adviser greets you, tells you a bit about the bank and its services and then, in hushed tones, he leans across and tells you that you'd actually be better off signing up to this cheaper plan. Sure, it means he won't get commission, but it's the best deal for you and he wants your business to get off to a great start. The rates are comparable, but you feel like this guy actually cares and is willing to put your needs before his own profits. Whether you're aware of it or not, at a subconscious level this interaction elicits a trust response from you and you come away feeling a sense of kinship—an emotional bond has been forged. You're already pretty swayed by this second adviser (after all, he has your best interests at heart), but you've made a commitment to chat to the third bank, so you go along for your final appointment.

Again, the adviser sits you down and tells you about all the perks of that bank's specific bank account and, like the two before, the rates and benefits are pretty comparable.

Having "done your research," you come away from your last appointment with a clear winner in mind—you're going to go for the middle guy. Why? Because, at a time of uncertainty, and especially when it comes to your hard-earned cash, you're going to give your business to the person whom you feel you can count on. It just so happens that he's the one who got your emotional, or affective, trust.

BOOSTING YOUR CREDIBILITY

When it comes to boosting your website's overall credibility, factors such as a website's usability[19] and its "aesthetic beauty"[20] can have a significant impact on trust and (as any good designer will attest) attractive websites are generally viewed as more trustworthy[21] and easy to use than less attractive ones.[22] With regards to isolated components of a website, there is evidence to show that you can boost the perceived expertise and trustworthiness of (for instance) a web article by adding a formal photograph of its author to the page (as compared to using an informal photo or none at all).[23]

However, if you want to boost the credibility of an *entire* website and, by extension, the brand and business behind it, the process becomes much more complex. Add to this the fact that people express huge variances in the kinds of faces and photographs that they prefer and the challenge becomes harder still.

Let's consider the world of e-commerce for a moment. Since the birth of the online marketplace, companies have been falling over themselves in a bid to find the Holy Grail of e-retail: those elusive, cast-iron conversion principles that, once implemented, are guaranteed to attract and convert the hordes of global online shoppers eager to blow their hard-earned cash. While there *are* key principles for conversion (as we've already seen) the success of these principles does vary according to the contexts in which they are applied.

For example, adding a photo to an e-commerce website (as opposed to a web article) can, in two different contexts, have completely opposite effects on perceived credibility. In a study designed to investigate this phenomenon, psychologists found that people were able to *accurately* judge a vendor's trustworthiness when no photos were added to its website.[24] Show me no photos and I'll tell you no lies. When a few photos were thrown into the mix, however, it was an entirely different story. Visitors were less able to distinguish between those vendors who had good reputations and those who had bad ones. The very simple act of including photographs was enough to artificially level the reputational playing field.

In an unpredictable turn of fortunes, adding photos actually *increased* the perceived trustworthiness of vendors who had bad reputations, while simultaneously *decreasing* the credibility of those vendors who had good ones.[25] Yes, it is weird, but it does tell us one thing: credibility is a fragile notion and one that rests not on reason alone but also on a whole host of factors, of which many exert their influence below the level of our conscious awareness.

MAKE THIS WORK FOR YOU

Designing trust

- **Website** If you are serious about attracting new customers online, invest in your website. Users tend to prefer and trust websites that are of high quality and designed to a professional standard.[26]

- **Picture perfect** While photos are not a guaranteed way to build trust across all websites, research has shown that simply using a photo of a person on *one* web page can have a significant, positive effect on trust.[27] Choose wisely and only use photographs on the pages that really need it—such as the testimonials page.

- **Stay away from stock** When adding photos, don't cut corners by using stock photographs—customers can spot them a mile away, so they are more likely to harm your reputation than raise your credibility. Instead, ensure that any photos you do use are congruent with your brand's identity and that they reflect and sit comfortably within the design of your website.[28]

- **Usability** If you want loyal, happy customers, improve your website's usability. Research has found we tend to trust websites that have good usability and that this can also increase our website loyalty and user satisfaction.[29]

- **Competence** Satisfy your clients' need for cognitive trust by showing them that your shop is competent and can deliver safely and on time (testimonials always help here).

▶

- **Be coherent** As in the real world, when we're online, we look for cues to assess if we can trust a website or not. In the case of e-commerce, coherence is key[30]—so make sure your website and all its components (design, text, images, layout, privacy policies) align with the core values of your brand and its identity.

- **Free P&P** To elicit emotional trust, express your sense of goodwill by having a free postage and returns policy. You can also show that you offer value and integrity by providing benefits such as live customer care.

- **Congruence** If you are selling a particular product or showcasing an article about a particular topic, make sure any accompanying photo of that source of information is congruent to the topic in question. For instance, if you are a website dedicated to health products, using an image of a doctor will be more congruent and credible than, say, a photo of a chef.

- **Conversation** Make the time to engage your clients in conversation and, where possible, create solutions that show your clients that their needs trump yours. This can be as simple as offering a choice of payment plans, a free no strings attached consultation or a comparison service giving them a transparent view of how you stack up against your competitors.

- **Similarity** Bear in mind that we tend to find people and sources of information similar to ourselves more credible and the characteristics we identify as similar will vary from one demographic to the next. If in doubt, analyze your customer base (young moms, for example), identify the common traits of the majority (gender, age, ethnicity, income level) and reflect these characteristics in the photos you include in your website. As a rule of thumb, like attracts like.

DIFFERENT PRODUCTS REQUIRE DIFFERENT KINDS OF TRUST

In a study investigating the relationship between e-commerce, peer recommendations and social trust,[31] psychologists found that we're more likely to buy a product if we see that an unknown peer has recommended it. When it comes to "experience" items (such as bungee jumping or track days), however, peer recommendations tend to be most effective when accompanied by a photo of someone who appears trustworthy.

On the face of it, this may seem like common sense, since our real-world experiences confirm that we find people who seem honest and well-meaning as most persuasive, but, in an online context, these images are mere avatars—virtual (and sometimes even fictitious) representations of real people. Yet, we seem to consistently expect the same social rules to apply both off- and online, despite the clear differences between the two environments.

These results in themselves should come as no revelation, but the research did spit out one thing that was rather unexpected: for items in the "credence" category (such as vitamin and diet pills), positive recommendations actually tend to *decrease* our trust of the product. In this bizarre scenario, psychologists suspect that we may simply distrust the advice of our peers since they lack the expert knowledge required to reliably recommend the product.

Whatever the reason, when it comes to making purchasing decisions on websites, factors such as the reputation of your company and whether your website has a privacy policy can have a strong impact on whether or not visitors will trust your site enough to buy from you.

PERSUASIVE STRATEGIES FOR DATA COLLECTION

If you want your visitors to perform certain actions, especially those that require a greater degree of trust (such as entering their phone number or surname), you must take care to frame these requests within an acceptable form of transaction, so that they appear more reasonable, rewarding and legitimate.[32] This could mean asking clients to enter their details in order to receive better aftercare or requesting extra information when they are completing a payment (since at this point they are already entering their information in order to pay, so asking them for a little extra is typically seen as congruent and reasonable).

The common approach to collecting data from visitors is to offer rewards in exchange for information, which implies a trade of equal value. Although this tactic may work for the more opportunistic among us, it does frame the process as a simple transaction of gains to which there is no intrinsic motivation. This in itself can lower the perceived value of the trade, reducing its efficacy and, ultimately, turning clients off.

While it is well documented that website users are generally concerned about disclosing sensitive information (such as credit card details and their postal address), it may surprise you to learn that offering a reward in exchange for your customers' information can actually *heighten* their concern and have a detrimental impact on sales. In fact, in one study, 31 percent of online consumers actually regarded offers of reward with suspicion, indicating their mistrust in what they believed to be a coercive maneuver by companies to obtain sensitive personal information.[33] Not only that but exchanges based on reciprocity tend to result in a higher quality of participation than those based on reward. Since we essentially seek and value opportunities to connect, use this to your advantage and let it inform the way in which you collect data from your customers.

MAKE THIS WORK FOR YOU

Different strokes for different folks

- **Reciprocity** If you want to collect data from your customers but don't want to resort to rewards, use the powerful principle of reciprocity instead. By offering your visitors something valuable, with no conditions attached, you are likely to increase your credibility, their trust in you and, ultimately, your bottom line. In this scenario, the data collection comes at a later point, when the visitor becomes a paying customer— you collect their details at checkout.

- **Concessions** Increase your conversion rates by offering unilateral concessions and special discounts to your visitors. Research has shown that these kinds of offers are much more likely to result in purchases.[34]

- **Happy snaps** If you're selling an experience, such as a tour or scuba-diving lessons, maximize your selling power by including a few images of trustworthy-looking customers alongside their reviews. If you're not sure which clients to approach, ask yourself this—if you met them at a café, would you trust them to keep an eye on your things while you were in the bathroom?

- **Call in the experts** When selling products that concern health and well-being, consider including a few recommendations from trusted, recognizable experts in that field to add credibility to your products (for example, an actual doctor or well-respected nutritionist).

- **Share the love** Make your knowledge-collecting website seem more friendly and inhabited by adding social media share buttons (the ones that show how many people have "Liked," "Stumbled," "Digged," "Google+1ed" and "tweeted" your website to their friends).

- **Emotion by numbers** You can also include an RSS feed subscription counter and a forum for existing customers—this will help humanize your website and add to its emotional accessibility. It will also help to activate the principle of social proof, encouraging new visitors to trust you as so many customers before them have done.

- **First contact** If you are requesting contact information from your website visitors, make the first move by providing them with a quick, easy and reliable way to contact you. If you're asking for their name, email address and postal information, include all of this information for your business so that your customers feel that they are on an equal footing.

- **Be reasonable** Make sure you frame any requests for customer information with a clear reason for your needing it and how it will be used (for example, to send out offers that are relevant to them). Your customers are more likely to comply with your request if it seems appropriate and reasonable.[35]

- **In confidence** If you need to collect data from your website visitors, do so transparently and highlight that any data collected will be treated with the utmost confidentiality.

- **Anti-spam** If you are wanting people to sign up to your newsletter, make it clear that you hate spam as much as your clients do by providing clearly marked option boxes so that they can set what communications they wish to receive from you.

- **Data protection** Make sure your website complies with the Data Protection Act for your country (the UK guidelines can be found at ico.gov.uk/for_organisations/data_protection.aspx).

A CLOSING NOTE

Thank you for choosing to pick up this book. I hope you have found our foray into the vast world of online persuasion at turns exciting, intriguing and useful.

New insights into the ways in which technology shapes and changes us are unearthed every day, but, in the face of all our advances, one thing is certain: no matter how things progress, we will always exploit technology to meet our human desires. Whoever understands these desires and the drivers behind them will hold the key to online influence. Here's yours.

NOTES

Introduction

1 E. B. Weiser (2000) "Gender differences in Internet use patterns and Internet application preferences: A two-sample comparison," *Cyberpsychology and Behavior*, 3 (2): 167–78.

2 F. La Rue (2011) "Report of the Special Rapporteur on the promotion and protection of the right to freedom of opinion and expression." United Nations General Assembly. Available online at: www2.ohchr.org/english/bodies/hrcouncil/docs/17session/A. HRC.17.27_en.pdf (accessed 23 January 2012).

3 Cisco (2011) "Connected world technology report." Available online at: www.cisco. com/en/US/netsol/ns1120/index.html (accessed 23 January 2012).

Chapter 1

1 C. C. Camerer, L. G. Loewenstein and D. P. Prelec (2005) "Neuroeconomics: How neuroscience can inform economics," *Journal of Economic Literature*, 43: 9–64.

2 R. Kurzweil (1999) *The Age of Spiritual Machines*. New York: Viking.

3 E. R. Kandel, J. H. Schwartz and T. M. Jessell (eds) (2000) *Principles of Neural Science*. New York: McGraw-Hill.

4 A. Siegel, T. A. Roeling, T. R. Gregg and M. R. Kruk (1999) "Neuropharmacology of brain-stimulation-evoked aggression," *Neuroscience and Biobehavioral Reviews*, 23 (3): 359–89.

5 R. Sutherland (2012) "Influence," a talk given at The School of Life, 25 March.

6 J. S. Winston, B. A. Strange, J. O'Doherty and R. J. Dolan (2002) "Automatic and intentional brain responses during evaluation of trustworthiness of faces," *Nature Neuroscience*, 5: 277–83.

7 R. D. Lane, E. M. Reiman, M. M. Bradley, P. J. Lang, G. L. Ahern, R. J. Davidson and G. E. Schwartz (1997) "Neuroanatomical correlates of pleasant and unpleasant emotion," *Neuropsychologia*, 35 (11): 1437–44.

8 P. W. Burgess and T. Shallice (1996) "Response suppression, initiation and strategy use following frontal lobe lesions," *Neuropsychologia*, 34 (4): 263–72.

9 E. B. Keverne, F. L. Martel and C. M. Nevison (1996) "Primate brain evolution: Genetic and functional considerations," *Proceedings: Biological Sciences*, 263 (1371): 689–96.

10 P. Aggarwal and A. L. McGill (2007) "Is that car smiling at me?: Schema congruity as a basis for evaluating anthropomorphized products," *Journal of Consumer Research*, 34 (4): 468–79.

11 D. W. Zaidel, S. M. Aarde and K. Baig (2005) "Appearance of symmetry, beauty, and health in human face," *Brain and Cognition*, 57 (3): 261–3.

12 S. Djamasbia, M. Siegelb and T. Tullis (2010) "Generation Y, web design, and eye tracking," *International Journal of Human–Computer Studies*, 68: 307–23.

13 E. O'Brien and P. C. Ellsworth (2012) "Saving the last for best: A positivity bias for end experiences," *Psychological Science*, 23 (2): 163–5.

14 G. di Pellegrino, L. Fadiga, L. Fogassi, V. Gallese and G. Rizzolatti (1992) "Understanding motor events: a neurophysiological study," *Experimental Brain Research*, 91 (1): 176–80.

15 T. R. Bacon (2011) *The Elements of Power: Lessons on leadership and influence*. New York: AMACOM. p 76.

Chapter 2

1 F. Crick (1995) *Astonishing Hypothesis: The scientific search for the soul*. Chicago, IL: Scribner.

2 B. Libet (1985) "Unconscious cerebral initiative and the role of conscious will in voluntary action," *Behavioral and Brain Sciences*, 8 (4): 529–66.

3 D. M. Wegner and T. Wheatley (1999) "Apparent mental causation: Sources of the experience of will," *American Psychologist*, 54 (7): 480–92.

4 L. E. Williams and J. A. Bargh (2002) "Experiencing physical warmth promotes interpersonal warmth," *Science*, 322 (5901): 606–7.

5 F. Strack, L. L. Martin and S. Stepper (1988) "Inhibiting and facilitating conditions of the human smile: A nonobtrusive test of the facial feedback hypothesis," *Journal of Personality and Social Psychology*, 54 (5): 768–77.

6 N. Eisenberger, M. Lieberman and K. Williams (2003) "Does rejection hurt?: An FMRI study of social exclusion," *Science*, 302 (5643): 290–2.

7 E. Kross, T. Egner, K. Ochsner, J. Hirsch and G. Downey (2007) "Neural dynamics of rejection sensitivity," *Journal of Cognitive Neuroscience*, 19 (6): 945–56.

8 D. T. Gilbert and J. E. J. Ebert (2002) "Decisions and revisions: The affective forecasting of changeable outcomes," *Journal of Personality and Social Psychology*, 82 (4): 503–14.

9 Coloribus (2003) "'Desert' print ad for Pure Life water by D'arcy Shanghai." Available online at: www.coloribus.com/adsarchive/prints/pure-life-water-desert-5252605 (accessed 3 January 2012).

10 M. De Pittà, V. Volman, H. Berry, E. Ben-Jacob (2011) "A tale of two stories: Astrocyte regulation of synaptic depression and facilitation," *PLoS Computational Biology*, 7 (12): e1002293.

11 R. Boyd (2008) "Do people only use 10 percent of their brains?," *Scientific American Mind*. Available online at: www.scientificamerican.com/article.cfm?id=people-only-use-10-percent-of-brain (accessed 28 March 2012).

12 E. A. Maguire, D. G. Gadian, I. S. Johnsrude, C. D. Good, J. Ashburner, R. S. J. Frackowiak and C. D. Frith (2000) "Navigation-related structural change in the hippocampi of taxi drivers," *Proceedings of the National Academy of Sciences of the United States of America*, 97 (8): 4398–403.

13 E. A. Maguire, K. Woollett and H. J. Spiers (2006) "London taxi drivers and bus drivers: A structural MRI and neuropsychological analysis," *Hippocampus*, 16: 1091–101.

14   C. C. Camerer, L. G. Loewenstein and D. P. Prelec (2005) "Neuroeconomics: How neuroscience can inform economics," *Journal of Economic Literature*, 43 (1): 9–64.

15   D. Kahneman (2011) *Thinking Fast and Slow*. New York: Farrar, Straus & Giroux.

16   W. Schneider and R. M. Shiffrin (1977) "Controlled and automatic human information processing: I. Detection, search and attention," *Psychological Review*, 84 (1): 1–66.

17   M. D. Lieberman, R. Gaunt, D. T. Gilbert and Y. Trope (2002) "Reflection and reflexion: A social cognitive neuroscience approach to attributional inference," in M. Zanna (ed.), *Advances in Experimental Social Psychology*. New York: Academic Press. pp. 199–249.

18   D. Kahneman (2011).

19   L. Cosmides and J. Tooby (2004) "Evolutionary psychology and the emotions," in M. Lewis and J. M. Haviland-Jones (eds) *Handbook of Emotions*. New York: Guilford Press.

20   R. B. Zajonc (1998) "Emotions," in D. T. Gilbert, S. T. Fiske and G. Lindzey (eds) *Handbook of Social Psychology*. New York: Oxford University Press. pp. 591–632.

21   R. Carter (1999) *Mapping the Mind*. Berkeley, CA: University of California Press.

22   J. E. LeDoux (1996) *The Emotional Brain: The mysterious underpinnings of emotional life*. New York: Simon & Schuster.

23   J. S. Lemer and D. Keltner (2001) "Fear, anger, and risk," *Journal of Personality and Social Psychology*, 81 (1): 146–59.

24   S. L. Master, N. I. Eisenberger, S. E. Taylor, B. D. Naliboff, D. Shirinyan and M. D. Lieberman (2009) "A picture's worth: Partner photographs reduce experimentally induced pain," *Psychological Science*, 20 (11): 1316–18.

25   T. D. Wilson, D. J. Lisle, J. W. Schooler, S. D. Hodges, K. J. Klaaren and S. J. LaFleur (1993) "Introspecting about reasons can reduce post-choice satisfaction," *Personality and Social Psychology Bulletin*, 19: 331–9.

Chapter 3

1   J. Donne (1624) *Devotions upon emergent occasions and seuerall steps in my sicknes*, Meditation XVII.

2   Internet World Stats (2011) "Internet usage statistics: The Internet big picture: World Internet users and population stats." Available online at: www.internetworldstats.com/stats.htm (accessed 12 April 2012).

3   J. Turner (2011) "Are there REALLY more mobile phones than toothbrushes?," 60 Second Marketer. Available online at: 60secondmarketer.com/blog/2011/10/18/more-mobile-phones-than-toothbrushes (accessed 6 January 2012).

4   Internet World Stats (2011).

5   D. Bryson (2012) "Banks see opportunity in Africa," Huffington Post. Available online at: www.huffingtonpost.com/huff-wires/20120323/af-banking-on-africa (accessed 4 April 2012).

6   eMarketers (2011) "Millennials more comfortable with m-commerce." Available online at: www.emarketer.com/Article.aspx?R=1008593 (accessed 6 January 2012).

7   Cisco (2011) "Connected world technology report." Available online at: www.cisco.com/en/US/netsol/ns1120/index.html (accessed 23 January 2012).

8   S. Coughlan (2012) "Children switching from TV to mobile internet," *BBC News*. Available online at: www.bbc.co.uk/news/education-16475278 (accessed 12 April 2012).

9   ComScore (2012) "The European perspective: The rise of the iPad." Available online at: www.comscoredatamine.com/2012/03/the-european-perspective-the-rise-of-the-ipad (accessed 12 April 2012).

10 L. Indvik (2011) "Tablets drive deeper news consumption," Mashable. Available online at: http://mashable.com/2011/10/14/tablet-ipad-news-study (accessed 9 January 2012).

11 ComScore (2012) "More than half of people that access social networks on their smartphone do so on a near daily basis." Available online at: www.comscoredatamine.com/2012/02/more-than-half-of-people-that-access-social-networks-on-their-smartphone-do-so-on-a-near-daily-basis (accessed 16 April 2012).

12 ComScore (2012) "1 in 3 smartphone buyers made purchase on their phone while in a store." Available online at: www.comscoredatamine.com/2011/12/1-in-3-smartphone-buyers-made-purchase-on-their-phone-while-in-a-store (accessed 12 April 2012).

13 ComScore (2012) "Online retail attracts highest number of Europeans to date." Available online at: www.comscoredatamine.com/2012/02/online-retail-attracts-highest-number-of-europeans-to-date (accessed 12 April 2012).

14 ComScore (2012) "Majority of mobile deal-a-day audience from upper income segments." Available online at: www.comscoredatamine.com/2012/01/majority-of-mobile-deal-a-day-audience-from-upper-income-segments (accessed 12 April 2012).

15 Digital Strategy Consulting (2012) "4pm Wednesday 'is peak-time for workplace shopping'." Available online at: www.digitalstrategyconsulting.com/intelligence/2010/09/4pm_wednesday_is_peaktime_for.php (accessed 12 April 2012).

16 Compete Pulse (2011) "It's 10pm; do you know where your shoppers are?." Available online at: http://blog.compete.com/2011/04/25/it%E2%80%99s-10pm-do-you-know-where-your-shoppers-are (accessed 12 April 2012).

17 Nielsen Wire (2012) "Ads with friends: Analyzing the benefits of social ads." Available online at: http://blog.nielsen.com/nielsenwire/online_mobile/ads-with-friends-analyzing-the-benefits-of-social-ads (accessed 12 April 2012).

18 Pew Research (2011) "Search and email still the most popular online activities." Available online at: www.pewinternet.org/Reports/2011/Search-and-email/Report.aspx?src=prc-headline (accessed 6 January 2012).

19 ComScore (2012) "European engagement with news/information sites ascends."Available online at: www.comscoredatamine.com/2012/03/european-engagement-with-newsinformation-sites-ascends-with-age (accessed 12 April 2012).

20 eMarketers (2011).

21 Nielsen Wire (2012) "Double vision: Global trends in tablet and smartphone use while watching TV." Available online at: http://blog.nielsen.com/nielsenwire/online_mobile/double-vision-global-trends-in-tablet-and-smartphone-use-while-watching-tv (accessed 16 April 2012).

22 S. Lohr (2011) "Google schools its algorithm," *New York Times*. Available online at: www.nytimes.com/2011/03/06/weekinreview/06lohr.html?_r=2&pagewanted=1&hpw (accessed 6 January 2012).

23 C. Bartolozzi (2012) "Pinterest becomes first major social networking site driven by women." Available online at: www.policymic.com/articles/3306/pintrest-becomes-first-major-social-networking-site-driven-by-women (accessed 12 April 2012).

24 V. Chowney (2012) "More male Pinterest users in UK than female: Infographic," eConsultancy. Available online at: http://econsultancy.com/uk/blog/9021-more-male-pinterest-users-in-uk-than-female-infographic (accessed 12 April 2012).

25 ComScore (2012) "People spent 6.7 billion hours on social networks in October." Available online at: www.comscoredatamine.com/2012/01/people-spent-6-7-billion-hours-on-social-networks-in-october (accessed 12 April 2012).

26 S. Livingstone, K. Ólafsson and E. Staksrud (2011) "Social networking, age and privacy: EU kids online." Available online at: http://www2.lse.ac.uk/media@lse/research/EUKidsOnline/ShortSNS.pdf (accessed 9 January 2012).

27 J. McCombe (2012) "TGI: Digital kids," MediaTel. Available online at: http://mediatel.co.uk/newsline/2010/11/18/tgi-digital-kids (accessed 9 January 2012).

28 MarketWatch (2012) "Global online gaming report 2012." Available online at: www.marketwatch.com/strong/global-online-gaming-report-2012.

29 http://sharethis.com

Chapter 4

1 Dr. Seuss (1990) *Oh, the Places You'll Go!* New York: Random House.

Chapter 5

1 D. Cyra, M. Head and H. Larios (2010) "Colour appeal in website design within and across cultures: A multi-method evaluation," *International Journal of Human–Computer Studies*, 68: 1–21.

2 S. Komin (1991) *Psychology of the Thai People: Values and behavioral patterns.* Bangkok, Thailand: Magenta.

3 S. S. Robbins and A. C. Stylianou (2002) "A study of cultural differences in global corporate websites," *Journal of Computer Information Systems*, Winter: 3–9.

4 M. H. Segall, P. R. Dasen, J. W. Berry, Y. H. Poortinga (1999) *Human Behavior in Global Perspective: An introduction to cross-cultural psychology* (2nd edn). New York: Simon & Schuster.

5 R. Robertson (1994) "Mapping the global condition: Globalization as the central concept," in M. Featherstone (ed.), *Global Culture: Nationalism, globalization and modernity.* Newbury Park, CA: Sage. p. 36.

6 M. Helft (2010) "Google's computing power refines translation tool." Available online at: www.nytimes.com/2010/03/09/technology/09translate.html?_r=1 (accessed 12 April 2012).

7 M. S. Roth (1995) "Effects of global market conditions on brand image customization and brand performance," *Journal of Advertising*, 24 (4): 55–75.

8 www.virtualvender.coca-cola.com/ft/index.jsp (accessed 28 June 2011).

9 www.coke.co.nz/assets/img/aboutcocacola/aboutcoca-cola.pdf (accessed 28 June 2011).

10 http://geert-hofstede.com/countries.html (accessed 29 March 2012).

11 G. Hofstede (2010) *Cultures and Organizations: Software of the mind.* Maidenhead: McGraw Hill.

12 Based on scores for Ethiopia, Kenya, Tanzania, Zambia.

13 Data sourced from G. Hofstede (2010). Also, http://geert-hofstede.com/countries.html (accessed 29 March 2012).

14 http://geert-hofstede.com/countries.html (accessed 29 March 2012).

15 www.obanmultilingual.com (accessed 1 May 2012).

16 www.cocacola.co.jp (accessed 16 April 2012).

17 R. Kanai, T. Feilden, C. Firth and G. Rees (2011) "Political orientations are correlated with brain structure in young adults," *Current Biology*, 21: 1–4.

18 G. Hofstede (2010).

19 www.stumbleupon.com/home (accessed 2 April 2012).

20 http://geert-hofstede.com/india.html (accessed 2 April 2012).

21 http://repskan.com (accessed 2 April 2012).

22 G. Hofstede (2010).

23 www.carling.com/ipint_details.html (accessed 4 April 2012).

Chapter 6

1 M. G. Hoy and G. Milne (2010) "Gender differences in privacy-related measures for young adult Facebook users," *Journal of Interactive Advertising*, 10 (2): 28–45.

2 C. Aguiton, D. Cardon, A. Castelain, P. Fremaux, H. Girard, F. Granjon *et al.* (2009) Does showing off help to make friends? *Proceedings of the Third International ICWSM Conference*. Menlo Park, CA: AAAI. pp. 10–17.

3 I. Oomen and R. Leenes (2008) "Privacy risk perception and privacy protection strategies," in E. de Leeuw, S. Fischer Hubner, J. Tseng and J. Borking (eds), *Policies and Research in Identity*. Boston, MA: Springer. pp. 121–38.

4 M. Madden and A. Smith (2010) "Reputation management and social media: How people monitor their identity and search for others online," Pew Internet & American Life Project, 26 May. Available online at: http://pewinternet.org/Reports/2010/Social-Media-and-Young-Adults.aspx (accessed 7 March 2012).

5 Z. Tufekci (2008) "Can you see me now?: Audience and disclosure regulation in online social network sites," *Bulletin of Science, Technology and Society*, 28 (1): 20–36.

6 A. Acquisti and R. Gross (2006) "Imagined communities: Awareness, information sharing, and privacy on the Facebook," *Lecture Notes in Computer Science*, 4258: 36–58.

7 M. G. Hoy and G. Milne (2010).

8 Z. Tufekci (2008) "Grooming, gossip, Facebook and MySpace: What can we learn about these sites from those who won't assimilate?," *Information, Communication & Society*, 11 (4): 544–64.

9 D. Rosen, M. A. Stefanone and D. Lackaff (2010) "Online and offline social networks: Investigating culturally-specific behavior and satisfaction," *Proceedings of the 43rd Hawai`i International Conference on System Sciences*. New Brunswick, NJ: Institute of Electrical and Electronics Engineers. Available online at: www.communication.buffalo.edu/contrib/people/faculty/documents/Stefanone_HICSS2010.pdf (accessed 7 March 2012).

10 M. Thelwall (2009) "Social network sites: Users and uses," in M. Zelkowitz (ed.), *Advances in Computers*. Amsterdam: Elsevier. pp. 19–73.

11 Nielsen (2011) "State of the media: The social media report." Available online at: www.nielsen.com/content/dam/corporate/us/en/reports-downloads/2011-Reports/nielsen-social-media-report.pdf (accessed 9 January 2012).

12 E. B. Weiser (2000) "Gender differences in Internet use patterns and Internet application preferences: A two-sample comparison," *Cyberpsychology and Behavior*, 3 (2): 167–78.

13 L. A. Jackson, K. S. Ervin, P. D. Gardner and N. Schmitt (2001) "Gender and the Internet: Women communicating and men searching," *Sex Roles*, 44: 363–79.

14 H. Fisher (2009) *Why Him? Why Her?: Finding real love by understanding your personality type*. New York: Henry Holt & Co.

15 http://wish.co.uk/zombie-boot-camp (accessed 17 April 2012).

16 M. Zuckerman and D. Kuhlman (2000) "Personality and risk-taking: Common bisocial factors," *Journal of Personality*, 68 (6): 999–1029.

17 P. Smith, N. Smith, K. Sherman, K. Kriplani, I. Goodwin, A. Bell and C. Crothers (2008) "The Internet: Social and demographic impacts in Aotearoa, New Zealand," *Observatorio Journal*, 6: 307–30.

18 I. Akman and A. Mishra (2010) "Gender, age and income differences in Internet usage among employees in organizations," *Computers in Human Behavior*, 26: 482–90.

19 A. J. A. M. van Deursen, J. A. G. M. van Dijk and O. Peters (2011) "Rethinking Internet skills: The contribution of gender, age, education, Internet experience, and hours online to medium- and content-related Internet skills," *Poetics*, 39 (2): 125–44.

20 S. Djamasbia, M. Siegelb and T. Tullis (2010) "Generation Y, web design, and eye tracking," *International Journal of Human-Computer Studies*, 68: 307–23.

Chapter 7

1 G. R. Miller (1980) "On being persuaded: Some basic distinctions," in M. E. Roloff and Miller, M. E. (eds) *Persuasion: New directions in theory and research*. Beverly Hills, CA: Sage. pp. 11–28.

2 T. M. Y. Lin, H. Wu, C. Liao and T. Liu (2006) "Why are some emails forwarded and others not?," *Internet Research*, 16 (1): 81–93.

3 J. D. O'Keefe (1990) *Persuasion: Theory and research*. Newbury Park, CA: Sage.

4 J. B. Stiff (1994) *Persuasive Communication*. New York: Guilford Press.

5 E. Aronson (2004) *The Social Animal*. New York: Worth.

6 S. Chaiken (1979) "Communicator physical attractiveness and persuasion," *Journal of Personality and Social Psychology*, 37: 1387–97.

7 J. A. Goguen (2005) "Semiotics, compassion and value-centered design," in K. Liu (ed.), *Virtual, Distributed and Flexible Organisations*. New York: Springer. pp. 3–14.

8 S. Singh (2006) "Impact of color on marketing," *Management Decision*, 44 (6): 783–9.

9 http://wemakewebsites.com (accessed 17 April 2012).

Chapter 8

1 S. C. Chen and G. S. Dhillon (2002) "Interpreting dimensions of consumer trust in e-commerce," *Information Management and Technology*, 4: 303–18.

2 Ibid.

3 M. Featherstone (1991) *Consumer Culture and Postmodernism*. London: Sage.

4 M. Gommans, K. S. Krishan and K. B. Scheddold (2001) "From brand loyalty to e-loyalty: A conceptual framework," *Journal of Economic and Social Research*, 3 (1): 43–58.

5   C. N. Wathan and J. Burkell (2002) "Believe it or not: Factors influencing credibility on the web," *Journal of the American Society for Information Science and Technology*, 53 (2): 134–44.

6   C. L. Sia, K. H. Lim, K. Leung, M. K. Lee, W. W. Huang and I. Benbasat (2009) "web strategies to promote Internet shopping: Is cultural-customization needed?," *MIS Quarterly*, 33 (3): 491–512.

7   V. Venkatesh, M. G. Morris, G. B. Davis and F. D. Davis (2003) "User acceptance of information technology: Toward a unified view," *MIS Quarterly*, 27 (3): 425–78.

8   M. Bauerly (2008) "Effects of symmetry and number of compositional elements on interface and design aesthetics," *International Journal of Human–Computer Interaction*, 24 (3): 275–87.

9   T. Jacobsen, R. Schubotz, L. Höfel and D. Cramon (2006) "Brain correlates of aesthetic judgment of beauty," *Neuroimage*, 29 (1): 276–85.

10 E. Papachristos, N. Tselios and N. Avouris (2005) "Inferring relations between color and emotional dimensions of a website using Bayesian networks," *Proceedings of INTERACT '05*. Berlin: Springer-Verlag. pp. 1075–8.

11 J. Avrahami, T. Argaman and D. Weiss-Chasum (2004) "The mysteries of the diagonal: Gender-related perceptual asymmetries," *Perception and Psychophysics*, 66 (8): 1405–17.

12 C. K. Coursaris, E. Lansing, S. J. Swierenga, E. Watrall, I I. A. Letters and S. S. Online (2008) "An empirical investigation of color temperature and gender effects on web aesthetics," *Journal of Usability Studies*, 3 (3): 103–17.

13 S. Simon (2001) "The impact of culture and gender on websites: An empirical study," *ACM SIGMIS DataBase*, 32 (1): 18–37.

14 D. Cyr and C. Bonanni (2005) "Gender and website design in e-business," *International Journal of Electronic Business*, 3 (6): 565–82.

15 S. Simon (2001).

16 E. Garbarino and M. Strahilevitz (2004) "Gender differences in the perceived risk of buying online and the effects of receiving a site recommendation," *Journal of Business Research*, 57: 768–75.

17 S. Simon (2001).

18 H. Dittmar, K. Long and R. Meek (2004) "Buying on the Internet: Gender difference in online and conventional buying motivations," *Sex Roles*, 50 (5–6): 423–44.

19 Ibid.

20 L. A. Jackson, K. S. Ervin, P. D. Gardner and N. Schmitt (2001) "Gender and the Internet: Women communicating and men searching," *Sex Roles*, 44: 363–79.

21 J. Holland and S. Menzel-Baker (2001) "Customer participation in creating site brand loyalty," *Journal of Interactive Marketing*, 15 (4): 34–45.

22 M. Koufaris (2002) "Applying the technology acceptance model and flow theory to online consumer behavior," *Information Systems Research*, 13 (2): 205–23.

23 V. Postrel (2003) *The Substance of Style*. New York: HarperCollins.

24 D. Pfaff (2006) *Brain Arousal and Information Theory: Neural and genetic mechanisms*. Cambridge, MA: Harvard University Press.

25 R. Cialdini (2007) *Influence: The psychology of persuasion*. New York: HarperCollins.

26   J. Y. Chen, A. T. W. Whitfield, A. Robertson and Y. Chen (2010) "The effect of cultural and educational background in the aesthetic responses of website users." Tainan City, Taiwan: Kun Shan University. Available online at: http://ir.lib.ksu.edu.tw/handle/987654321/12274 (accessed 16 April 2012).

27   V. Evers, A. Kukulska-Hulme and A. Jones (1999) "Cross-cultural understanding of interface design: A cross-cultural analysis of icon recognition." Paper presented at the International Workshop on Internationalisation of Products and Systems, 21–22 May. Rochester, New York.

28   D. Block (2004) "Globalization, transnational communication and the Internet," *International Journal on Multicultural Societies*, 6 (1): 13–28.

29   Internet World Stats (2010) "Internet world users by language: Top 10 languages." Available online at: www.internetworldstats.com/stats7.htm (accessed 16 April 2012).

30   K. Allmann (2009) "Arabic language use online: Social, political, and technological dimensions of multilingual Internet communication," *The Monitor: Journal of International Studies*, 15 (1): 61–76.

31   P. Lambert-Diesbach and D. F. Midgley (2007) "Embodied agents on a website: Modelling an attitudinal route of influence," *Persuasive*, *LNCS*, 4744: 223–30.

32   C. Nass and Y. Moon (2000) "Machines and mindlessness: Social responses to computers," *Journal of Social Issues*, 56 (1): 81–103.

33   C. Nass and B. Reeves (1996) *The Media Equation*. Cambridge: SLI and Cambridge University Press.

34   L. L. Constantine and L. A. D. Lockwood (1999) *Software for Use: A Practical Guide to the Models and Methods*. Reading, MA: Addison-Wesley/Longman.

35   J. Noiwana and A. F. Norcio (2006) "Cultural differences on attention and perceived usability: Investigating color combinations of animated graphics," *International Journal of Human–Computer Studies*, 64: 103–22.

36   V. A. Zeithaml, A. Parasuraman and A. Malhotra (2000) "A conceptual framework for understanding e-service quality: Implications for future research and managerial practice." Marketing Science Institute, Working Paper Series, No. 00-115. Cambridge, MA. pp. 1–49.

37   A. M. Aladwani and P. C. Palvia (2002) "Developing and validating an instrument for measuring user-perceived web quality," *Information and Management*, 39: 467–76.

38   P. Katerattanakul and K. Siau (1999) "Measuring information quality of websites: Development of an instrument," *Proceedings of the 20th International Conference on Information Systems*. Atlanta, GA: Association for Information Systems. pp. 279–85.

39   G. W. Tan and K. K. Wei (2006) "An empirical study of Web browsing behaviour: Towards an effective website design," *Electronic Commerce Research and Applications*, 5: 261–71.

40   E. Huizingh (2000) "The content and design of websites: An empirical study," *Information and Management*, 37: 123–34.

41   N. Bevan (1999) "Usability issues in website design," London: Serco ExperienceLab. Available online at: www.serco.com/Images/Usability%20issues%20in%20website%20design_tcm3-34013.pdf (accessed 20 March 2012).

42   R. Agarwal and V. Venkatesh (2002) "Assessing a firm's web Presence: A heuristic evaluation procedure for measurement of usability," *Information Management Research*, 13 (2): 168–21.

43 B. J. Fogg, C. Soohoo and D. Danielson (2002) "How people evaluate a website's credibility: Results from a large study." Persuasive Technology Lab, Stanford University. Available online at: www.consumerwebwatch.org/news/report3_credibilityresearch/stanfordPTL.pdf (accessed 20 March 2012).

44 P. J. Lynch and S. Horton (2009) *web Style Guide: Basic design principles for creating websites*. New Haven, CT: Yale University Press.

45 N. Tractinsky, A. Shoval-Katz and D. Ikar (2000) "What is beautiful is usable," *Interacting with Computers*, 13 (2): 127–45.

46 G. Fernandes, G. Lindgaard, R. Dillon and J. Wood (2003) "Judging the appeal of websites," *Proceedings 4th World Congress on the Management of Electronic Commerce*, McMaster University, Hamilton, ON, 15–17, January.

47 J. Nielsen and M. Tahir (2002) *Homepage Usability: 50 websites deconstructed*. Indianapolis, IN: New Riders.

48 G. W. Tan and K. K. Wei (2006).

49 Nielsen (2011) "State of the media: The social media report." Available online at: www.nielsen.com/content/dam/corporate/us/en/reports-downloads/2011-Reports/nielsen-social-media-report.pdf (accessed 9 January 2012).

50 G. W. Tan and K. K. Wei (2006).

51 B. Cugelman, M. Thelwall and P. Dawes (2007) "Can brotherhood be sold like soap … online?: An online social marketing and advocacy pilot study synopsis." *Persuasive*, *LNCS*, 4744: 144–7.

52 D. L. Hoffman, T. P. Novak and P. Chatterjee (1995) "Commercial scenarios for the web: Opportunities and challenges," *Journal of Computer-Mediated Communication*, 1 (3): 1–21.

53 Z. Yanga, S. Caib, Z. Zhouc and N. Zhou (2005) "Development and validation of an instrument to measure user perceived service quality of information presenting web portals," *Information and Management*, 42: 575–89.

54 T. Raykov (1997) "Scale reliability: Cronbach's coefficient alpha, and violations of essential tau-equivalence for fixed congeneric components," *Multivariate Behavioral Research*, 32: 329–54.

55 J. V. Saraph, P. G. Benson and R. G. Schroeder (1989) "An instrument for measuring the critical factors of quality management," *Decision Sciences*, 20 (4): 810–29.

56 G. W. Tan and K. K. Wei (2006).

57 M. K. Campbell, J. M. Bernhardt, M. Waldmiller, B. Jackson, D. Potenziani, B. Weathers and S. Demissie (1999) "Varying the message source in computer-tailored nutrition education," *Patient Education & Counseling*, 36: 157–69.

58 C. N. Wathan and J. Burkell (2002).

59 www.obanmultilingual.com (accessed 10 May 2012).

60 S. J. McMillan (1999) "Health communication and the Internet: Relations between interactive characteristics of the medium and site creators, content, and purpose," *Health Communication*, 11: 375–90.

61 R. Agarwal and V. Venkatesh (2002).

62 B. J. Fogg, C. Soohoo and D. Danielson (2002).

63 B. Eisenberg (2009) *Always Be Testing: The complete guide to Google Website Optimizer*. Indianapolis, IN: Sybex/Wiley.

Chapter 9

1 F. R. Barnard (1921) "One look is worth a thousand words," *Printers' Ink*, 8 December, 96–7.

2 V. S. Ramachandran and W. Hirstein (1999) "The science of art: A neurological theory of aesthetic experience," *Journal of Consciousness Studies*, 6 (6–7): 15–51.

3 T. Ishizu and S. Zeki (2011) "Toward a brain-based theory of beauty," *PLoS ONE*, 6 (7): e21852.

4 J. Wypijewski (ed.) (1999) *Painting by Numbers: Komar and Melamid's scientific guide to art.* Berkeley, CA: University of California Press.

5 S. Kaplan (1992) "Environmental preference in a knowledge-seeking, knowledge-using organism," in J. Barkow, L. Cosmides and J. Tooby (eds), *The Adapted Mind: Evolutionary psychology and the generation of culture.* New York: Oxford University Press.

6 G. H. Orians and J. H. Heerwagen (1992) "Evolved responses to landscapes," in ibid.

7 J. Breeze (2009) "You look where they look." Available online at: http://usableworld.com.au/2009/03/16/you-look-where-they-look (accessed 6 February 2012).

8 S. R. H. Langton, R. J. Watt and V. Bruce (2000) "Do the eyes have it?: Cues to the direction of social attention," *Trends in Cognitive Sciences*, 4 (2): 50–9.

Chapter 10

1 www.communicatetv.co.uk/media/files/1340964671gauging-video-effectiveness-28-6-12.pdf

2 J. L. Derrick, S. Gabriel and K. Hugenberg (2009) "Social surrogacy: How favored television programs provide the experience of belonging," *Journal of Experimental Social Psychology*, 45 (2): 352–62.

3 *What makes a masterpiece? Stories and Film* (2012), Channel 4, UK, 7 January.

4 www.neurofocus.com (accessed 18 April 2012).

5 *Jaws* (1975), Universal.

6 *The Bourne Identity* (2002), Universal.

7 *Love Actually* (2003), Universal

8 www.neuro-insight.com (accessed 18 April 2012).

9 *What Makes a Masterpiece? Stories and Film* (2012).

10 U. Hasson (2012) interview in ibid.

11 *Casino Royale* (2006), Columbia.

12 R. Ohme (2012) study in *What Makes a Masterpiece? Stories and Film*, Channel 4, UK, 7 January.

13 P. Skalskia, R. Tamborinib, E. Glazerb and S. Smith (2009) "Effects of humor on presence and recall of persuasive messages," *Communication Quarterly*, 57 (2): 136–53.

14 M. Eisend (2011) "How humor in advertising works: A meta-analytic test of alternative models," *Marketing Letters*, 22 (2): 115–32.

Chapter 11

1 M. M. Aslam (2006) "Are you selling the right colour?: A cross-cultural review of colour as a marketing cue," *Journal of Marketing Communications*, 12 (1): 15–30.

2 T. J. Madden, K. Hewitt and M. S. Roth (2000) "Managing images in different cultures: A cross-national study of color meanings and preferences," *Journal of International Marketing*, 8 (4): 90–107.

3   D. Cyra, M. Head and H. Larios (2010) "Colour appeal in website design within and across cultures: A multi-method evaluation," *International Journal of Human–Computer Studies*, 68: 1–21.

4   A. J. Elliot and M. A. Maier (2007) "Color and psychological functioning," *Current Directions in Psychological Science*, 16 (5): 250–4.

5   H. Triandis (2007) "Culture and psychology: A history of the study of their relationship," in S. Kitayama and D. Cohen (eds), *Handbook of Cultural Psychology*. New York: Guilford Press. pp. 59–76.

6   L. Eiseman (2000) *Pantone Guide to Communicating with Color*. Cincinnati, OH: North Light Books.

7   Ibid.

8   S. Kerfoot, B. Davies and P. Ward (2003) "Visual merchandising and the creation of discernible retail brands," *International Journal of Distribution and Retail Management*, 31 (3): 143–52.

9   Ibid.

10 W. J. Stanton, M. J. Etzel and B. J. Walker (1994) *Fundamentals of Marketing* (10th edn). New York: McGraw-Hill.

11 L. Randall (1991) "Does orange mean cheap?," *Forbes*, 23 December, 144–7.

12 Ibid.

13 T. J. Madden, K. Hewitt and M. S. Roth (2000).

14 A. J. Elliot, M. A. Maier, M. J. Binser, R. Friedman and R. Pekrun (2009) "The effect of red on avoidance behavior in achievement contexts," *Personality and Social Psychology Bulletin*, 35 (3): 365–75.

15 A. J. Elliot, M. A. Maier, A. C. Moller, R. Friedman and J. Meinhardt (2007) "Color and psychological functioning: The effect of red on performance attainment," *Journal of Experimental Psychology: General*, 136: 154–168.

16 Cheskin & Masten Inc. (1987) "Color information package: A non-proprietary color research report," Palo Alto, CA: Cheskin & Masten Inc.

17 R. P. Grossman and J. Z. Wisenblit (1999) "What we know about consumers' color choices," *Journal of Marketing Practice: Applied Marketing Science*, 5 (3): 78–88.

18 Cheskin & Masten Inc. (1987).

19 N. Bonnardel, A. Piolat and L. Le Bigot (2011) "The impact of colour on website appeal and users" cognitive processes', *Displays*, 32 (2): 69–80.

20 J. P. Guilford and P. C. Smith (1959) "A system of color-preferences," *The American Journal of Psychology Human–Computer Interaction*, 72 (4): 487–502.

21 B. J. Fogg, J. Marshall, O. Laraki, A. Osipovich, C. Varma, N. Fang, J. Paul, A. Rangnenkar, J. Shon, P. Swani and M. Treinen (2001) "What makes websites credible?: A report on a large quantitative study," *SIGCHI'01*, 3 (1): 61–8.

22 P. Zhang and N. Li (2005) "The importance of affective quality," *Communications of the ACM*, 48 (9): 105–8.

23 F. Seitel (1993) "The colors of banking," *Communications*, 123 (May): 79.

24 C. M. Conway, J. E. Pelet, P. Papadopoulou and M. Limayem (2010) "Coloring in the lines: Using color to change the perception of quality in e-commerce sites," *ICIS 2010 Proceedings*, Paper 224.

25 D. Cyra, M. Head and H. Larios (2010).

26 H. J. Eysenck (1941) "A critical and experimental study of color preferences," *American Journal of Psychology*, 54 (3): 385–94.

27 P. Valdez and A. Mehrabian (1994) "Effects of color on emotions," *Journal of Experimental Psychology: General*, 123 (4): 394–409.

28 M. De Bortoli and J. Maroto (2001) "Translating colours in website localization," *Proceedings of the European Languages and the Implementation of Communication and Information Technologies (Elicit) Conference*, University of Paisley, Scotland.

29 J. -E. Pelet (2010) "Effets de la couleur des sites web marchands sur la mémorisationet sur l'intention d'achat," *Systèmes d'Informationet Management*, 15 (1): 97–131.

30 C. M. Neal, P. G. Quester and D. I. Hawkins (2002) *Consumer Behaviour: Implications for marketing strategy* (3rd edn). Roseville, NSW: McGraw-Hill.

31 G. Hofstede (1991) *Cultures and Organizations: Software of the mind*. Maidenhead: McGraw-Hill.

32 L. van den Berg-Weitzel and G. van den Laar (2001) "Relation between culture and communication in packaging design," *Journal of Brand Management* 8 (3): 171–84.

33 Color Marketing Group, cited in J. Lambert (2004) "Colour schemers," *Canadian Business*, 77 (18): 76–82.

34 E. Yee, S. Z. Ahmed and S. L. Thompson-Schill (2012) "Colorless green ideas (can) prime furiously," *Psychological Science*, 23 (4): 364–9.

35 R. Wallace (2002) "Icons: Your brand's visual language," *Point of Purchase*, 8 (2): 18.

36 B. H. Schmitt and Y. Pan (1994) "Managing corporate and brand identities in the Asian-Pacific region," *California Management Review*, 36 (summer): 32–48.

37 P. F. Kilmer (1995) "Trade dress protection 1995: A U.S. perspective," *Journal of Brand Management*, 3 (1): 95–103.

38 G. Ward (1995) "Colors and employee stress reduction," *Supervision*, 56 (February): 3–5.

39 G. Torkzadeh and G. Dhillon (2002) "Measuring factors that influence the success of Internet commerce," *Information Systems Research*, 13 (2): 187–204.

40 N. Tractinsky, A. Cokhavi, M. Kirschenbaum and T. Sharfi (2006) "Evaluating the consistency of immediate aesthetic perceptions of web pages," *International Journal of Human-Computer Studies*, 64 (11): 1071–83.

41 J.-E. Pelet and P. Papadopoulou (2010) "The effect of e-commerce websites" colors on consumer trust', *International Journal of E-Business Research*, 7 (3): 34–55.

42 Ibid.

43 R. H. Hall and P. Hanna (2004) "The impact of web page text-background color combination on readability, retention, aesthetics, and behavioral intention," *Behaviour Information Technology*, 23 (3): 183–95.

44 K. Shieh and C. Lin (2000) "Effects of screen type, ambient illumination, and color combination on VDT visual performance and subjective preference," *International Journal of Industrial Ergonomics*, 26: 527–36.

45 A. L. Hill and L. V. Scharff (1997) "Readability of screen displays with various foreground/background color combinations, font styles, and font types," *Proceedings of the 11th National Conference on Undergraduate Research*, pp. 742–6.

46 R. H. Hall and P. Hanna (2004) "The impact of web page text-background color combination on readability, retention, aesthetics, and behavioral intention," *Behaviour Information Technology*, 23 (3): 183–95.

47 N. Singh, H. Xhao and X. Hu (2003) "Cultural adaptation on the web: A study of American companies" domestic and Chinese website', *Journal of Global Information Management*, 11 (3): 63–80.

48 C. M. Neal, P. G. Quester and D. I. Hawkins (2002) *Consumer Behaviour: Implications for marketing strategy* (3rd edn). Roseville, NSW: McGraw-Hill.

49 R. M. Rider (2010) "Color psychology and graphic design applications," Unpublished Senior Honors thesis, Liberty University, Lynchburg, VA.

50 J. Dettmer (2003) "Orange stakes its claim as color du jour," *Insight on the News*, 19 (19): 55.

51 P. Paul (2002) "Color by numbers," *American Demographics*, February, pp. 30–4.

52 W. R. Crozier (1999) "The meanings of colour: Preferences among hues," *Pigment and Resin Technology*, 28 (1): 6–14.

53 A. Choungourian (1968) "Color preferences and cultural variation: Perceptual and motor skills," *Perceptual and Motor Skills*, 26 (3c): 1203–6.

54 P. Paul (2002).

55 W. R. Crozier (1999) "The meanings of colour: Preferences among hues," *Pigment and Resin Technology*, 28 (1): 6–14.

56 R. P. Nelson (1994) *The Design of Advertising*. Dubuque, IA: WCB Brown & Benchmark.

57 M. M. Aslam (2006).

58 M. Berman (2007) *Street Smart Advertising: How to win the battle of the buzz*. Lanham, MD: Rowman & Littlefield.

59 R. A. Hill and R. A. Barton (2005) "Red enhances human performance in contests," *Nature*, 435 (19): 293.

60 J. M. Setchell and E. J. Wickings (2005) "Dominance, status signals, and coloration in male mandrills (Mandrillus sphinx)," *Ethology*, 111: 25–50.

61 A. J. Elliot and M. A. Maier.

62 F. Birren (1997). *The Power of Color: How it can reduce fatigue, relieve monotony, enhance sexuality, and more*. Secaucus, NJ: Carol.

63 A. J. Elliot and D. Niesta (2008) "Romantic red: Red enhances men's attraction to women," *Journal of Personality and Social Psychology*, 95 (5): 1150–64.

64 J. Grimm and W. Grimm (1812) "Rotkäppchen, kinderund hausmärchen" [Children's and household tales, known as Grimms' fairy tales], no. 26, translated by D. L. Ashliman, 2000–2002.

65 *Battlestar Gallactica* (2004), British Sky Broadcasting (BSkyB), David Eick Productions, NBC Universal Television (2004–2007), R&D TV, Stanford Pictures (II), Universal Media Studios (UMS) (2007–2009).

66 *The Matrix* (1999), Warner Brothers.

67 S. Ahmed (2008) "Saudi Arabia bans all things red ahead of Valentine's Day," *CNN*, 12 February. Available online at: http://edition.cnn.com/2008/WORLD/meast/02/12/saudi.valentine/index.html (accessed 20 April 2012).

68 A. D. Pazdaa, A. J. Elliota and T. Greitemeyerb (2012) "Sexy red: Perceived sexual receptivity mediates the red–attraction relation in men viewing woman," *Journal of Experimental Social Psychology*, 48 (3): 787–90.

69 C. Barelli, M. Heistermann, C. Boesch and U. H. Reichard (2007) "Sexual swellings in wild white-handed gibbon females (Hylobateslar) indicate the probability of ovulation," *Hormones and Behavior*, 51: 221–30.

70 P. Valdez and A. Mehrabian (1994) "Effects of color on emotions," *Journal of Experimental Psychology: General*, 123 (4): 394–409.

71 T. J. Madden, K. Hewitt and M. S. Roth (2000).

72 P. Valdez and A. Mehrabian (1994).

73 C. M. Conway, J. -E. Pelet, P. Papadopoulou and M. Limayem (2010) "Coloring in the lines: Using color to change the perception of quality in e-commerce sites," *ICIS 2010 Proceedings*, Paper 224.

74 M. Lichtlé (2007) "The effect of an advertisement's colour on emotions evoked by an ad and attitude towards the ad," *International Journal of Advertising*, 26 (1): 37–62.

75 B. H. Schmitt (1995) "Language and visual imagery: Issues of corporate identity in East Asia," *Journal of World Business*, 30 (4): 28–36.

76 W. E. Simon and L. H. Primavera (1972) "Investigation of the "blue seven phenomenon" in elementary and junior high school children," *Psychological Reports*, (31): 128–30.

77 L. G. Schiffman, D. Bednall, E. Cowley, A. O'Cass, J. Watson and L. Kanuk (2001) *Consumer Behaviour* (2nd edn). Frenchs Forest, NSW: Prentice Hall.

78 M. Lichtlé (2007).

79 J. A. Bellizzi and R. E. Hite (1992) "Environmental color, consumer feelings, and purchase likelihood," *Psychology and Marketing*, 9 (5): 347–63.

80 R. Mehta and R. Zhu (2009) "Blue or red?: Exploring the effect of color on cognitive task performances," *Science*, 323 (5918): 1226–9.

81 S. Bleicher (2005) *Contemporary Color Theory and Use*. Clifton Park, NY: Thomson/ Delmar Learning.

82 F. Birren (1997) *The Power of Color: How it can reduce fatigue, relieve monotony, enhance sexuality, and more*. Secaucus, NJ: Carol.

83 D. J. Sturgess (2008) "A spectrum of missed opportunity," *Brandweek*, 49 (29): 15.

84 G. J. Gorn, A. Chattopadhyay, J. Sengupta and S. Tripathi (2004) "Waiting for the web: How screen color affects time perception," *Journal of Marketing Research*, 41 (2): 215–25.

85 M. Hemphill (1996) "A note on adults" color–emotion associations', *The Journal of Genetic Psychology*, 157 (3): 275–80.

86 S. Lehrl, K. Gerstmeyer, J. H. Jacob, H. Frieling, A. W. Henkel, R. Meyrer, J. Wiltfang, J. Kornhuber and S. Bleich (2007) "Blue light improves cognitive performance," *Journal of Neural Transmissions*, 114 (4): 457–60.

87 W. R. Crozier (1999).

88 M. Hemphill (1996).

89 R. S. Cimbalo, K. L. Beck and D. S. Sendziak (1978) "Emotionally toned pictures and color selection for children and college students," *Journal of Genetic Psychology*, 133 (2): 303–4.

90 F. Adams and C. Osgood (1973) "Cross-cultural study of affective meanings of color," *Journal of Cross-Cultural Psychology*, 4 (2): 135–56.

91 F. Birren (1997).

92 M. Hemphill (1996).

93 M. Berman (2007) *Street Smart Advertising: How to win the battle of the buzz.* Lanham, MD: Rowman & Littlefield.

94 C. Fehrman and K. Fehrman (2004) *Color: The secret influence.* Upper Saddle River, NJ: Prentice Hall.

95 T. J. Madden, K. Hewitt and M. S. Roth (2000).

96 L. K. Peterson and C. D. Cullen (2000) *Global Graphics: Color: A guide to design with color for an international market.* Gloucester, MA: Rockport.

97 T. J. Madden, K. Hewitt and M. S. Roth (2000).

98 M. G. Frank and T. Gilovich (1988) "The dark side of self and social perception: Black uniforms and aggression in professional sports," *Journal of Personality and Social Psychology,* 54: 74–85.

Chapter 12

1 ComScore (2011) "It's a social world: Top 10 need-to-knows about social networking and where it's headed." Available online at: www.comscore.com/Press_Events/ Presentations_Whitepapers/2011/it_is_a_social_world_top_10_need-to-knows_about_ social_networking (accessed 20 January 2012).

2 Tech Journal (2011) "Many B2B marketers don't measure social media impact." Available online at: www.techjournalsouth.com/2011/11/many-b2b-marketers-dont-measure-social-media-impact/ (accessed 9 January 2012).

3 E. Keller (2007) "Unleashing the power of word of mouth: Creating brand advocacy to drive growth," *Journal of Advertising Research,* 47 (4): 448–52.

4 B. J. Jansen, M. Zhang, K. Sobeland and A. Chowdury (2009) "Twitter power: Tweets as electronic word of mouth," *Journal of the American Society for Information Science and Technology,* 60 (11): 2169–88.

5 L. Fisher (2011) "44% of companies track employees" social media use in AND out of the office'. Available online at: thenextweb.com/socialmedia/2011/08/17/44-of-companies-track-employees-social-media-use-in-and-out-of-the-office (accessed 9 January 2012).

6 ComScore (2011).

7 www.alexa.com/topsites/countries (accessed 20 April 2012).

8 ComScore (2011).

9 ComScore (2011).

10 Cisco (2011) "Connected world technology report." Available online at: www.cisco. com/en/US/netsol/ns1120/index.html (accessed 9 January 2012).

11 C. Vollmer and K. Premo (2011) "Campaigns to capabilities: Social media and marketing." Booz & Co. Available online at: www.booz.com/media/file/BoozCo-Campaigns-to-Capabilities-Social-Media-and-Marketing-2011.pdf (accessed 9 January 2012).

12 National Restaurant Association (2011) "Inside the mind of today's consumer: Why restaurants are poised for success in 2011 and beyond." Restaurant Industry Forecast. Available online at: www.restaurant.org/pdfs/research/forecast_2011.pdf (accessed 9 January 2012).

13 T. Wasserman (2011) "What drives brand sociability?" (infographic). Mashable. Available online at: http://mashable.com/2011/10/12/brand-sociability-infographic/ (accessed 9 January 2012).

14   S. Bennet (2011) "34% of marketers have generated leads using Twitter" (infographic), Media Bistro. Available online at: www.mediabistro.com/alltwitter/digital-marketing-2011_b15395 (accessed 9 January 2012).

15   M. Stelzner (2012) "2012 social media marketing industry report: How marketers are using social media to grow their businesses," *Social Media Examiner*. Available online at: www.socialmediaexaminer.com/social-media-marketing-industry-report-2012/ (accessed 12 April 2012).

16   R. A. Hill and R. I. M. Dunbar (2003) "Social network sizes in humans," *Human Nature*, 14 (1): 53–72.

17   www.facebook.com/press/info.php?statistics (accessed 6 January 2012).

18   ComScore (2012) "Media Metrix ranks top 50 U.S. web properties for January 2012." Available online at: www.comscore.com/Press_Events/Press_Releases/2012/2/comScore_Media_Metrix_Ranks_Top_50_U.S._Web_Properties_for_January_2012 (accessed 11 April 2012).

19   http://blog.bitly.com/post/9887686919/you-just-shared-a-link-how-long-will-people-pay?utm_campaign=Argyle%2BSocial-2011-09&utm_medium=Argyle%2BSocial&utm_source=twitter&utm_term=2011-09-07-09-34-00 (accessed 9 January 2012).

20   ComScore (2011).

21   www.dmnews.com/corona-light-to-take-over-times-square-billboard-in-digital-initiative/article/181005/ (accessed 25 January 2012).

22   R. B. Cialdini and N. J. Goldstein (2004) "Social influence: Compliance and conformity," *Annual Review of Psychology*, 55: 591–621.

23   N. Harbison (2011) "Corona's epic Facebook campaign," The Next web. Available online at: http://thenextweb.com/socialmedia/2011/05/31/coronas-epic-facebook-campaign (accessed 25 January 2012).

24   S. Mahmud (2010) "Corona Light to take over Times Square billboard in digital initiative," *Direct Marketing News*. Available online at: www.dmnews.com/corona-light-to-take-over-times-square-billboard-in-digital-initiative/article/181005 (accessed 25 January 2012).

25   www.quantcast.com/facebook.com#!demo (accessed 14 May 2012).

26   www.psychometrics.cam.ac.uk/page/321/preference-tool.htm (accessed 26 April 2012).

27   R. Burn-Callander (2012) "Twitter hits 500 million users," *Management Today*. Available online at: www.managementtoday.co.uk/features/1118751/twitter-hits-500-million-users/ (accessed 23 February 2012).

28   Twitter (2011) "One hundred million voices." http://blog.twitter.com/2011/09/one-hundred-million-voices.html (accessed 9 January 2012).

29   J. Meikle (2012) "Twitter is harder to resist than cigarettes and alcohol, study finds," *The Guardian*, 3 February. www.guardian.co.uk/technology/2012/feb/03/twitter-resist-cigarettes-alcohol-study (accessed 3 February 2012).

30   L. Rao (2011) "Beyonce pregnancy news at MTV VMAs births new Twitter record of 8,868 tweets per second," Tech Crunch. Also available online at: http://techcrunch.com/2011/08/29/beyonce-pregnancy-news-at-the-mtv-vmas-births-new-twitter-record-with-8868-tweets-per-second (accessed 9 January 2012).

31 S. Asur and B. A. Huberman (2010) "Predicting the future with social media." 2010 IEEE/WIC/ACM International Conference on web Intelligence and Intelligent Agent Technology. pp. 492–9.

32 L. Menchaca (2012) "Expanding connections with customers through social media," Dell. Available online at: http://en.community.dell.com/dell-blogs/direct2dell/b/direct2dell/archive/2009/12/08/expanding-connections-with-customers-through-social-media.aspx (accessed 17 January 2012).

33 H. Mehta (2009) "Isn't the value of social media what business is all about?," Huffington Post. Available online at: www.huffingtonpost.com/manish-mehta/isnt-the-value-of-social_b_383320.html (accessed 17 January 2012).

34 L. Menchaca (2012).

35 H. Mehta (2009).

36 M. Georgiera (2011) "Action-oriented tweets get more shares," (data) Hubspot Blog. Available online at: http://blog.hubspot.com/blog/tabid/6307/bid/26764/Action-Oriented-Tweets-Get-More-Shares-Data.aspx#ixzz1dGSEUrTA (accessed 6 January 2012).

37 M. Monsen (2011) "Twitter psychology for marketers," White Fire. Available online at: www.whitefireseo.com/infographics/twitter-psychology-for-marketers (accessed 9 January 2012).

38 W. A. Kahn (1990) "Psychological conditions of personal engagement and disengagement at work," *Academy of Management Journal*, 33 (4): 692–724.

39 www.youtube.com/t/press_statistics (accessed 11 April 2012).

40 www.youtube.com/watch?v=XQcVllWpwGs (accessed 9 January 2012).

41 www.eurorscg.com (accessed 9 January 2012).

42 www.unrulymedia.com (accessed 9 January 2012).

43 Unruly (2008) "Evian – Roller Babies." Available online at: www.unrulymedia.com/case-studies/evian-roller-babies.html (accessed 9 January 2012).

44 www.youtube.com/watch?v=Vdgl0j1odkY (accessed 11 January 2012).

45 M. Sweney (2008) "Cadbury brings back gorilla ad with Bonnie Tyler remix," *The Guardian*, 5 September. www.guardian.co.uk/media/2008/sep/05/advertising.marketingandpr (accessed 11 January 2012).

46 M. Lindstrom (2011) *Brandwashed: Tricks companies use to manipulate our minds and persuade us to buy*. New York: Crown Business.

47 www.youtube.com/watch?v=lUlC79KBfmA&feature=player_embedded (accessed 9 March 2012).

48 A. Palmer, R. Beggs and C. Keown-McMullan (2000) "Equity and repurchase intention following service failure," *Journal of Services Marketing*, 14 (6): 513–28.

49 S. Kwon and S. Jang (2011) "The effectiveness of compensation for service recovery: Roles of perceived equity and relationship level." Paper presented at the 16th Graduate Students Research Conference, Houston, Texas, 6–8 January.

Chapter 13

1 L. Gamberini, G. Petrucci, A. Spoto and A. Spagnolli (2007) "Embedded persuasive strategies to obtain visitors" data: Comparing reward and reciprocity in an amateur, knowledge-based website', *Persuasive, LNCS*, 4744: 187–98.

2   A. Spagnolli, D. Varotto and G. Mantovani (2003) "An ethnographic, action-based approach to human experience in virtual environments," *International Journal of Human–Computer Studies,* 59 (6): 797–822.

3   B. P. Davis and E. S. Knowles (1999) "A disrupt-then-reframe technique of social influence," *Journal of Personality and Social Psychology,* 76: 192–9.

4   D. Dolinski and M. Nawrat (1998). "'Fear-then-relief' procedure for producing compliance: Beware when the danger is over," *Journal of Experimental Social Psychology,* 34: 27–50.

5   J. M. Burger (1999) "The foot-in-the-door compliance procedure: A multiple-process analysis and review," *Personality and Social Psychology Review,* 3: 303–25.

6   R. B. Cialdini and N. J. Goldstein (2004) "Social influence: Compliance and conformity," *Annual Review of Psychology,* 55: 591–621.

7   M. A. Whatley, M. J. Webster, R. H. Smith and A. Rhodes (1999) "The effect of a favor on public and private compliance: How internalized is the norm of reciprocity?," *Basic Applied Social Psychology,* 21: 251–59.

8   B. Rind and D. Strohmetz (1999) "Effect on restaurant tipping of a helpful message written on the back of customers" checks', *Journal of Applied Social Psychology,* 29: 139–44.

9   www.silvermanresearch.com/ (accessed 29 February 2012).

10 http://opinion.berkeley.edu/1.0/# (accessed 29 February 2012).

11 P. Newhouse (2011) "Capturing the employee voice to reshape reward policies," *Strategic Communication Management,* 16 (1): 20–3.

12 www.surveymonkey.com/mp/tour/realtimeresults/ (accessed 29 February 2012).

13 www.instantpresenter.com/ (accessed 29 February 2012).

Chapter 14

1   R. Cialdini (1993) *Influence: Science and practice* (3rd edn). New York: HarperCollins.

2   R. Leakey and R. Lewin (1978) *People of the Lake.* New York: Anchor Press/ Doubleday.

3   P. S. Adler and S. Kwon (2002) "Social capital: Prospects for a new concept," *Academy of Management Review,* 27: 17–40.

4   P. Seabright (2004) *The Company of Strangers: A natural history of economic life.* Princeton, NJ: Princeton University Press.

5   R. Cialdini (1993).

6   R. B. Cialdini and M. R. Trost (1998) "Social influence: Social norms, conformity, and compliance," in D. T. Gilbert, S. T. Fiske and G. Lindzey (eds), *The Handbook of Social Psychology* (4th edn). Boston, MA: McGraw-Hill.

7   R. B. Cialdini, M. R. Trost and J. T. Newsom (1995) "Preference for consistency: The development of a valid measure and the discovery of surprising behavioral implications," *Journal of Personality and Social Psychology,* 69: 318–28.

8   R. B. Cialdini and M. R. Trost (1998).

9   D. Cioffi and R. Garner (1996) "On doing the decision: Effects of active versus passive choice on commitment and self-perception," *Personality and Social Psychology Bulletin,* 22: 133–44.

10 R. B. Cialdini and M. R. Trost (1998).

11 J. M. Burger and T. Cornelius (2003) "Raising the price of agreement: Public commitment and the low-ball compliance procedure," *Journal of Applied Social Psychology*, 33 (5): 923–34.

12 http://codecanyon.net/item/viral-lock-like-google1-or-tweet-to-unlock/1486602 (accessed 2 March 2012).

13 M. Deutsch and H. B. Gerard (1955) "A study of normative and informative social influences upon individual judgment," *Journal of Abnormal Social Psychology*, 51: 629–36.

14 R. B. Cialdini and N. J. Goldstein (2004) "Social influence: Compliance and conformity," *Annual Review of Psychology*, 55: 591–621.

15 R. Spears, T. Postmes, M. Lea and S. E. Watt (2001) "A SIDE view of social influence," in J. P. Forgas and K. D. Williams (eds), *Social Influence: Direct and indirect processes*. Philadelphia/Hove, UK: Psychology Press. p. 336.

16 R. Cialdini (1993).

17 R. B. Cialdini (2001) *Influence: Science and Practice* (4th edn). Boston, MA: Allyn & Bacon.

18 R. B. Cialdini and N. J. Goldstein (2004).

19 R. Martin and M. Hewstone (2001) "Determinants and consequences of cognitive processes in majority and minority influence," in J. Forgas and K. Williams (eds), *Social Influence: Direct and indirect processes*. Philadelphia, PA: Psychology Press.

20 B. Latané (1981) "The psychology of social impact," *American Psychologist*, 36 (4): 343–56.

21 B. Latané (1996) "Dynamic social impact: The creation of culture by communication," *Journal of Communication*, 46 (4): 13–25.

22 R. B. Cialdini, W. Wosinska, D. W. Barrett, J. Butner and M. Gornik-Durose (1999) "Compliance with a request in two cultures: The differential influence of social proof and commitment/consistency on collectivists and individualists," *Personality and Social Psychology Bulletin*, 25: 1242–53.

23 R. Bond and P. B. Smith (1996) "Culture and conformity: A meta-analysis of studies using Asch's (1952, 1956) line judgment task," *Psychological Bulletin*, 119: 111–37.

24 H. S. Kim and H. R. Markus (1999) "Deviance or uniqueness, harmony or conformity?: A cultural analysis," *Journal of Personality and Social Psychology*, 77: 785–800.

25 N. Ravindran (2007) "Asia's love for luxury brands," Business Library. Available online at: http://findarticles.com/p/articles/mi_m1NDC/is_2007_Feb-March/ai_n25006642 (accessed 6 March 2012).

26 A. Wiederhecker (2008) "China: Rapid growth fuelled by the super-rich," *Financial Times*, 18 June.

27 H. S. Kim and H. R. Markus (1999).

28 R. B. Cialdini and N. J. Goldstein (2004).

29 B. J. Fogg and D. Eckles (2007) "The behavior chain for online participation: How successful web services structure persuasion," *Persuasive, LNCS*, 4744: 199–209.

30 L. L. Jacoby (1983) "Perceptual enhancement: Persistent effects of an experience," *Journal of Experimental Psychology: Learning, Memory, and Cognition*, 9: 21–38.

31 J. A. Bargh, M. Chen and L. Burrows (1996) "Automaticity of social behavior: Direct effects of trait construct and stereotype activation on action," *Journal of Personality and Social Psychology*, 71 (2): 230–44.

32   www.whit.li/ (accessed 26 April 2012).

33   www.psychometrics.cam.ac.uk/page/321/preference-tool.htm (accessed 26 April 2012).

34   T. L. Chartrand and J. A. Bargh (1999) "The chameleon effect: The perception behavior link and social interaction," *Journal of Personality and Social Psychology*, 76: 893–910.

35   Ibid.

36   R. Dunbar (2011) "How many 'friends' can you really have?," Spectrum IEEE. Available online at: http://spectrum.ieee.org/telecom/internet/how-many-friends-can-you-really-have (accessed 6 March 2012).

37   R. B. Cialdini and M. R. Trost (1998).

38   M. McCall (1997) "Physical attractiveness and access to alcohol: What is beautiful does not get carded," *Journal of Applied Social Psychology*, 27: 453–62.

39   M. Lynn and T. Simons (2000) "Predictors of male and female servers" average tip earnings', *Journal of Applied Social Psychology*, 30: 241–52.

40   J. M. Burger, S. Soroka, K. Gonzago, E. Murphy and E. Somervell (2001) "The effect of fleeting attraction on compliance to requests," *Personality and Social Psychology Bulletin*, 27: 1578–86.

41   D. Dolinski, M. Nawrat and I. Rudak (2001) "Dialogue involvement as a social influence technique," *Personality and Social Psychology Bulletin*, 27: 1395–406.

42   Ibid.

43   S. E. Cross and L. Madson (1997) "Models of the self: self-construals and gender," *Psychology Bulletin*, 122: 5–37.

44   D. J. Howard, C. E. Gengler and A. Jain (1997) "The name remembrance effect: A test of alternative explanations," *Journal of Social Behavior and Personality*, 12: 801–10.

45   R. A. Gordon (1996) "Impact of ingratiation on judgments and evaluations: A meta-analytic investigation," *Journal of Personality and Social Psychology*, 71: 54–70.

46   R. B. Cialdini and N. J. Goldstein (2004).

47   G. Yukl and C. F. Seifert (2002) "Preliminary validation research on the extended version of the influence behavior questionnaire." Paper presented at the Annual Conference of the Society for Industrial and Organizational Psychology, Toronto, 12–14 April.

48   M. Koslowsky, J. Schwarzwald and S. Ashuri (2001) "On the relationship between subordinates" compliance to power sources and organizational attitudes', *Applied Psychology: International Review*, 50: 455–76.

49   C. M. Falbe and G. Yukl (1992) "Consequences for managers of using single influence tactics and combinations of tactics," *Academy of Management Journal*, 35: 638–52.

50   Ibid.

51   M. Koslowsky, J. Schwarzwald and S. Ashuri (2001).

52   G. Yukl (2002) *Leadership in Organizations* (5th edn). Upper Saddle River, NJ: Prentice Hall.

53   www.groupon.com/ (accessed 2 March 2012).

54   www.achica.com/promotions.aspx (accessed 15 May 2012).

55   www.gilt.com/ (accessed 2 March 2012).

56 www.dalani.co.uk/ (accessed 2 March 2012).

57 M. Eisend (2008) "Explaining the impact of scarcity appeals in advertising: The mediating role of perceptions of susceptibility," *Journal of Advertising*, 37 (3): 33–40.

58 M. Lynn and J. Harris (1997) "Individual differences in the pursuit of self-uniqueness through consumption," *Journal of Applied Social Psychology*, 27: 1861–83.

59 www.net-a-porter.com (accessed 2 March 2012).

60 S. Worchel, J. Lee and A. Adewole (1975) "Effects of supply and demand on rating of object value," *Journal of Personality and Social Psychology*, 32 (5): 906–14.

Chapter 15

1 K. T. Jackson (2004) *Building Reputational Capital: Strategies for integrity and fair play that improve the bottom line.* New York: Oxford University Press.

2 D. Gelles and A. Rappeport (2006) "Domino's eats humble pie to boost sales," FT.com, May. Available online at: http://www.ft.com/cms/s/0/f8178fa2-7804-11e0-b90e-00144feabdc0.html#axzz1uwqbr9Ju (accessed 11 April 2012).

3 Nielsen (2012) "Global trust in advertising and brand messages." Available online at: www.nielsen.com/us/en/insights/reports-downloads/2012/global-trust-in-advertising-and-brand-messages.html (accessed 11 April 2012).

4 J. Ahrens and M. A. Strahilevitz (2007) "Can companies initiate positive word of mouth?: A field experiment examining the effects of incentive magnitude and equity, and ereferral mechanisms," *Persuasive, LNCS*, 4744: 160–3.

5 E. Bakshy (2012) "Rethinking information diversity in networks," Facebook Data. Available online at: www.facebook.com/notes/facebook-data-team/rethinking-information-diversity-in-networks/10150503499618859 (accessed 7 February 2012).

6 M. McPherson, L. Smith-Lovin and J. M. Cook (2001) "Birds of a feather: Homophily in social networks," *Annual Review of Sociology*, 27: 415–44.

7 E. Bakshy (2012).

8 http://codecanyon.net/item/viral-lock-like-google1-or-tweet-to-unlock/1486602 (accessed 7 February 2012).

9 S. Y. Rieh (2002) "Judgment of information quality and cognitive authority in the web," *Journal of the American Society for Information Sciences and Technology*, 53 (2): 145–61.

10 D. M. Mackie, L. T. Worth and A. G. Asuncion (1990) "Processing of persuasive in-group messages," *Journal of Personality and Social Psychology*, 58: 812–22.

11 J. K. Burgoon, J. A. Bonito, B. Bengtsson, C. Cederberg, M. Lundeberg and L. Allspach (2000) "Interactivity in human–computer interaction: A study of credibility, understanding, and influence," *Computers in Human Behavior*, 16: 553–74.

12 J. Kim and J. Y. Moon (1997) "Designing towards emotional usability in customer interfaces: Trustworthiness of cyber-banking system interfaces," *Interacting with Computers*, 10: 1–29.

13 C. N. Wathan and J. Burkell (2002) "Believe it or not: Factors influencing credibility on the web," *Journal of the American Society for Information Science and Technology*, 53 (2): 134–144.

14 C. N. Wathan and J. Burkell (2002).

15 Ibid.

16 S. Ferebee (2007) "An examination of the influence of involvement level of website users on the perceived credibility of websites," *Persuasive, LNCS*, 4744: 176–86.

Chapter 16

1 M. Bonera (2011) "The propensity of e-commerce usage: The influencing variables," *Management Research Review*, 34 (7): 821–37.

2 G. L. Lohse and P. Spiller (1998) "Electronic shopping," *Communications of ACM*, 41 (7): 81–9.

3 J. Reynolds (2000) "eCommerce: A critical review," *International Journal of Retail and Distribution Management*, 28 (10): 417–44.

4 M. Bonera (2011).

5 Ibid.

6 W. Schultz (2002) "Getting formal with dopamine and reward," *Neuron*, 36 (2): 241–63.

7 H. C. Breiter, I. Aharon, D. Kahneman, A. Dale and P. Shizgal (2001) "Functional imaging of neural responses to expectancy and experience of monetary gains and losses," *Neuron*, 30 (2): 619–39.

8 I. Aharon, N. Etcoff, D. Ariely, C. F. Chabris, E. O'Connor and H. C. Breiter (2001) "Beautiful faces have variable reward value: fMRI and behavioral evidence," *Neuron*, 32 (3): 537–51.

9 S. Erk, M. Spitzer, A. P. Wunderlich, L. Galley and H. Walter (2002) "Cultural objects modulate reward circuitry," *Neuroreport*, 13 (18): 2499–503.

10 Future Foundation Research (2011) "Social network site users per country aged 16–64." Base: 261–3, 299.

11 D. Mobbs, M. D. Greicius, E. Abdel-Azim, V. Menon and A. L. Reiss (2003) "Humor modulates the mesolimbic reward centers," *Neuron*, 40 (5): 1041–48.

12 http://bodymetrics.com/home.php (accessed 7 March 2012).

13 D. Aamoth (2012) "Kinect camera tech lets you try on clothes without trying on clothes," Time, Techland, 12 January. Available online at: http://techland.time.com/2012/01/13/kinect-camera-tech-lets-you-try-on-clothes-without-trying-on-clothes (accessed 8 March 2012).

14 G. L. Lohse and P. Spiller (1998) "Electronic shopping," *Communications of ACM*, 41 (7): 81–9.

15 H. Nguyen, J. Masthoff and P. Edwards (2007) "Persuasive effects of embodied conversational agent teams," *Proceedings of the 12th International Conference on Human–Computer Interaction: Intelligent Multimodal Interaction Environments (HCI'07)*. Berlin: Springer-Verlag. 176–85.

16 J. Alba, J. Lynch, B. Weitz, C. Janiszewski, R. Lutz, A. Sawyer and S. Wood (1997) "Interactive home shopping: Consumer, retailer, and manufacturer incentives to participate in electronic marketplaces," *Journal of Marketing*, 61: 38–53.

17 www.joinred.com/red/ (accessed 8 March 2012).

18 R. A. Peterson, S. Balasubramanian and B. J. Bronnenberg (1997) "Exploring the implications of the Internet for consumer marketing," *Journal of the Academy of Management Science*, 25 (4): 329–46.

19 J. G. Lynch and D. Ariely (2000) "Wine online: Search costs affect competition on price, quality, and distribution," *Marketing Science*, 19 (1): 83–103.

20 J.-E. Pelet and P. Papadopoulou (2010) "The effect of e-commerce websites" colors on consumer trust', *International Journal of E-Business Research*, 7 (3): 1–18.

21 www.google.com/ads/preferences/html/about.html (accessed 8 March 2012).

22 http://klout.com/home (accessed 23 April 2012).

23 http://repskan.com/ (accessed 23 April 2012).

Chapter 17

1 G. Naylor and K. E. Frank (2001) "The effect of price bundling on consumer perceptions of value," *Journal of Services Marketing*, 15 (4): 270–81.

2 E. T. Anderson and D. I. Simester (2003) "Effects of $9 price endings on retail sales: evidence from field experiments," *Quantitative Marketing and Economics*, 1 (1): 93–110.

3 R. M. Schindler and L. S. Warren (1988) "Effect of odd pricing on choice of items from a menu," *Advances in Consumer Research*, 15: 348–53.

4 R. M. Schindler and T. Kibarian (1993) "Testing for perceptual underestimation of 9-ending prices," *Advances in Customer Research*, 20: 580–5.

5 M. Stiving (2000) "Price-endings: When prices signal quality," *Management Science*, 46 (12): 1617–29.

6 D. Kahneman and A. Tversky (1979) "Prospect theory: An analysis of decisions under risk," *Econometrica*, 47 (2): 263–91.

7 R. Thaler (1980) "Toward a positive theory of consumer choice," *Journal of Economic Behavior and Organization*, 1: 39–60.

8 W. Samuelson and R. Zeckhauser (1988) "Status quo bias in decision making," *Journal of Risk and Uncertainty*, 1 (1): 7–59.

9 A. Lambrecht and B. Skiera (2006) "Paying too much and being happy about it: Causes and consequences of tariff choice–bias," *Journal of Marketing Research*, 43 (2): 212–23.

10 *Secrets of the Superbrands*, BBC Three television documentary, 17 May 2011.

11 D. Ariely and I. Simonson (2003) "Buying, bidding, playing, or competing?: Value assessment and decision dynamics in online auctions," *Journal of Consumer Psychology*, 13: 113–23.

12 R. Dhar and K. Wertenbroch (2000) "Consumer choice between hedonic and utilitarian goods," *Journal of Marketing Research*, 37 (February): 60–71.

13 www.psychometrics.cam.ac.uk/page/321/preference-tool.htm (accessed 26 April 2012).

14 Think Insights (2011) "The zero moment of truth macro study," Google. www.thinkwithgoogle.com/insights/library/studies/the-zero-moment-of-truth-macro-study (accessed 11 April 2012).

15 E. Bachisa and C. A. Pigab (2011) "Low-cost airlines and online price dispersion," *International Journal of Industrial Organization*, 29 (6): 655–67.

16 C. Bicknell (2000) "Online prices not created equal," *Wired*. Available online at: www.wired.com/techbiz/media/news/2000/09/38622 (accessed 7 March 2012).

17 O. Hinz, I. Hann and M. Spann (2011) "Price discrimination in e-commerce?: An examination of dynamic pricing in name-your-own-price markets," *MIS Quarterly and the Society for Information Management*, 35 (1): 81–98.

18 A. Ramasastry (2005) "Websites change prices based on customers" habits', *CNN*. Available online at: www.cnn.com/2005/LAW/06/24/ramasastry.website.prices/index.html (accessed 7 March 2012).

19 A. Pigou (1920) *The Economics of Welfare*. London: Macmillan.

20 M. Spann and G. J. Tellis (2006) "Does the Internet promote better consumer decisions?: The case of name-your-own-price auctions," *Journal of Marketing*, 70 (1): 65–78.

21 M. Joo, T. Mazumdar and S. P. Raj (2012) "Bidding strategies and consumer savings in NYOP auctions," *Journal of Retailing*, 88 (1): 180–8.

22 K. Nicole (2007) "Radiohead kicks the middleman to the curb: 1 week, 1.2m albums sold," Mashable. Available online at: http://mashable.com/2007/10/19/radiohead-album-sales/ (accessed 10 January 2012).

23 G. Naylor and K. E. Frank (2001) "The effect of price bundling on consumer perceptions of value," *Journal of Services Marketing*, 15 (4): 270–81.

Chapter 18

1 B. J. Fogg and D. Eckles (2007) "The behavior chain for online participation: How successful web services structure persuasion," *Persuasive, LNCS*, 4744: 199–209.

2 Ibid.

3 Ibid.

4 http://en.wikipedia.org (accessed 14 February 2012).

5 http://pinterest.com/wholefoods (accessed 14 February 2012).

6 J. Falls (2012) "How Pinterest is becoming the next big thing in social media for business," *Entrepreneur*. Available online at: www.entrepreneur.com/article/222740 (accessed 14 February 2012).

7 T. Ries (2012) "Pin-commerce?: 21% of Pinterest users have purchased a product they found on the site," The Realtime Report. Available online at: http://therealtimereport.com/2012/04/02/pin-commerce-21-of-pinterest-users-have-purchased-a-product-they-found-on-the-site/ (accessed 12 April 2012).

8 www.linkedin.com (accessed 14 February 2012).

9 S. Y. Lam, V. Shankar, M. K. Erramilli and B. Murthy (2004) "Customer value, satisfaction, loyalty, and switching costs: An illustration from a business-to-business service context," *Academy of Marketing Science*, 32 (3): 293–311.

10 A. Fitzpatrick (2012) "The U.S. Army uses Pinterest?: Sir, yes sir!," Mashable. Available online at: http://mashable.com/2012/02/17/us-army-on-pinterest_n_1284383.html (accessed 17 February 2012).

Chapter 19

1 P. de Vries and A. Pruyn (2007) "Source salience and the persuasiveness of peer recommendations: The mediating role of social trust," *Persuasive, LNCS*, 4744: 164–75.

2 H. Van der Heijden, T. Verhagen and M. Creemers (2003) "Understanding online purchase intentions: Contributions from technology and trust perspectives," *European Journal of Information Systems*, 12: 41–8.

3 Y. H. Tan and W. Thoen (2001) "Toward a generic model of trust for electronic commerce," *International Journal of Electronic Markets*, 5 (2): 61–74.

4 J. Riegelsberger, M. A. Sasse and J. D. McCarthy (2003) "Shiny happy people building trust?: Photos on e-commerce websites and consumer trust," *Proceedings of CHI 2003*. pp. 121–8.

5   E. Andrade, V. Kaltcheva and B. Weitz (2002) "Self-disclosure on the web: The impact of privacy policy, reward and brand reputation," *Advances in Consumer Research*, 29: 350–3.

6   M. Ahuja, B. Gupta, P. Raman (2003) "An empirical investigation of online consumer purchasing behaviour," *Communications of the ACM*, 46: 145–51.

7   D. H. McKnight and N. L. Chervany (2002) "What trust means in e-commerce customer relationships: An interdisciplinary conceptual typology," *International Journal of Electronic Commerce*, 6, 35–59.

8   M. F. Wolfinbarger and M. C. Gilly (2002) ".comQ: Dimensionalizing, measuring and predicting quality of the e-tailing experience." MSI Working Paper Series, No. 02-100.

9   D. Cyr and C. Bonanni (2005) "Gender and website design in e-business," *International Journal of Electronic Business*, 3 (6): 565–82.

10 Z. Tufekci (2008) "Can you see me now?: Audience and disclosure regulation in online social network sites," *Bulletin of Science, Technology and Society*, 28 (1): 20–36.

11 A. Acquisti and R. Gross (2006) "Imagined communities: Awareness, information sharing, and privacy on the Facebook," *Lecture Notes in Computer Science*, 4258: 36–58.

12 E. Garbarino and M. Strahilevitz (2004) "Gender differences in the perceived risk of buying online and the effects of receiving a site recommendation," *Journal of Business Research*, 57: 768–75.

13 H. Dittmar, K. Long and R. Meek (2004) "Buying on the Internet: Gender difference in online and conventional buying motivations," *Sex Roles*, 50 (5-6): 423–44.

14 D. Cyr and C. Bonanni (2005).

15 G. B. Murphy and N. Tocher (2011) "Gender differences in the effectiveness of online trust building information cues: An empirical examination," *The Journal of High Technology Management Research*, 22 (1): 26–35.

16 C. Moorman, G. Zaltman and R. Deshpande (1992) "Relationship between providers and users of marketing research: The dynamics of trust within and between organizations," *Journal of Marketing Research*, 29 (August): 314–28.

17 Ibid.

18 D. Johnson and K. Grayson (2005) "Cognitive and affective trust in service relationships," *Journal of Business Research*, 58, 500–7.

19 C. Flaviàn, M. Guinaliu and R. Gurrea (2006) "The role played by perceived usability, satisfaction and consumer trust on website loyalty," *Information and Management*, 43 (1): 1–14.

20 K. Karvonen (2000) "The beauty of simplicity," *ACM Proceedings of the Conference on Universal Usability*. pp. 85–90.

21 D. Gefen, E. Karahanna and D. W. Straub (2003) "Trust and TAM in online shopping: An integrated model," *MIS Quarterly*, 27 (1): 51–90.

22 T. Lavie and N. Tractinsky (2004) "Assessing dimensions of perceived visual aesthetics of websites," *International Journal of Human–Computer Studies*, 60 (3): 269–98.

23 B. J. Fogg, J. Marshall, T. Kameda, J. Solomon, A. Rangnekar, J. Boyd and B. Brown (2001) "web credibility research: A method for online experiments and early study results," *CHI 2001*: 295–6.

24 J. Riegelsberger, M. A. Sasse and J. D. McCarthy (2003).
25 Ibid.
26 Ibid.
27 Ibid.
28 Ibid.
29 C. Flavián (2006).
30 J. Riegelsberger, M. A. Sasse and J. D. McCarthy (2003).
31 P. de Vries and A. Pruyn (2007).
32 L. Gamberini, G. Petrucci, A. Spoto and A. Spagnolli (2007) "Embedded persuasive strategies to obtain visitors" data: Comparing reward and reciprocity in an amateur, knowledge-based website', *Persuasive, LNCS*, 4744: 187–98.
33 E. Andrade, V. Kaltcheva and B. Weitz (2002).
34 R. B. Cialdini, J. E. Vincent, S. K. Lewis, J. Catalan, D. Wheeler and B. L. Darby (1975) "Reciprocal concessions procedure for inducing compliance: The door in the face technique," *Journal of Personality and Social Psychology*, 31: 206–15.
35 L. Gamberini, G. Petrucci, A. Spoto and A. Spagnolli (2007).

GLOSSARY

A/B split testing in relation to websites, when you design two versions of the same site and direct half your visitors to website A and half to website B. By splitting your audience in this way, you can analyze their interactions with each version and use this information to design a website that is more compelling.

DTI (Diffusion Tensor Imaging) is a new technique that exploits the fact that water flows rapidly through myelinated (sheathed) neural axons.

EEG (electro-encephalogram) is one of the oldest techniques, in which electrodes are attached to the scalp to measure electrical activity synchronized to stimulus events or behavioral responses (known as Event Related Potentials or ERPs).

fMRI (functional magnetic resonance imaging) is the newest and currently most popular imaging method. It tracks blood flow in the brain using changes in magnetic properties due to blood oxygenation.

PET (positron emission topography) scanning is also an old technique but remains useful. It measures neural activity by measuring blood flow in the brain (a reasonable proxy since neural activity in a region leads to increased blood flow to that region).

SEO search engine optimization.

Single neuron measurements involve the insertion of tiny electrodes into the brain, each of which measures a single neuron's firing.

TMS (transcranial magnetic stimulation) uses pulsed magnetic fields to temporarily disrupt brain function in specific regions. It has been used successfully to treat some cases of chronic depression and recurring migraine.

INDEX